REPORT OF A SUMMIT

THE 1ST ANNUAL CROSSING THE QUALITY CHASM SUMMIT

A Focus on Communities

Committee on the Crossing the Quality Chasm:
Next Steps Toward a New Health Care System

Board on Health Care Services

Karen Adams, Ann C. Greiner, and Janet M. Corrigan, *Editors*

INSTITUTE OF MEDICINE
OF THE NATIONAL ACADEMIES

THE NATIONAL ACADEMIES PRESS
Washington, D.C.
www.nap.edu

THE NATIONAL ACADEMIES PRESS   500 Fifth Street, N.W.   Washington, DC 20001

NOTICE: The project that is the subject of this report was approved by the Governing Board of the National Research Council, whose members are drawn from the councils of the National Academy of Sciences, the National Academy of Engineering, and the Institute of Medicine. The members of the committee responsible for the report were chosen for their special competences and with regard for appropriate balance.

This study was supported by Contract No. 046718 between the National Academy of Sciences and The Robert Wood Johnson Foundation. It was also supported by a subcontract from The Johns Hopkins Bloomberg School of Public Health with funds provided by Grant No. 037049 from the Robert Wood Johnson Foundation. Any opinions, findings, conclusions, or recommendations expressed in this publication are those of the author(s) and do not necessarily reflect the view of the organizations or agencies that provided support for this project.

International Standard Book Number 0-309-09303-1 (Book)
International Standard Book Number 0-309-54535-8 (PDF)
Library of Congress Control Number: 002004112492

Additional copies of this report are available from the National Academies Press, 500 Fifth Street, N.W., Lockbox 285, Washington, DC 20055; (800) 624-6242 or (202) 334-3313 (in the Washington metropolitan area); Internet, http://www.nap.edu.

For more information about the Institute of Medicine, visit the IOM home page at: www.iom.edu.

Copyright 2004 by the National Academy of Sciences. All rights reserved.

Printed in the United States of America.

The serpent has been a symbol of long life, healing, and knowledge among almost all cultures and religions since the beginning of recorded history. The serpent adopted as a logotype by the Institute of Medicine is a relief carving from ancient Greece, now held by the Staatliche Museen in Berlin.

*"Knowing is not enough; we must apply.
Willing is not enough; we must do."*
—Goethe

INSTITUTE OF MEDICINE
OF THE NATIONAL ACADEMIES

Adviser to the Nation to Improve Health

THE NATIONAL ACADEMIES
Advisers to the Nation on Science, Engineering, and Medicine

The **National Academy of Sciences** is a private, nonprofit, self-perpetuating society of distinguished scholars engaged in scientific and engineering research, dedicated to the furtherance of science and technology and to their use for the general welfare. Upon the authority of the charter granted to it by the Congress in 1863, the Academy has a mandate that requires it to advise the federal government on scientific and technical matters. Dr. Bruce M. Alberts is president of the National Academy of Sciences.

The **National Academy of Engineering** was established in 1964, under the charter of the National Academy of Sciences, as a parallel organization of outstanding engineers. It is autonomous in its administration and in the selection of its members, sharing with the National Academy of Sciences the responsibility for advising the federal government. The National Academy of Engineering also sponsors engineering programs aimed at meeting national needs, encourages education and research, and recognizes the superior achievements of engineers. Dr. Wm. A. Wulf is president of the National Academy of Engineering.

The **Institute of Medicine** was established in 1970 by the National Academy of Sciences to secure the services of eminent members of appropriate professions in the examination of policy matters pertaining to the health of the public. The Institute acts under the responsibility given to the National Academy of Sciences by its congressional charter to be an adviser to the federal government and, upon its own initiative, to identify issues of medical care, research, and education. Dr. Harvey V. Fineberg is president of the Institute of Medicine.

The **National Research Council** was organized by the National Academy of Sciences in 1916 to associate the broad community of science and technology with the Academy's purposes of furthering knowledge and advising the federal government. Functioning in accordance with general policies determined by the Academy, the Council has become the principal operating agency of both the National Academy of Sciences and the National Academy of Engineering in providing services to the government, the public, and the scientific and engineering communities. The Council is administered jointly by both Academies and the Institute of Medicine. Dr. Bruce M. Alberts and Dr. Wm. A. Wulf are chair and vice chair, respectively, of the National Research Council.

www.national-academies.org

COMMITTEE ON CROSSING THE QUALITY CHASM:
NEXT STEPS TOWARD A NEW HEALTH CARE SYSTEM

REED V. TUCKSON *(Chair)*, Senior Vice President, Consumer Health and Medical Care Advancement, UnitedHealth Group, Minnetonka, MN

RON J. ANDERSON, President and Chief Executive Officer, Parkland Memorial Health and Hospital System, Dallas, TX

REGINA M. BENJAMIN, Founder and Chief Executive Officer, Bayou La Batre Rural Health Clinic, Inc., Bayou La Batre, AL

LINDA BURNES BOLTON, Vice President and Chief Nursing Officer, Cedars-Sinai Medical Center and Burns and Allen Research Institute, Los Angeles, CA

BRUCE E. BRADLEY, Director Health Plan Strategy and Public Policy, Health Care Initiatives, General Motors Corporation, Detroit, MI

ALLEN S. DANIELS, Chief Executive Officer, Alliance Behavioral Care, University of Cincinnati Department of Psychiatry, Cincinnati, OH

LILLEE S. GELINAS, Vice President and Chief Nursing Officer, VHA Inc., Irving, TX

CHARLES J. HOMER, President and Chief Executive Officer, National Initiative for Children's Healthcare Quality, Boston, MA

DAVID C. KIBBE, Director of the Center for Health Information Technology, American Academy of Family Physicians, Chapel Hill, NC

MARY ANNE KODA-KIMBLE, Professor and Dean, School of Pharmacy, University of California San Francisco, San Francisco, CA

PETER V. LEE, President and Chief Executive Officer, Pacific Business Group on Health, San Francisco, CA

KATE R. LORIG, Professor of Medicine, Stanford University, Stanford, CA

JOANNE LYNN, Director, The Washington Home Center for Palliative Care Studies, and Senior Scientist with The RAND Corporation, Washington, DC

DAVID M. NATHAN, Director, Diabetes Center, Massachusetts General Hospital and Professor of Medicine, Harvard Medical School, Boston, MA

CHERYL M. SCOTT, President and CEO, Group Health Cooperative, Seattle, WA

JOHN A. SPERTUS, Director of Cardiovascular Education and Outcomes Research, Mid America Heart Institute and Professor of Medicine at the University of Missouri-Kansas City, Kansas City, MO

I. STEVEN UDVARHELYI, Senior Vice President and Chief Medical Officer, Independence Blue Cross, Philadelphia, PA

Study Staff

KAREN ADAMS, Co-Study Director
ANN C. GREINER[1], Co-Study Director
DANITZA VALDIVIA, Senior Project Assistant

Board on Health Care Services

JANET M. CORRIGAN, Senior Director, Board on Health Care Services
ANTHONY BURTON, Administrative Assistant

Auxiliary Staff

THOMAS M. MADDOX[2], Gustav Leinhard Fellow in Health Sciences Policy
PATSY O'MEARA[3], Project Intern

Editorial Consultants

RONA BRIERE, Briere Associates, Inc.
ALISA DECATUR, Briere Associates, Inc.

---

[1] Served through January, 2004.
[2] Served through May, 2003.
[3] Served through December, 2003.

Reviewers

This report has been reviewed in draft form by individuals chosen for their diverse perspectives and technical expertise, in accordance with procedures approved by the NRC's Report Review Committee. The purpose of this independent review is to provide candid and critical comments that will assist the institution in making its published report as sound as possible and to ensure that the report meets institutional standards for objectivity, evidence, and responsiveness to the study charge. The review comments and draft manuscript remain confidential to protect the integrity of the deliberative process. We wish to thank the following individuals for their review of this report:

GEORGE ISHAM, HealthPartners, Inc., Bloomington, MN
ARTHUR AARON LEVIN, Center for Medical Consumers, New York, NY
ANGELA BARRON MCBRIDE, Indiana University; Institute of Medicine Scholar-in-Residence
JOSEPH E. SCHERGER, University of California, San Diego, CA
LISA SIMPSON, All Children's Hospital; University of South Florida, St. Petersburg, FL

Although the reviewers listed above have provided many constructive comments and suggestions, they were not asked to endorse the conclusions or recommendations nor did they see the final draft of the report before its release. The review of this report was overseen by **Elaine L. Larson**, Columbia University, and **Don E. Detmer**, University of Cambridge and University of Virginia. Appointed by the National Research Council and Institute of Medicine, they were responsible for making certain that an independent examination of this report was carried out in accordance with institutional procedures and that all review comments were carefully considered. Responsibility for the final content of this report rests entirely with the authoring committee and the institution.

Preface

This report represents an important addition to a series of studies generated by the Institute of Medicine dedicated to improving the quality and safety of health care. It is firmly grounded in the principles articulated in *Crossing the Quality Chasm: A New Health System for the 21st Century* as a guide for the transformation of our current health care delivery system—namely the six aims of safety, effectiveness, patient-centeredness, timeliness, efficiency, and equity.

The 1st Annual Crossing the Quality Chasm Summit was convened specifically to address the redesign of the nation's currently broken health care delivery system. As recommended in the *Quality Chasm* report, the summit was focused on improving care processes for a targeted set of priority areas, in this case five common, high-burden chronic conditions: asthma, depression, diabetes, heart failure, and pain control in advanced cancer.

The summit benefited from the contributions and expertise of more than 200 local and national health care leaders who convened to collaborate on the development of strategies for improving the quality of care for individuals with these five chronic illnesses. As described in this report, significant progress is being made toward implementing the above six aims in communities across the country. It is our hope that readers will be encouraged by the support of the national champions who participated in the summit and expressed their support for efforts to facilitate the broad achievement of key strategic priorities.

The reader of this report will also appreciate how much more is required from every stakeholder in the American health care system if the goals of optimal quality and safety are to be achieved.

I am deeply appreciative of the support of our sponsor, The Robert Wood Johnson Foundation; my colleagues on the Institute of Medicine committee who helped organize and lead the summit; and all who so generously contributed their experience, judgment, and expertise to this effort.

Reed V. Tuckson, M.D.
Chair
August 2004

Foreword

In January 2004, the Institute of Medicine (IOM) was pleased to convene the 1st Annual Crossing the Quality Chasm Summit. This was a high-energy endeavor designed to move us closer to realizing the vision for the nation's health care system described in the 2001 IOM report *Crossing the Quality Chasm: A New Health System for the 21st Century*. That report called for fundamental redesign of the current system. To begin this transformation, the report recommended focusing on a set of priority conditions, taking into account frequency, burden, and resource use. A subsequent IOM report, *Priority Areas for National Action: Transforming Health Care Quality* identified 20 such areas, 5 of which—asthma, depression, diabetes, heart failure, and pain control in advanced cancer—were initially targeted for the summit's work.

At the summit, representatives of innovative communities from across the country joined forces with national leaders and organizations to identify strategies for achieving high-quality care for patients burdened with these five chronic illnesses. The synergy between local and national leaders at the summit was strong, and the strategies put forth are actionable now. The essential goal is to close the gap between what we know to be best practice and how care is routinely delivered today.

Although much work remains to achieve the kind of fundamental change called for in the *Quality Chasm* report, it is apparent that we are well on our way. I applaud the communities and national champions who participated in the summit for their creative approaches and their dedication to improving the quality and safety of health care for all Americans.

Harvey V. Fineberg, M.D., Ph.D.
President, Institute of Medicine
August 2004

Acknowledgments

The Committee on the Crossing the Quality Chasm Summit wishes to acknowledge the many people whose contributions made this report possible. We appreciate how willingly and generously these individuals contributed their time and expertise to assist the committee.

The committee benefited from the knowledge and input of members of the liaison panel: Brian Austin, MacColl Institute for Health Care Innovation at Group Health Cooperative; Donald M Berwick, Institute for Healthcare Improvement; Maureen Bisognano, Institute for Healthcare Improvement; Carolyn M. Clancy, Agency for Healthcare Research and Quality; Lisa M. Koonin, Centers for Disease Control and Prevention; Dan Stryer, Agency for Healthcare Research and Quality; Ed Wagner, MacColl Institute for Health Care Innovation at Group Health Cooperative; and Stephanie Zaza, Centers for Disease Control and Prevention.

Presenters and panelists helped inform and enlighten summit participants: Donald M. Berwick, Institute for Healthcare Improvement; William L. Bruning, Mid-America Coalition on Health Care Community Initiative on Depression; Albert D. Charbonneau, Rochester Health Commission; Helen Darling, President, National Business Group on Health; Jack C. Ebeler, Alliance of Community Health Plans; Harvey V. Fineberg, Institute of Medicine; Henry Gaines, United Automobile Workers/General Motors Community Health Initiatives; George J. Isham, HealthPartners, Inc.; Sylvia Drew Ivie, The Help Everyone Clinic, Inc.; John Lumpkin, The Robert Wood Johnson Foundation; Jay M. Portnoy, Children's Mercy Hospital; and Martha Whitecotton, Carolinas Medical Center.

Facilitators for the cross-cutting strategy sessions were invaluable to a successful and productive summit: Gerard F. Anderson, The Johns Hopkins University; David Brailer, Health Technology Center; Christine K. Cassel, American Board of Internal Medicine; Russell E. Glasgow, Kaiser Permanente Colorado; Judith Hibbard, University of Oregon; Arnold Milstein, Pacific Business Group on Health; Shoshanna Sofaer, Baruch College; and David M. Stevens, Agency for Healthcare Research and Quality.

Summit scribes provided timely and vital recording of work produced during the strategy sessions: Shari M. Erickson, Institute of Medicine; Beverly Lunsford, The Washington Home; Elizabeth McCann, medical student at Columbia College of Physicians and Surgeons; Sydney Morss Dy, the Johns Hopkins Bloomberg School of Public Health; Hsien Seow, The Washington Home; Lynne Page Snyder, Institute of Medicine; and Anne Wilkinson, the RAND Corporation. Special thanks also go to Joanne Lynn of The Washington Home Center for Palliative Care Studies for providing the student volunteers to help with recording.

Webcasts and transcripts of the summit were graciously facilitated by the Kaiser Family Foundation. They are freely accessible at <http://www.kaisernetwork.org/healthcast/iom/06jan04>.

Support for this project was generously provided by The Robert Wood Johnson Foundation. We are also grateful to the Johns Hopkins Bloomberg School of Public Health for its support of the summit's cross-cutting strategy sessions.

Contents

EXECUTIVE SUMMARY 1
  Abstract 1
  Priority Areas for Focusing and Implementing the *Quality Chasm* Vision 2
  1st Annual Crossing the Quality Chasm Summit 2
  Setting the Context for the Summit 6
  Cross-Cutting Sessions 6
  Condition-Specific Action Plans 10
  Next Steps 11

1 INTRODUCTION 13
  Background 13
  The Quality Chasm Summit 15
  Scope and Organization of the Report 24

2 MEASUREMENT 27
  Definition and Overarching Themes 27
  Key Strategies 28
  Closing Statement 35

3 INFORMATION AND COMMUNICATIONS TECHNOLOGY 37
  Definition and Overarching Themes 37
  Key Strategies 38
  Closing Statement 44

4 CARE COODINATION 47
  Definition and Overarching Themes 47
  Key Strategies 48
  Closing Statement 55

5 PATIENT SELF-MANAGEMENT SUPPORT 57
  Definition and Overarching Themes 57
  Key Strategies 58
  Closing Statement 65

6 FINANCE 67
  Definition and Overarching Themes 67
  Key Strategies 69
  Closing Statement 75

7	**COALITION BUILDING** 77
	Definition and Overarching Themes 77
	Key Strategies 78
	Closing Statement 83

8	**CONDITION-SPECIFIC ACTION PLANS** 85
	Asthma 86
	Depression 88
	Diabetes 90
	Heart Failure 91
	Pain Control in Advanced Cancer 93

9	**NEXT STEPS** 97
	Synopsis of Reactor Panel and Audience Feedback 97
	Commitments of National Champions 99
	Closing Statement 108

APPENDIX A—BIOGRAPHICAL SKETCHES OF COMMITTEE MEMBERS 111
APPENDIX B—*QUALITY CHASM* SELECTED BIBLIOGRAPHY 117
APPENDIX C—DESCRIPTIONS OF SUMMIT COMMUNITIES 119
APPENDIX D—COMMUNITY SELECTION CRITERIA 125
APPENDIX E—SUMMIT ATTENDEES 129
APPENDIX F—CONFERENCE PREWORK AND SAMPLE MATRICES 139
APPENDIX G—SUMMIT PLANNING 149
APPENDIX H—SUMMIT AGENDA 151
APPENDIX I—FACILITATING THE SUMMIT WORKING GROUPS 155
APPENDIX J—CONDITION-SPECIFIC WORKING GROUP QUESTIONS 157

Executive Summary

ABSTRACT

On January 6 and 7, 2004, the Institute of Medicine (IOM) hosted the 1st Annual Crossing the Quality Chasm Summit, convening a group of national and community health care leaders to pool their knowledge and resources with regard to strategies for improving patient care for five common chronic illnesses. This summit was a direct outgrowth and continuation of the recommendations put forth in the 2001 IOM report *Crossing the Quality Chasm: A New Health System for the 21st Century*. The summit's purpose was to offer specific guidance at both the community and national levels for overcoming the challenges to the provision of high-quality care articulated in the *Quality Chasm* report and for moving closer to achievement of the patient-centered health care system envisioned therein.

The Institute of Medicine's (IOM) 2001 report *Crossing the Quality Chasm: A New Health System for the 21st Century* rose out of a series of studies conducted by the IOM and others documenting serious and widespread quality problems in the nation's health care system (Chassin and Galvin, 1998; IOM, 2000; President's Advisory Commission on Consumer Protection and Quality in the Health Care Industry, 1998; Schuster et al., 1998). Disturbing examples of *overuse* of procedures that cannot help, *underuse* of procedures known to be beneficial, and *misuse* or errors of execution of care are pervasive (Bates et al., 1995; Berwick, 2004; Leatherman and McCarthy, 2002; Wang et al., 2000; Wennberg et al., 2004). And despite more than a decade of alarming statistics, the quality of care the average American receives is still unacceptable. This observation is supported by a recent study published in the *New England Journal of Medicine* revealing that on average, Americans have just over a 50 percent chance of receiving recommended care for a host of acute and chronic conditions, as well as preventive services (McGlynn et al., 2003).

Given the magnitude and urgency of this problem, the *Quality Chasm* report called not for incremental tentative steps, but a major overhaul of the current health care delivery system. Though reforming a system as vast and complex as American health care is a daunting task, the *Quality Chasm* report distilled the principles of change into six guiding aims: health care should be *safe, effective, patient-centered, timely, efficient, and equitable* (IOM, 2001:5).

PRIORITY AREAS FOR FOCUSING AND IMPLEMENTING THE *QUALITY CHASM* VISION

As a starting point for translating the above six aims into clinical reality, the *Quality Chasm* report recommended focusing on a set of common chronic conditions that account for the majority of the nation's health care burden and resource consumption (Druss et al., 2002, 2001; Hoffman et al., 1996; Partnership for Prevention, 2002). In response, an IOM committee was convened to select at least 15 priority conditions for which reform strategies should be implemented. After carefully analyzing such criteria as impact on the population, potential for improvement, and inclusiveness for a broad range of individuals, health care settings, and providers, the committee identified 20 priority clinical areas for national action. These 20 areas represent the full spectrum of health care, including preventive care, acute and chronic disease management, and palliative care (IOM, 2003).

1ST ANNUAL CROSSING THE QUALITY CHASM SUMMIT

The 1st Annual Crossing the Quality Chasm Summit was charged with catalyzing the transformation of the health care delivery system as delineated in the *Quality Chasm* report. A diverse committee representing a wide range of perspectives from many health care sectors was assembled to organize and lead this activity. While the committee is responsible for the overall quality and accuracy of this report as a record of what transpired at the summit, the views contained herein are not necessarily those of the committee.

In an effort to manage this enormous undertaking, the committee decided to narrow its focus to 5 of the original 20 priority areas—asthma, depression, diabetes, heart failure, and pain control in advanced cancer—with the goal that lessons learned from this initial summit would then be disseminated and further applied to the remaining 15 priority areas and beyond. The committee then identified 6 critical cross-cutting topics applicable to all of these priority areas: measurement, information and communications technology, care coordination, patient self-management support, finance, and community coalition building.

EXECUTIVE SUMMARY

It was decided that the summit should have a community focus, as successful community innovations can provide a lens for viewing how to redesign care delivery systems, and involving community stakeholders would help mobilize the next round of quality improvement efforts. Communities can also serve as "laboratories of innovation" to assess what does and does not work before a policy is adopted nationally. Additionally, working at the community level can strengthen the interface between the personal and the population-based health systems.

Having laid this groundwork, the committee identified three objectives for the summit:

- To stimulate and further local and national quality improvement efforts, consistent with the IOM's *Crossing the Quality Chasm* report, focusing on five priority areas—asthma, depression, diabetes, heart failure, and pain control in advanced cancer.

- To describe measurable aims and appropriate strategies for improving care in the five targeted priority areas, including endorsing performance measures necessary to assess progress over 3 to 5 years.[1]

- To stimulate supportive interrelationships and synergies between locally based efforts and resources at the national level, and to make highly visible the resulting commitments.

To achieve these objectives, the committee solicited the input and advice of several liaison groups, including the Centers for Disease Control and Prevention; the Institute for Healthcare Improvement; the MacColl Institute for Healthcare Innovation at Group Health Cooperative; and the Agency for Healthcare Research and Quality. The committee also identified summit attendees who would best serve to inform and advance the *Quality Chasm* vision. More than 200 individuals participated in this event, including nationally recognized experts in the five clinical conditions and six cross-cutting areas; representatives of 15 local communities (see Box ES-1), chosen from a pool of 90 across the country; and leaders from national organizations referred to as "national champions" (see Box ES-2), which through their influence could expedite progress at the local level.[2] The design of the summit is unique in the IOM's experience in that it brought together innovative local and regional providers ("doers") and national leaders, as well as representatives of national public, voluntary, and private organizations ("environments").

"Each of the communities that are participating is a building block. Each is an experimental center. Each is a place of innovation. And if we take advantage of our mutual learning in the course of this day to renew our own sense of possibility and direction then the objectives of our meeting will have been accomplished."

—Harvey Fineberg, President, IOM

---

[1] Although performance measurement standards for each condition were called for by the participants—as noted at a number of points in this report—the summit itself did not endorse any specific performance measures for the targeted conditions.

[2] There are many champions of health care quality improvement around the nation. Some play on a national stage in the scope of their work, while some are regional and others are located in communities. Those listed are a number of key players who work at the national level; some of them, as well as others not listed, make an impact at the international level as well. It is hoped that others will join this list, and we emphasize that any omissions are unintentional.

> **Box ES-1. Summit Communities**
>
> - Asthma communities
>   - Children's Mercy Hospital/Kansas City Asthma Coalition
>   - Controlling Asthma in the Richmond Metropolitan Area (CARMA)
>   - The Pediatric/Adult Asthma Coalition of New Jersey
>   - Philadelphia Department of Health
>
> - Depression communities
>   - Intermountain Health Care–Depression in Primary Care Initiative
>   - Mid-America Coalition on Health Care Community Initiative on Depression
>
> - Diabetes communities
>   - The Asheville Project
>   - County of Santa Cruz, California
>   - Madigan Army Medical Center
>   - The Washington State Diabetes Collaborative
>
> - Heart failure communities
>   - Grand Rapids Medical Education and Research Center
>   - Greater Flint Health Coalition
>   - The Oregon Heart Failure Project
>
> - Pain control in advanced cancer communities
>   - Kaiser-Bellflower
>   - Rochester Health Commission

Box ES-2. National Champions

- Agency for Healthcare Research and Quality
- Alliance of Community Health Plans
- American Association of Retired Persons
- American Board of Internal Medicine
- American Cancer Society
- American Diabetes Association
- American Heart Association
- American Hospital Association
- American Pain Foundation
- America's Health Insurance Plans
- Blue Cross and Blue Shield Association
- Bridges to Excellence
- Centers for Disease Control and Prevention
- Centers for Medicare and Medicaid Services
- General Electric Company
- Grantmakers in Health
- Institute for Healthcare Improvement
- Institute of Medicine
- Joint Commission on Accreditation of Healthcare Organizations
- Leapfrog Group
- MacColl Institute for Healthcare Innovation at Group Health Cooperative
- National Association of Community Health Centers
- National Business Coalition on Health
- National Business Group on Health
- National Cancer Institute
- National Center for Healthcare Leadership
- National Committee for Quality Assurance
- National Quality Forum
- Pacific Business Group on Health
- Substance Abuse and Mental Health Services Administration
- The Robert Wood Johnson Foundation
- UnitedHealth Group
- URAC
- VHA, Inc.

SETTING THE CONTEXT FOR THE SUMMIT

In launching the summit, Reed Tuckson, chair of the IOM committee that organized this event, set the stage by positioning the patient as "true north"—serving as a compass to steer and guide health care reform efforts (Berwick, 2002). In this vein, the summit was organized to reinforce the *Quality Chasm* report's core tenet of patient-centered health care. Patient-centered care has different meanings for each patient. For some patients it may mean care only for themselves; for others it includes both patients and their families; while for others it comprises non–professionally trained caregivers who serve as a safety net. When the "patient" is referred to in this report, the term implicitly represents this full range of circumstances.

At the summit, participants first heard from Martha Whitecotton, a registered nurse, who poignantly described the shortfalls of the current health care delivery system by relaying her family's experiences in trying to obtain high-quality care for a child with major depression. She highlighted gaps and deficiencies in care relevant not only to depression, but to all chronic conditions. Examples included lack of a well-coordinated care plan, poor communication among multiple clinicians involved in a patient's care, and failure to inform patients and their families about best practices. Redressing these deficiencies became the focus of the work at the summit.

Continuing on this theme during his keynote speech, Don Berwick, President of the Institute for Healthcare Improvement, reiterated the emphasis on honoring the patient—respecting patients' preferences, needs, ethnicity, and diversity, and viewing them as the ultimate source of control. He translated the *Quality Chasm* aims from the patient's perspective: "to have health care with no needless deaths, no needless pain or suffering, no unwanted waiting, no helplessness, and no waste" (Berwick, 2004). Embracing this approach requires not segregating patients into silos as defined by their disease, but taking a more holistic approach to their care. The summit was deliberately structured to reflect this philosophy, emphasizing solutions that transcend any one chronic illness, in the belief that applying lessons from the core set of five priority conditions to other conditions would be expedited if the cross-cutting areas were the central focus.

"The ultimate judge of the quality of our work is the patient, end of story."

—Don Berwick, summit keynote speaker

CROSS-CUTTING SESSIONS

The confirmed diagnosis of a broken, fragmented health care delivery system led directly to the identification of the six cross-cutting areas enumerated above. These areas largely reflect those discussed in the *Quality Chasm* series of reports, with one exception—community coalition building, added to reflect the interests and needs of summit participants from communities. The purpose of the sessions in these six areas was to identify strategies and opportunities for overcoming barriers to high-quality care, learning from communities that have made promising advances, as well as from distinguished individuals and organizations recognized as leaders in these fields. Following is a synthesis of the key strategies to be explored as identified by the summit participants (summarized in Boxes ES-3 through ES-8).

> **Box ES-3. Measurement: Key Strategies**
>
> - Integrating measurement into the delivery of care to benefit patient care
> - Improving information and communications technology infrastructure to reduce the burden of data collection
> - Focusing on longitudinal change in performance and patient-centered outcomes in addition to point-in-time measures
> - Improving public reporting by effectively disseminating results to diverse audiences

Measurement

Summit participants called for national organizations, accrediting agencies, and appropriate subspecialty providers to agree on a defined, well-validated set of performance measures for the 5 chronic conditions featured at the summit, subsequently to be expanded to the other 15 priority areas. At present, clinicians collect different data for multiple parties, making the process not only overwhelming, but often infeasible in a climate of limited resources. A parsimonious set of measures would:

- Reduce redundancy and ease the load of data collection.
- Permit benchmarking and meaningful comparisons within organizations, across communities, and nationally.
- Allow for longitudinal patient-focused measures that appraise changes in health status and function over time.
- Capture community-based measures derived from actionable community-wide aims.

To create relevant measurement sets, participants advanced the idea of a matrix, with the six *Quality Chasm* aims on one axis and the priority areas on the other, whose cells would be populated with appropriate measures. They also supported public reporting of quality outcomes, including patient-centered measures of experience. Dissemination of this information must be done in a way that is meaningful and useful to different audiences.

> **Box ES-4. Information and Communications Technology: Key Strategies**
>
> - Using standardized systems
> - Leveraging federal leadership to accelerate the adoption of electronic health records
> - Creating a public utility that holds data at the local level

Information and Communications Technology

The importance of patients' access to and control of their health records was reiterated during many of the sessions at the summit. Ideally, patient health information would be stored in a transportable electronic format, easily retrieved from any computer regardless of software or system requirements. A companion goal would be for all providers' offices to have electronic health records. Both of these visions highlight the urgent need for national data standards, as transmitting health information across organizational and regional boundaries is severely stymied today by the inability of different computer systems to "talk" to each other in a common language—referred to as lack of interoperability. Accelerating the uptake of information and communications technology would involve a dual strategy of new financial incentives for clinicians from the private sector to invest in the necessary infrastructure, such as the Bridges to Excellence program (Bridges to Excellence, 2004), and federal leadership in promulgating national data standards (IOM, 2002a). Additionally, participants characterized health data as a public good and suggested creating a public utility that would store these data, making them accessible at the community level.

and holding each team member accountable for ensuring that a patient's care is properly managed. Participants emphasized that practicing clinicians, managers, educational leaders, and current students will need preparation and guidance on care coordination principles, such as working in interdisciplinary teams, in both the didactic and clinical components of their initial and ongoing professional training.

> **Box ES-5. Care Coordination: Key Strategies**
>
> - Aligning financial incentives
> - Providing educational supports, including multidisciplinary health professions education, teaching of care coordination principles in academic settings, and development of care teams
> - Instituting patient-centered health records, supported by information and communications technology
> - Ensuring accountability and defining roles for care

> **Box ES-6. Patient Self-Management Support: Key Strategies**
>
> - Identifying and disseminating evidence-based self-management practices
> - Recognizing the centrality of self-management to good patient care and incorporating it into health care culture
> - Developing programs and tools applicable to diverse populations
> - Providing incentives for the appropriate use of self-management supports integrated into the delivery of health care
> - Making better use of all members of the health care team

Care Coordination

To address the problem of care coordination not being routinely reimbursed under most payment schemes today, participants emphasized the need for a shared vision around an operational construct—consistent with the evidence base—defining what good care coordination would be. Once operationalized, care coordination could then be measured, with the goal of quickly disseminating successful reimbursement models.

Effective management of chronic conditions requires the delivery of many services, hand-offs to other specialists, and aggressive follow-up. To address these challenges, participants suggested a two-pronged approach: (1) empowering patients and families to play a central role in the diffusion and exchange of their health information, and (2) formulating clearly defined roles for health care practitioners

Patient Self-Management Support

Despite the strong evidence base for many self-management practices, it is often difficult for practitioners to assess best practices or to distinguish between those that are grounded in evidence and those that are not (Bodenheimer et al., 2002; Lorig et al., 1999, 2001). Participants suggested consolidating this information and disseminating it to providers, patients, and their families through a centralized clearinghouse. Additionally, they favored aggressive expansion of the existing evidence base—both learning from rapid-cycle practical models and, in parallel, using these experiences to inform and develop a firmer scientific base.

It was suggested that if self-management is to be recognized as an integral component of high-quality care, demand for these services must be created among clinicians and patients and incorporated into the mainstream health care culture. Barriers to widespread adoption of self-management practices include brief, rigidly scheduled office visits, which are not conducive to more labor-intensive interactions, such as completing a patient-generated action plan, and the lack of reimbursement for self-management support. Additionally, self-management programs must be flexible enough to allow for tailoring to individual patient preferences, as well as culturally, linguistically, age, gender, and lifestyle appropriate. Particular attention should be paid to health literacy and the ability to assimilate and process medical information (IOM, 2004). As with care coordination, defining roles and making more efficient use of the talents and skills of all members of the health care team are necessary, along with teaching these principles in academic and clinical settings. Families and other caregivers also need to be supported and provided adequate resources to assist patients in managing their condition.

Box ES-7. Finance: Key Strategies

- Instituting performance-based payment models
- Implementing evidence-based benefit design
- Providing payment for proven quality support services—care coordination and patient self-management support
- Engaging consumers with information and incentives

Finance

As a core strategy, participants proposed shifting to performance-based payment models that pay for performance and align incentives with evidence-based high-quality care. This approach assumes that the problem may not be one of insufficient resources, but of substantial waste and variation in the current health care system (Fisher et al., 2003a,b). Thus any changes to the present finance system would be budget neutral—redirecting and redistributing revenue streams in the many organizations that make up the larger health care system, rather than adding to the total funding for that system.

Infusing evidence-based medicine into benefit design was identified as another way to apply resources toward more effective care. For example, benefit packages could be created that would cover bundles of high-value services known to work clinically for chronic illnesses—such as HbA_1c monitoring, annual eye and foot exams, lipid testing, and blood pressure control for diabetics.

The strategy of empowering consumers to modify their behavior by using monetary incentives or providing them with information important to their health was also proposed. As with all of the proposals in this area, the aim is not to simply shift costs to consumers—as is the growing trend—but instead to institute cost sharing with consumers, designed with the specific intent of encouraging them to obtain the right care at the right time. Finally, as discussed by participants addressing care coordination and self-management, reimbursement for these support services will require a shift from the current piecemeal approach of paying for individual clinician encounters to paying for elements linked to systems of care involving a team of diverse practitioners.

> **Box ES-8. Community Coalition Building: Key Strategies**
>
> - Determining who is going to be involved in the coalition
> - Getting people to agree on a common objective and determining how to measure whether this objective has been achieved

Community Coalition Building

Coalitions are organizational structures that integrate and support the work of multiple diverse stakeholders on a focused, shared goal. Input from participants prior to the summit revealed the desire for additional knowledge and skills in developing community engagement. In response, a session in this area was added to identify strategies that communities might use to establish and sustain a coalition, with particular attention to public–private partnerships and ways to gather the necessary human and financial resources. For the purposes of the summit, the aim of coalition building was identified as improving the quality and efficiency of care at the community level.

The first step in the process of activating a coalition is to ensure a proper balance among stakeholder groups—at both the community and organizational levels. Often this entails bringing together groups with competing interests. To minimize conflicts and avoid potential gridlock once the coalition has been assembled, it is critical to identify a common objective that supercedes differences in perspectives. Transparency regarding biases and conflicts of interest is paramount. Early on in the process, it is prudent to determine what issues are most important to each participant and then negotiate a workable solution that is sensitive to those concerns (Sofaer, 2003).

Once consensus has been reached around an actionable and manageable goal, the coalition must establish objectives and agree on how its impact on the community will be measured, both quantitatively and qualitatively. Care must be taken in selecting metrics that are meaningful to diverse members of the community and relevant to multiple stakeholder groups. Measurement has the dual purpose of documenting progress while also supporting a shared accountability that solidifies community cohesion and directs the rational use of coalition resources to areas of need. Documenting positive outcomes—and reasons for negative ones—helps coalitions acquire additional support and resources.

CONDITION-SPECIFIC ACTION PLANS

The cross-cutting sessions helped prepare summit participants for the condition-specific work that followed. The composition of the condition-specific working groups balanced local- and national-level stakeholder groups, individuals with proficiency in the cross-cutting areas, and nationally recognized experts in the chronic conditions represented. Before the summit, the participating communities completed substantial preparatory work to identify gaps in their current care programs as compared with "ideal" evidence-based care. As a result, it was possible to minimize the time spent reviewing past accomplishments and obstacles during the summit and to focus on shared learning and collaborative problem solving.

In identifying strategies most relevant to each priority condition, participants acknowledged that for these five conditions, health care disparities persist for minority/underserved populations within communities and that addressing this issue should be a high priority (IOM, 2002b). Several overlapping strategies were proposed across the condition-specific working groups, echoing the themes that emerged during the cross-cutting sessions.

Restructuring the current finance system to reward well-integrated care and providing supports for patient self-management, for example, was a recurring topic. Information and communications technology figured prominently as an enabling tool for data collection, decision support, and improved flow of communication across providers. Measurement was a theme for all the strategies—particularly to establish short- and long-term goals. Proposals to support a patient-centered health environment ranged from research to better understand the wants and needs of patients with diabetes, to concrete actions such as ensuring that every patient has portable electronic health summaries.

Two working groups—addressing asthma and heart failure—targeted community collaborations to establish partnerships and build capacity and to create mechanisms for patients and families to take control of their chronic illness(es). Training and education on appropriate screening and treatment was a salient issue for the depression group, since depression is a major comorbidity for many chronic conditions, such as diabetes and heart failure. The heart failure group called for greater clinical engagement, focusing on the creation of methods that would make it easier for clinicians to provide efficient evidence-based care, such as dissemination of guidelines and the development and maintenance of registries. For the group addressing pain control in advanced cancer, a tactic proposed was to raise the bar on public awareness—making it inconceivable to tolerate bad cancer pain. This group expressed the need for strong coordinated leadership to "carry the ball" and convene key stakeholder groups. In addition, clinicians' fears of legal or professional retribution for prescribing opioids—even when warranted— need to be addressed at the regulatory level.

NEXT STEPS

The central message emerging from the 1st Annual Crossing the Quality Chasm Summit is that, despite environmental obstacles to system redesign, some communities are making headway in the struggle to deliver health care that embodies, at least in part, the six aims set forth in the *Quality Chasm* report. Other communities can learn from and build on those experiences. The summit offered a public forum for "national champions" to step up and announce what they are willing to do to help facilitate community efforts, while also bringing national experts into the discussion to help translate local experiences to speak to a larger audience. It is hoped that the summit will be the first of many such efforts dedicated to further implementing the vision laid out in the *Quality Chasm* report.

REFERENCES

Bates DW, Cullen DJ, Laird N, Petersen LA, Small SD, Servi D, Laffel G, Sweitzer BJ, Shea BF, Hallisey R. 1995. Incidence of adverse drug events and potential adverse drug events: Implications for prevention. ADE Prevention Study Group. *The Journal of the American Medical Association* 274(1):29–34.

Berwick DM. 2002. A User's Guide for the IOM's 'Quality Chasm' Report. *Health Affairs (Millwood, VA)* 21(3):80–90.

Berwick DM. 2004. *Crossing the Quality Chasm: Health Care for the 21st Century*. Powerpoint Presentation.

Bodenheimer T, Lorig K, Holman H, Grumbach K. 2002. Patient self-management of chronic disease in primary care. *The Journal of the American Medical Association* 288(19):2469–2475.

Bridges to Excellence. 2004. *Bridges to Excellence: Rewarding Quality across the Health Care System*. [Online]. Available: http://www.bridgestoexcellence.org/bte/ [accessed April 29, 2004].

Chassin MR, Galvin RW. 1998. The urgent need to improve health care quality. Institute of Medicine National Roundtable on Health Care Quality. *The Journal of the American Medical Association* 280(11):1000–1005.

Druss BG, Marcus SC, Olfson M, Pincus HA. 2002. The most expensive medical conditions in America: This nationwide study found that the most disabling conditions are not necessarily the ones we spend the most to treat. *Health Affairs (Millwood, VA)* 21(4):105–111.

Druss BG, Marcus SC, Olfson M, Tanielian T, Elinson L, Pincus HA. 2001. Comparing the national economic burden of five chronic conditions. *Health Affairs (Millwood, VA)* 20(6):233–241.

Fisher ES, Wennberg DE, Stukel TA, Gottlieb DJ, Lucas FL, Pinder EL. 2003a. The implications of regional variations in Medicare spending. Part 2: Health outcomes and satisfaction with care. *Annals of Internal Medicine* 138(4):288–298.

Fisher ES, Wennberg DE, Stukel TA, Gottlieb DJ, Lucas FL, Pinder EL. 2003b. The implications of regional variations in Medicare spending. Part 1: The content, quality, and accessibility of care. *Annals of Internal Medicine* 138(4):273–287.

Hoffman C, Rice D, Sung HY. 1996. Persons with chronic conditions: Their prevalence and costs. *The Journal of the American Medical Association* 276(18):1473–1479.

IOM (Institute of Medicine). 2000. *To Err Is Human: Building a Safer Health System.* Kohn LT, Corrigan JM, Donaldson MS, eds. Washington, DC: National Academy Press.

IOM. 2001. *Crossing the Quality Chasm: A New Health System for the 21st Century.* Washington, DC: National Academy Press.

IOM. 2002a. *Leadership by Example: Coordinating Government Roles in Improving Health Care Quality.* Corrigan JM, Eden J, Smith BM, eds. Washington, DC: National Academy Press.

IOM. 2002b. *Unequal Treatment: Confronting Racial and Ethnic Disparities in Health Care.* Smedley BS, Stith AY, Nelson BD, eds. Washington, DC: National Academy Press.

IOM. 2003. *Priority Areas for National Action: Transforming Health Care Quality.* Adams K, Corrigan JM, eds. Washington, DC: National Academy Press.

IOM. 2004. *Health Literacy: A Prescription to End Confusion.* Nielsen-Bohlman L, Panzer AM, Kindig DA, eds. Washington, DC: National Academy Press.

Leatherman S, McCarthy D. 2002. *Quality of Health Care in the United States: A Chartbook.* New York, NY: The Commonwealth Fund.

Lorig KR, Ritter P, Stewart AL, Sobel DS, Brown BW Jr, Bandura A, Gonzalez VM, Laurent DD, Holman HR. 2001. Chronic disease self-management program: 2-year health status and health care utilization outcomes. *Medical Care* 39(11):1217–1223.

Lorig, KR, Sobel DS, Stewart AL, Brown BW Jr, Bandura A, Ritter P, Gonzalez VM, Laurent DD, Holman HR. 1999. Evidence suggesting that a chronic disease self-management program can improve health status while reducing hospitalization: A randomized trial. *Medical Care* 37(1):5–14.

McGlynn EA, Asch SM, Adams J, Keesey J, Hicks J, DeCristofaro A, Kerr EA. 2003. The quality of health care delivered to adults in the United States. *New England Journal of Medicine* 348(26):2635–2645.

Partnership for Prevention. 2002. *Better Lives for People with Chronic Conditions.* Baltimore, MD: John Hopkins University, Robert Wood Johnson Foundation.

President's Advisory Commission on Consumer Protection and Quality in the Health Care Industry. 1998. *Quality First: Better Health Care for All Americans—Final Report to the President of the United States.* Washington, DC: U.S. Government Printing Office.

Schuster MA, McGlynn EA, Brook RH. 1998. How good is the quality of health care in the United States? *Milbank Quarterly* 76(4):509, 517–563.

Sofaer S. 2003. *Working Together, Moving Ahead.* New York, NY: School of Public Affairs, Baruch College.

Wang PS, Berglund P, Kessler RC. 2000. Recent care of common mental disorders in the United States: Prevalence and conformance with evidence-based recommendations. *Journal of General Internal Medicine* 15(5):284–292.

Wennberg JE, Fisher ES, Stukel TA, Skinner JS, Sharp SM, Bronner KK. 2004. Use of hospitals, physician visits, and hospice care during last six months of life among cohorts loyal to highly respected hospitals in the United States. *British Medical Journal* 328(7440):607–612.

Chapter 1
Introduction

During the last decade, there has been growing recognition among organizations, experts, health professionals, and more recently the American public that serious, widespread, and unacceptable quality problems exist in the nation's health care system (Blendon et al., 2001, 2002; Davis et al., 2002). Numerous studies have documented the scope of this problem and its many facets, including disparities based on race and ethnicity (Chassin, 1998; IOM, 2000, 2001, 2003a; Leatherman and McCarthy, 2002; McGlynn et al., 2003). The 1st Annual Crossing the Quality Chasm Summit was part of a series of efforts undertaken by the Institute of Medicine (IOM) to address this pervasive problem.

BACKGROUND

The IOM report *To Err Is Human: Building a Safer Health System* (IOM, 2000) is credited with helping to raise the public's consciousness about the nation's broken health care system. Its troubling bottom-line finding—that tens of thousands of Americans die each year and hundreds of thousands more suffer not because of their illnesses, but because of the care they are receiving in our nation's hospitals—elevated the quality problem from scientific journals to the evening news and the policy arena. Both *To Err Is Human* and the subsequent IOM report *Crossing the Quality Chasm: A New Health System for the 21st Century* (IOM, 2001) emphasize that placing the blame on physicians, nurses, pharmacists, and others or asking them to just try harder will not solve this critical problem. Patients are needlessly suffering and dying as a result of a faulty system that undermines clinicians' best efforts or does not help them succeed.

To address this urgent national issue, the *Quality Chasm* report challenges the country to undertake a comprehensive reform of the health care delivery system and the policy environment that shapes and influences it. To this end, the report provides overall guidance for the systemic reforms it proposes, setting forth six quality aims for the health care system: it should be safe, effective, patient-centered, timely, efficient, and equitable (see Box 1-1).

Numerous private-sector organizations, the federal and local governments, and communities across the country have launched efforts to redesign the nation's health care system, guided by the vision laid out in the *Quality Chasm* report (AHRQ, 2004; CMS, 2004; JCAHO, 2004; NCQA, 2004; The Leapfrog Group, 2004). These efforts are not always coordinated to the extent they might be for maximum leverage. And despite what they have accomplished, the system's level of performance remains inadequate, some would say even unjust, given the resources our country expends on health care (Millenson, 2003).

The 1st Annual Crossing the Quality Chasm Summit: A Focus on Communities was an effort by the IOM to bring together and catalyze the various committed and innovative leaders across the country toward a highly targeted purpose: improving care for a selected set of clinical conditions within the *Quality Chasm* framework. This report serves as a summary of that 2-day event, held January 6–7, 2004. The committee that planned the summit (see Appendix A for biographical sketches) hopes this report will serve to further activate, coordinate, and integrate the quality efforts of the leaders who attended, as well as other reform-minded individuals from around the nation. While the committee is responsible for the overall quality and accuracy of the report as a record of what transpired at the summit, the views contained herein are not necessarily those of the committee. It is also hoped that this summit will be the first of many such annual events bringing together diverse leaders from across the country to further their work in implementing the vision set forth in the *Quality Chasm* for a 21st-century health care system.

Box 1-1. Six Aims for Health Care Improvement

- *Safe*—avoiding injuries to patients from the care that is intended to help them.
- *Effective*—providing services based on scientific knowledge to all who could benefit and refraining from providing services to those not likely to benefit (avoiding underuse and overuse, respectively).
- *Patient-centered*—providing care that is respectful of and responsive to individual patient preferences, needs, and values and ensuring that patient values guide all clinical decisions.
- *Timely*—reducing waits and sometimes harmful delays for both those who receive and those who give care.
- *Efficient*—avoiding waste, in particular waste of equipment, supplies, ideas, and energy.
- *Equitable*—providing care that does not vary in quality because of personal characteristics such as gender, ethnicity, geographic location, and socioeconomic status.

SOURCE: IOM, 2001:39–40.

INTRODUCTION

THE QUALITY CHASM SUMMIT

Since *Crossing the Quality Chasm* was released in 2001, the IOM has issued six reports focused on implementing various facets of that report's vision for a 21st-century health system (IOM, 2002a,b, 2003a,b,c, 2004). Each of these reports helped lay the foundation for the summit, with two of them being particularly germane: *Priority Areas for National Action: Transforming Health Care Quality* (IOM, 2003c) and *Fostering Rapid Advances in Health Care: Learning from System Demonstrations* (IOM, 2002a). (See Appendix B for a list of references and websites related to the *Quality Chasm* series.)

At the behest of the Agency for Healthcare Research and Quality (AHRQ), the *Priority Areas* report identifies 20 areas—which account for the majority of the nation's health care burden and expenditures—to be the focus of national and local efforts to redesign health care. Five of these 20 areas were selected to be the focus of the summit: asthma, diabetes, heart failure, major depression, and pain control in advanced cancer. These five areas were chosen at the advice of many experts in the field because collectively they touch on all age groups from children to the elderly, are important to a diverse set of payers, and encompass the full spectrum of care delivery; moreover, many existing community efforts addressing these areas can be shared, supported, and disseminated. The committee anticipates that subsequent summits will focus on additional priority areas. Finally, in addition to selecting the priority areas on which to focus at the summit, the committee identified six cross-cutting topics applicable to all of these areas: measurement, information and communications technology, care coordination, patient self-management support, finance, and community coalition building.

Fostering Rapid Advances, written in response to a request from Health and Human Services Secretary Thompson, lays out ideas for health system reform in the form of demonstrations that draw on many of the ideas developed in the *Quality Chasm* series. One of the central premises of that report is that we must support innovations at the local level, which can inform and guide comprehensive national policy. This was also a central premise behind the design of the summit, and one that informed many of its deliberations.

Goal and Objectives

At the start of the summit, Reed Tuckson, chair of the IOM organizing committee, asked participants to "envision this summit as a practical and tangible next step in the process of crossing the quality chasm." Harvey Fineberg, president of the IOM, described the summit as "an effort to bring together agents of change who can work in their communities and with their colleagues to (re)make the health system." Tuckson delineated what the committee hoped the summit would engender: an active dialogue—and even alliances—between local leaders involved in shaping community health systems and national leaders who influence the quality of the nation's health care infrastructure, which he described as a "two-way street." Tuckson expressed what the committee hoped would result from such a dialogue: articulation of on-the-ground experiences to inform and influence national-level policies, and the fostering of national action and policy directed at the local level to sustain and encourage innovators or early adopters (Berwick, 2003). Box 1-2 presents the objectives of the summit.

We are motivated by the reality of what is at stake…whether people shall live or whether they shall prematurely die….And we have all been learning as we go, learning as we lay the tracks and run the trains over the chasms in our health care system. But much more progress is needed, and much more quickly."

—Reed Tuckson, committee chair

> **Box 1-2. 1st Annual Crossing the Quality Chasm Summit: Objectives**
>
> - To stimulate and further local and national quality improvement efforts, consistent with the IOM's *Crossing the Quality Chasm* report, focusing on five priority areas—asthma, depression, diabetes, heart failure, and pain control in advanced cancer.
> - To describe measurable aims and appropriate strategies for improving care in the five targeted priority areas, including endorsing performance measures necessary to assess progress over 3 to 5 years.[1]
> - To stimulate supportive interrelationships and synergies between locally based efforts and resources at the national level, and to make highly visible the resulting commitments.

The summit participants included approximately 45 leaders from 15 communities across the country, selected from a pool of 90 communities identified as innovative in improving quality of care in at least one of the five targeted clinical areas (see Appendix C for a description of the communities and Appendix D for selection criteria). The 15 communities selected (see Box 1-3) are quite diverse, and while largely anchored in a geographic region, they are not solely defined by geography but rather by a "community of interest." For example, they include coalitions that encompass all of the stakeholders in a local market and others that comprise a more selective group; a state-level initiative involving providers, schools, and others focused almost entirely on patient and clinician education; and an integrated delivery system that has established links to community resources, including the public health department and community health centers.

Participants also included leaders from national organizations referred to as "national champions" (see Box 1-4), which through their influence could expedite progress at the local level.[2] These national leaders and other experts who attended the summit (see Appendix E) represented a broad range of organizations, including health plans, hospitals, physician groups, federal agencies, employer coalitions, consumer advocacy groups, quality groups, and disease-specific organizations, among others.

The participants worked together to identify key strategies for enhancing care in the five clinical areas that were the focus of the summit. These strategies had many common themes, the most prevalent being focused on information and communications technology, finance, and measurement. The strategies also addressed comorbidities or, as one summit participant, Bruce Bagley from the American Academy of Family Physicians, noted, "the necessity of taking care of the patient as a whole patient and not as a segment of disease."

---

[1] Although performance measurement standards for each condition were called for by the participants—as noted at a number of points in this report—the summit itself did not endorse any specific performance measures for the targeted conditions.

[2] There are many champions of health care quality improvement around the nation. Some play on a national stage in the scope of their work, while some are regional and others are located in communities. Those listed are a number of key players who work at the national level; some of them, as well as others not listed, make an impact at the international level as well. It is hoped that others will join this list, and we emphasize that any omissions are unintentional.

Box 1-3. Summit Communities

- Asthma communities
    - Children's Mercy Hospital/Kansas City Asthma Coalition
    - Controlling Asthma in the Richmond Metropolitan Area (CARMA)
    - The Pediatric/Adult Asthma Coalition of New Jersey
    - Philadelphia Department of Health

- Depression communities
    - Intermountain Health Care–Depression in Primary Care Initiative
    - Mid-America Coalition on Health Care Community Initiative on Depression

- Diabetes communities
    - The Asheville Project
    - County of Santa Cruz, California
    - Madigan Army Medical Center
    - The Washington State Diabetes Collaborative

- Heart failure communities
    - Grand Rapids Medical Education and Research Center
    - Greater Flint Health Coalition
    - The Oregon Heart Failure Project

- Pain control in advanced cancer communities
    - Kaiser-Bellflower
    - Rochester Health Commission

Box 1-4. National Champions

- Agency for Healthcare Research and Quality
- Alliance of Community Health Plans
- American Association of Retired Persons
- American Board of Internal Medicine
- American Cancer Society
- American Diabetes Association
- American Heart Association
- American Hospital Association
- American Pain Foundation
- America's Health Insurance Plans
- Blue Cross and Blue Shield Association
- Bridges to Excellence
- Centers for Disease Control and Prevention
- Centers for Medicare and Medicaid Services
- General Electric Company
- Grantmakers in Health
- Institute for Healthcare Improvement
- Institute of Medicine
- Joint Commission on Accreditation of Healthcare Organizations
- Leapfrog Group
- MacColl Institute for Healthcare Innovation at Group Health Cooperative
- National Association of Community Health Centers
- National Business Coalition on Health
- National Business Group on Health
- National Cancer Institute
- National Center for Healthcare Leadership
- National Committee for Quality Assurance
- National Quality Forum
- Pacific Business Group on Health
- Substance Abuse and Mental Health Services Administration
- The Robert Wood Johnson Foundation
- UnitedHealth Group
- URAC
- VHA, Inc.

Introduction

John Lumpkin of The Robert Wood Johnson Foundation, which funded the summit, characterized the larger environment in which the event was taking place in the spirit of Dickens' *A Tale of Two Cities*—as the best and worst of times. Among his characterization of what was the worst, he cited a recent *New England Journal of Medicine* article revealing that Americans receive only about 50 percent of the care that the evidence suggests they should get (McGlynn et al., 2003). He characterized the best as including the many more tools the field has to improve quality and the varied, committed, and talented stakeholders represented by the summit participants, who are developing community-based approaches to improving quality that hold promise for making a real difference.

Patients at the Center, with Community as a Focus

Reed Tuckson opened the 2-day summit by emphasizing that the patient must be at the center of all reform efforts. In this vein, he introduced the consumer panel, which began with a patient's story, relayed by a family member who is also a nurse. Martha Whitecotton told of her son's struggle with major depression, highlighting the gaps and dysfunctions that prevented him from receiving the best possible care. She touched on themes that are endemic to care not just for depression, but for all chronic conditions and across the entire health care system. In particular, Whitecotton stated, drawing from the *Quality Chasm* report, "patients' experiences should be the fundamental source of the definition of quality...[but] we have a long way to go." Patient-centered care has different meanings for each patient. For some patients it may mean care only for themselves; for others it includes both patients and their families; while for others it comprises non–professionally trained caregivers who serve as a safety net. When the "patient" is referred to in this report, the term implicitly represents this range of circumstances.

Don Berwick, president of the Institute for Healthcare Improvement and the summit's keynote speaker, echoed the notion that the patient must serve as the compass for the system. He asked the participants to develop a "fundamentally new view of the patient, not as the object of our care, not as a guest in our house, but as the host of our work and as the person who ultimately has the say in what we do or do not do." Berwick further challenged the group by saying that "we must learn to honor individual choices, respecting the variability in need, the variability in ethnicity and diversity, and the need for structures [that respect] the habits and spirits of the people we serve."

Henry Gaines of the Greater Flint Health Coalition in Genesee County, Michigan, provided an example of how one community put a program in place to change the culture for the delivery of maternal and child health care services. Friendly Access—developed to increase access, satisfaction, and utilization—is based in part on the well-regarded customer service model developed by the Disney Institute. Gaines described the model as making it possible to better understand the wants, needs, and emotions of the patients being served, and to translate those needs into policies and procedures, while motivating clinicians to provide care that exceeds patient expectations.

The Community Focus

With the patient as the central guiding force, the *Quality Chasm* report calls for systemic, simultaneous changes at four levels of the health system—the patient/family and other key non–professionally trained caregivers who may be involved with the patient; small-practice settings or microsystems; health care organizations; and the broader environment (e.g., payment, education, regulatory). These levels are nested within each other and interact in many complex ways (Berwick, 2002).

As Don Berwick noted, the community focus for the summit was particularly exciting because it encompasses each of these four levels, including the environment. Thus, he said, "You have a chance to actually raise issues which normally can't be raised because there aren't enough payers in the room." A community focus allows for a multiple-stakeholder approach to the complex set of issues posed by comprehensive redesign of the American health care system. John Lumpkin concurred, "If we're going to fix this system, we have to focus on quality. And if we're going to fix our system, communities are where we have to do the work."

> *"Each of the communities that are participating is a building block. Each is an experimental center. Each is a place of innovation. And if we take advantage of our mutual learning in the course of this day to renew our own sense of possibility and direction, then the objectives of our meeting will have been accomplished."*
>
> —Harvey Fineberg, President, IOM

Working at the community level also provides an opportunity for greater interaction between the personal health system and the public or population-based health system. Given that health care outcomes are determined by both health- and non-health-related factors—with behavioral patterns, social circumstances, environmental exposures and genetics playing substantial roles (McGinnis et al., 2002)—this interaction can maximize health for all by allowing individuals to obtain needed care and support for addressing broader health-related behaviors. This benefit is particularly relevant for children. For example, an approach to diabetes care that spans the personal and population-based systems might include individualized diabetic care, as well as programs in local schools and worksites designed to promote changes in diet and exercise, with the goal of reducing obesity and better managing or preventing the disease. Many summit participants echoed the need for such integration and for inclusion of a focus on primary prevention. Box 1-5 describes the Steps to a HealthierUS initiative, which is taking such an approach.

Box 1-5. Steps to a HealthierUS

The Department of Health and Human Services (DHHS) is currently supporting 12 communities in their efforts to promote better health and prevent disease through the newly launched Steps to a HealthierUS program. These DHHS awards, which totaled $13.7 million in fiscal year 2003, are focused on helping communities reduce the burden associated with diabetes, obesity, and asthma while addressing three related risk factors—physical inactivity, poor nutrition, and tobacco use. The overall goal of the effort is to help Americans live longer, better, and healthier lives. The grants are being used by leaders in small and large cities, rural communities, and one tribal consortium to implement community action plans that target racial and ethnic minorities, low-income populations, uninsured and underinsured persons, and others at high risk. Funded programs include those that focus on health care organizations, schools, workplaces, and other organizations, and are tailored to meet the needs of the particular community. In 2004, DHHS expects to award grants to additional communities and to continue funding existing efforts (Steps to a HealthierUS Initiative, 2004).

> *"In the case of asthma, it seems to me that if you are not dealing with the environmental determinants of health, you are then involved in a very Sisyphean task of rolling and rolling the rock up the hill, and then having it roll right back down on top of you."*
>
> —Shoshanna Sofaer, summit participant

Finally, there is value in working across communities as leaders share information about what does and does not work in their local health systems. Communities that collaborate may be able to learn from each other about transferable approaches and share strategies for delivering high-quality care.

Sustaining Community Innovators

Throughout the course of the summit, IOM committee members, speakers, participants, and others offered ideas about the best ways to catalyze and sustain systemic reform at the community level. National champions offered specific kinds of support (see Chapter 9). In addition, two of the five condition-specific plans that emerged from the summit deliberations included strategies for educating and activating communities. These strategies ranged from holding community-wide dialogues about issues associated with heart failure care, to supporting asthma coalitions, to developing innovative finance solutions that encompass both traditional and nontraditional methods of paying for services and span the personal and public health systems.

Don Berwick noted that communities must begin with a shared vision for reform that he described as a "change in purpose," and must focus the system on the experience of the people that it serves. He stated further that there must be an acceptance of responsibility that is beyond guilt, beyond blame, and beyond denial and is coupled with intense commitment. He noted that without this commitment, failure is more likely than success given the myths, belief systems, and habits, as well as system fragmentation, that undermine efforts at transformation.

Advance Work with the Communities and National Champions

To make the summit as action-oriented as possible, the IOM organizing committee worked in advance with leaders from the selected communities to summarize what they had accomplished and identify gaps in their current efforts. Committee members also contacted key national champions to inform them about the summit's objectives and ask them to consider in advance what they might commit to at the summit to further the vision of the *Quality Chasm* at both the community and national levels. Armed with the results of this substantial advance work, summit participants were able to minimize the time spent reviewing past accomplishments and focus more on shared learning and cooperative strategizing about future opportunities for improving care.

The community representatives shared the results of their considerable amount of advance work in one of five groups focused on the priority conditions cited above. Their efforts included the completion of two matrices, led by a clinical expert on the IOM committee. Sample matrices may be found in Appendix F. These two tools afforded the community leaders an evidence-based approach to self-evaluation and the chance to learn from others engaged in improving care for the same condition.

The first matrix aligned each component of the process of "ideal" care against the six aims of high-quality health care set forth in the *Quality Chasm* report and outlined above. The community representatives ranked where they thought they stood with regard to consistently providing the recommended care, and these scores were used to identify the areas most in need of improvement. The second matrix was adapted from the Chronic Care Model (CCM), developed by staff at the Improving Chronic Illness Care program of The Robert Wood Johnson Foundation (Improving Chronic Illness Care, 2004; Wagner, 2002). The CCM (see Figure 1-1) provides a scientific framework for organizing and delivering care at the level of the small-practice setting or microsystem. Under this model, patients are expected to participate actively in their care and play an integral role in both directing and managing their chronic condition. They are supported in their self-management efforts by their families and other key non–professionally trained caregivers who may be involved with the patient, as well as a proactive and well-prepared team of clinicians who provide regular follow-up.

The centerpiece of the CCM is facilitation of "productive interactions" between patients and their providers. To allow for greater specificity in the participants' advance work with respect to what infrastructure had been developed within their communities to support such interactions, the components of these interactions were explicitly compartmentalized. Team members from the 15 communities assessed what system elements they had in place to support evidence-based care for the chronic condition they were addressing (asthma, diabetes, depression, heart failure, or pain control in advanced cancer) consistent with the five elements of the CCM—clinical information systems, delivery system design, decision support, self-management support, and community resources and policies. This approach also provided a way to consider the interface between the health system and community resources so that, in the words of Reed Tuckson, public health is considered "not a competitive but a synergistic activity."

During the summit, Don Berwick described such evidence-based approaches to quality improvement as the way to be optimistic in the face of all that is wrong with our current system. He noted, "The optimism we have is science. It's the scientific understanding of what makes quality happen in the first place. The qualities

Chronic Care Model

Community — Resources and policies
Health System — Health care organization
- Self-management support
- Delivery system design
- Decision support
- Clinical information systems

Informed, activated patient ↔ **Productive Interactions** ↔ Prepared, proactive practice team

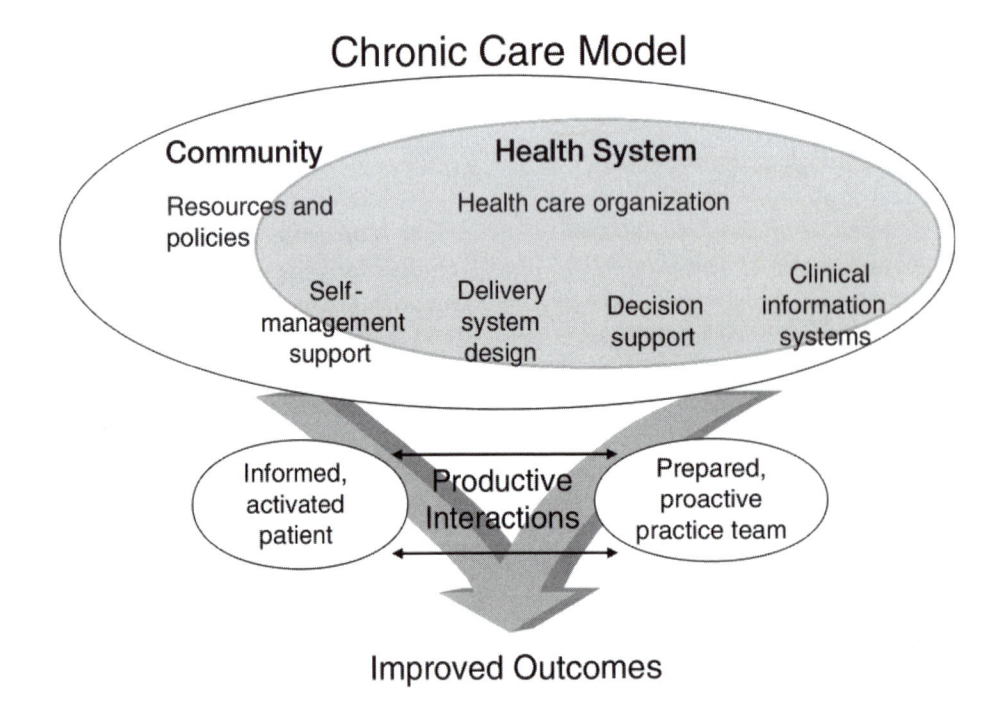

Improved Outcomes

Figure 1-1 Chronic Care Model
SOURCE: Reprinted with permission from *Effective Clinical Practice*. Copyright 1998 by Effective Clinical Practice. (Wagner, 1998)

INTRODUCTION

we care about...these are qualities of design." He further challenged the summit participants: "Every system is perfectly designed to achieve the results it gets....If you don't like your results, change your system."

Intensive planning by IOM committee members and input from the sponsor, liaisons, and others greatly contributed to the smooth execution and overall success of the summit. Appendix G details this extensive preparation.

The morning of the first day of the summit set the context for the event. It shone a spotlight on our broken health system from the patient's perspective, highlighted ways in which communities are working to overhaul the dysfunctional design of local health systems, and challenged participants—both local and national—to reach further and stretch higher in their efforts to remake American health care.

The summit welcome and introductions were shared by Reed Tuckson, IOM committee chair and senior vice president, UnitedHealth Group; Harvey Fineberg, president of the IOM; and John Lumpkin, senior vice president, The Robert Wood Johnson Foundation. (See Appendix H for the full summit agenda.) The consumer panel was chaired by Allen Daniels, an IOM committee member and CEO of Alliance Behavioral Care, and included Martha Whitecotton, R.N., Carolinas Medical Center; William Bruning, J.D., Mid-America Coalition on Health Care Community Initiative on Depression; Henry Gaines, Greater Flint Health Coalition; and Jay Portnoy, M.D., Children's Mercy Hospital/Kansas City Asthma Coalition. The keynote speaker was Don Berwick, President of the Institute for Healthcare Improvement.

In the afternoon, summit participants attended strategy sessions addressing the six cross-cutting topics. These sessions were intended to further prepare participants in the relevance of particular interventions to their ongoing quality improvement efforts so that the subsequent working groups focused on the priority areas could be maximally productive. For those with experience in such interventions, these sessions afforded an opportunity to share what they have learned with a larger group. The sessions were facilitated by subject experts and included short presentations from community representatives whose programs had focused on the particular interventions. The sessions and cofacilitators were as follows:

- Measurement, with facilitators Judith Hibbard, University of Oregon, and Arnold Milstein, Pacific Business Group on Health

- Information and Communications Technology, with facilitators David Kibbe, American Academy of Family Physicians, and David Brailer, Health Technology Center

- Care Coordination, with facilitators Gerard Anderson, the Johns Hopkins Bloomberg School of Public Health, and Christine Cassel, American Board of Internal Medicine

- Patient Self-Management, with facilitators Kate Lorig, Stanford University, and Russell Glasgow, Kaiser Permanente Colorado

- Finance, with facilitators Peter Lee, Pacific Business Group on Health, and Steve Udvarhelyi, Independence Blue Cross

- Community Coalition Building, with facilitators Shoshanna Sofaer, Baruch College, and David Stevens, Agency for Healthcare Research and Quality

The working groups addressing the priority areas met at the end of day one of the summit and for the first half of day two. The groups—which included community representatives, national champions, and other experts—used facilitation tools (see Appendix I) to develop plans incorporating key strategies at both the local and national levels for improving care for the targeted conditions. These plans describe who might spearhead such efforts, include time lines for implementation, and in most cases call for measures to gauge the effectiveness of the proposed strategies. These plans were presented at the plenary session, where initial feedback was received from summit participants. A diverse reactor panel—including moderator Bruce Bradley, an IOM committee member and Director of Health Plan Strategy and Policy, General Motors Corporation; Al Charbonneau, Rochester Health Commission; Helen Darling, National Business Group on Health; Sylvia Drew Ivie, The Help Everyone Clinic; and George J. Isham, HealthPartners, Inc.—provided further reflection on the plans and a candid reality check.

The final session of the summit, chaired by Reed Tuckson and described by many as a revival session, focused on commitments articulated by national champions for furthering the vision of the *Quality Chasm* report. These commitments targeted both the community and national levels, and included many that were announced for the first time at the summit, as well as others aimed at strengthening existing relevant efforts.

SCOPE AND ORGANIZATION OF THE REPORT

This report provides a synthesis of the outcomes of the summit, and is not intended to contain an exhaustive review of the literature for all of the topics discussed. Its content reflects the committee's commitment to carrying out its charge, which was to plan and execute a national summit focused on the vision of the *Quality Chasm* report for improving quality of care for a targeted set of conditions at both the community and national levels. A number of additional issues beyond this charge were discussed by the committee during its deliberations and by some summit participants, but are not captured in this follow-up report. Among others, these include how to enhance public health infrastructure and integrate it effectively into the personal health care system; how clinical education must be transformed so that health care professionals are best prepared to practice in a transformed system; and how clinicians, particularly physicians, can be engaged in quality improvement efforts.

In summarizing the summit outcomes, this report offers a vision, emerging from the summit deliberations, for how care for a targeted set of conditions can be improved by leveraging and integrating both community- and national-level strategies focused on key cross-cutting interventions:

- Chapters 2 through 7 focus on the cross-cutting strategies for improving care identified in the *Quality Chasm* report and by community leaders at the summit. These chapters highlight barriers and related solutions, based on discussions during the cross-cutting sessions and among the condition-specific working groups. They include examples from the participating communities illustrating how particular interventions can enhance care for one or more conditions.

- Chapter 8 provides a synopsis of the key strategies for change at the local and national levels proposed by the condition-specific working groups.

- Chapter 9 delineates next steps, calling for action on the part of both national and local leadership. It identifies the major commitments of the national champions and describes how they dovetail with the key strategies identified both in the cross-cutting sessions and by the five condition-specific working groups. It also includes comments from the reactor panel and summit participants.

- A series of appendices provides key summit documents, including the agenda, participant list, descriptions of participating communities, and other related materials.

REFERENCES

AHRQ (Agency for Healthcare Research and Quality). 2004. *Quality Research for Quality Healthcare*. [Online]. Available: http://www.ahrq.gov/ [accessed April 5, 2004].

Berwick DM. 2002. A User's Guide for the IOM's *Quality Chasm* Report. *Health Affairs (Millwood, VA)* 21(3):80–90.

Berwick DM. 2003. Disseminating innovations in health care. *The Journal of the American Medical Association* 289(15):1969–1975.

Blendon RJ, DesRoches CM, Brodie M, Benson JM, Rosen AB, Schneider E, Altman DE, Zapert K, Herrmann MJ, Steffenson AE. 2002. Views of practicing physicians and the public on medical errors. *New England Journal of Medicine* 347 (24):1933–1940.

Blendon RJ, Schoen C, Donelan K, Osborn R, DesRoches CM, Scoles K, Davis K, Binns K, Zapert K. 2001. Physicians' views on quality of care: A five-country comparison. *Health Affairs (Millwood, VA)* 20(3):233–243.

Chassin MR. 1998. Is health care ready for six sigma quality? *Milbank Quarterly* 76(4):510, 565–591.

CMMS (Centers for Medicare and Medicaid Services). 2004. *Centers for Medicare and Medicaid Services*. [Online]. Available: http://www.cms.hhs.gov/ [accessed April 5, 2004].

Davis K, Schoenbaum SC, Collins KS, Tenney K, Hughes DL, Audet AJ. 2002. *Room for Improvement: Patients Report on the Quality of Their Health Care*. Report 534. New York, NY: The Commonwealth Fund.

Improving Chronic Illness Care. 2004. *ICIC: Fostering Improvement: Learning Session #1*. [Online]. Available: http://www.improvingchroniccare.org/improvement/ls1.html#lstools8 [accessed April 6, 2004].

IOM (Institute of Medicine). 2000. *To Err Is Human: Building a Safer Health System*. Kohn LT, Corrigan JM, Donaldson MS, eds. Washington, DC: National Academy Press.

IOM. 2001. *Crossing the Quality Chasm: A New Health System for the 21st Century*. Washington, DC: National Academy Press.

IOM. 2002a. *Fostering Rapid Advances in Health Care: Learning from System Demonstrations*. Corrigan JM, Greiner AC, Erickson SM, eds. Washington, DC: National Academy Press.

IOM. 2002b. *Leadership by Example: Coordinating Government Roles in Improving Health Care Quality*. Corrigan JM, Eden J, Smith BM, eds. Washington, DC: National Academy Press.

IOM. 2003a. *Patient Safety: Achieving a New Standard for Care*. Aspden P, Corrigan JM, Wolcott J, Erickson SM, eds. Washington, DC: National Academy Press.

IOM. 2003b. *Health Professions Education: A Bridge to Quality*. Greiner AC, Knebel E, eds. Washington, DC: National Academy Press.

IOM. 2003c. *Priority Areas for National Action: Transforming Health Care Quality*. Adams K, Corrigan JM, eds. Washington, DC: National Academy Press.

IOM. 2004. *Keeping Patients Safe: Transforming the Work Environment of Nurses*. Page A, ed. Washington, DC: National Academy Press.

JCAHO (Joint Commission on Accreditation of Healthcare Organizations). 2004. *JCAHO Welcome Page*. [Online]. Available: http://www.jcaho.org/ [accessed April 5, 2004].

Leatherman S, McCarthy D. 2002. *Quality of Health Care in the United States: A Chartbook*. New York, NY: The Commonwealth Fund.

McGinnis MJ, Williams-Russo P, Knickman JR. 2002. The case for more active policy attention to health promotion: To succeed, we need leadership that informs and motivates, economic incentives that encourage change, and science that moves the frontiers. *Health Affairs (Millwood, VA)* 21(2):78–93.

McGlynn EA, Asch SM, Adams J, Keesey J, Hicks J, DeCristofaro A, Kerr EA. 2003. The quality of health care delivered to adults in the United States. *New England Journal of Medicine* 348 (26):2635–2645.

Millenson ML. 2003. The silence. *Health Affairs (Millwood, VA)* 22(2):103–112.

NCQA (National Committee for Quality Assurance). 2004. *NCQA: National Committee for Quality Assurance*. [Online]. Available: http://www.ncqa.org/index.asp [accessed April 5, 2004].

Steps to a HealthierUS Initiative. 2004. *Grantees, Steps to a HealthierUS Initiative.* [Online]. Available: http://www.healthierus.gov/steps/grantees.html [accessed March 24, 2004].

The Leapfrog Group. 2004. *The Leapfrog Group.* [Online]. Available: http://www.leapfroggroup.org [accessed April 5, 2004].

Wagner EH. 1998. Chronic disease management: What will it take to improve care for chronic illness? *Effective Clinical Practice* 1(1):2–4.

Wagner EH. 2002. *IOM Health Professions Education Summit.* Powerpoint Presentation. Washington, DC:

Chapter 2
Measurement

DEFINITION AND OVERARCHING THEMES

The aim of the cross-cutting session on measurement was to identify strategies communities might pursue for using performance measures to assess and improve quality of care, further the accountability of health care organizations, and inform payer and consumer purchasing and decision making. All of the communities participating in the summit had been involved in measuring the effectiveness of their efforts, although their objectives—whether for quality improvement purposes or public reporting—may have differed. Measurement was also an underlying assumption for all the condition-specific action plans.

The following definition of measurement served as the springboard for discussion during this session and had the general approval of the session's participants (IOM, 2002):

> To use quantitative indicators to identify the degree to which providers are delivering care that is consistent with standards or acceptable to customers of the delivery system. Performance measures may be used to support internal assessment and improvement, to further health care organization accountability, and to inform consumer and payer selection and purchasing based on performance.

KEY STRATEGIES

Overall, the participants view measurement as crucial to accelerating performance improvement in health care. Four key strategies emerged from this session: (1) integrate measurement into the delivery of care to benefit the patient whose care is measured, (2) improve information and communications technology (ICT) infrastructure to reduce the burden of data collection, (3) focus on longitudinal change in performance and patient-centered outcomes in addition to point-in-time measures, and (4) improve public reporting by effectively disseminating results to diverse audiences.

Integrate Measurement into the Delivery of Care

The underlying principle behind this strategy is that measurement should be integrated into routine clinical practice, so that the process of providing care also enables measurement to occur. Decreasing the burden of measurement and increasing the likelihood of data collection makes it possible to determine more accurately the quality of care being delivered. Once the necessary data are available, health care delivery systems can develop creative solutions to address suboptimal performance—thus continually improving the process of care.

In addition to posing a minimal data collection burden, performance measurement and reporting cannot be overly time-consuming or perceived as punitive. Moreover, as noted throughout the condition-specific working group sessions, national consensus on a core set of performance measures should simplify and bolster compliance with data collection by eliminating the collection of multiple conflicting measures collected against competing or conflicting standards. It was suggested that this common set of measures would include assessment of success in meeting the *Quality Chasm's* six aims for care—safe, effective, patient-centered, timely, efficient, and equitable—and do so in the most parsimonious manner possible so as to not be overwhelming (IOM, 2001). These key measures should be reviewed by professional societies and made readily available to purchasers and consumers.

"Institutional survival is not an aim of American health care. Patient well-being is the aim of American health care. Endorse the aims (IOM six aims) for improvement in measurable terms, and link it to measurement. If you don't know how you are doing you can't get better."

—*Don Berwick, summit keynote speaker*

The Washington State Diabetes Collaborative—one of the 15 community participants at the summit—candidly shared with the participants in the measurement session some lessons learned from that initiative regarding the need for standardized data collection of a discrete set of measures. See Box 2-1 for a brief overview of this ground-breaking state-level project.

Box 2-1. Washington State Diabetes Collaborative

The Washington State Diabetes Collaborative was established in 1999 to address the findings of a statewide project that identified significant gaps between existing and desirable diabetes care. Based on the Institute for Healthcare Improvement's Breakthrough Series approach, this first state-level collaborative on chronic disease has engaged more than 65 teams from urban and rural, public and private, and small to large care delivery systems and health plans in improving the delivery of patient-centered diabetes care.

Given the voluntary nature of the project—there were no external incentives for practitioners and facilities to participate—it was challenging at first to mandate a core set of measures to be collected, particularly across such a diverse set of stakeholders. As a result, during the first phase of the collaborative, considerable flexibility was allowed regarding what measures the team would use to assess progress related to glycemic control and blood pressure control. Although this flexibility was useful in that it permitted individual teams to follow their own internal quality improvement approach, it made meaningful comparisons or establishment of benchmarks difficult.

Adjustments were made during the second phase of the project, and teams were required to track the same four measures: HbA_1c <9.5 percent, LDL (low-density lipoprotein) cholesterol <130 mg/dl, blood pressure <140/90 mm Hg, and a documented self-management goal. With these standardized measures, it became possible to aggregate data more easily so the initiative could be evaluated as a whole. Overall, teams demonstrated improvement on these four measures, with higher gains in process-related than in outcome-related measures.

Note: A more detailed description of this collaborative and related case studies can be found in the February 2004 issue of the *Joint Commission Journal on Quality and Safety* (Daniel et al., 2004a,b).

The asthma working group suggested that national organizations such as the American Board of Internal Medicine (ABIM), the Centers for Medicare and Medicaid Services (CMS), the Leapfrog Group, the National Quality Forum (NQF), accrediting agencies, and appropriate subspecialty providers agree on a defined, well-validated set of quality performance measurement tools for chronic diseases—including patient self-management indicators—within 3 years. The depression and pain control working groups called on the NQF to serve as a convening body to bring together the appropriate experts to establish metrics for effective and efficient care in these areas. Many of the national champions at the summit weighed in on this issue and offered their support. Box 2-2 provides a snapshot of some of the commitments they made.

Improve Clinical ICT Infrastructure

Improving ICT infrastructure was identified as a key strategy to ease the burden of incorporating data collection, performance measurement, and results reporting into everyday clinical practice. Physician offices, hospitals, nursing homes, and health centers will require incentives to encourage the adoption of interoperable clinical information systems. A strategy suggested during this session was to reward practices that have clinical information systems in place—such as patient registries or partial/full electronic health records—that are used to collect data on their patient populations for quality measurement and improvement purposes. To this end, structural measures of ICT adoption by individual providers would have to be collected and reported.

Box 2-2. Commitments Made by National Champions Regarding Performance Measures

Steven Jencks, M.D., Centers for Medicare and Medicaid Services

"I want to be clear that CMS will work with you and other national partners and with the National Quality Forum to identify and implement a uniform standard national measure set involving the conditions discussed."

Arnold Milstein, M.D., Pacific Business Group on Health

"Within the two national purchaser organizations in whose leadership I participate, the Leapfrog Group and the Disclosure Project, I commit to accelerating national consensus on, and public reporting of, measures of quality, efficiency, and care redesign at multiple levels, including individual physician office teams, hospitals, larger health care organizations, and communities."

Greg Pawlson, M.D., National Committee for Quality Assurance

"We've been working already with the American Medical Association Consortium, the Joint Commission on Accreditation of Healthcare Organizations, the American Diabetes Association, the American Heart Association, the American Stroke Association, CMS, Leapfrog, the Pacific Business Group on Health, and many others to really try to populate the full spectrum of performance measures related to all six aims of the Institute of Medicine, and also to reduce duplication and redundancy."

Once this structural change occurs, measuring performance for multiple conditions can readily be achieved. Box 2-3 describes the Bridges to Excellence initiative, which recently launched a program to incentivize structural change in clinical ICT capability in physician offices.

Although incentives to build ICT capacity are certainly important, they are only a piece of a complex puzzle. Unresolved issues related to interoperability standards (addressed in detail in Chapter 3) and consensus on measures also figure prominently. There is a critical need for investment in this area, and participants called for the federal government to provide the necessary leadership. The federal government has provided grants to state mental health and substance abuse agencies to embark upon this effort, but limited resources impede the ability to reach all providers at the local level.

Participants generally believe that widespread adoption of ICT to assist measurement collection at the physician office level will necessitate partnering by public- and private-sector purchasers.

The condition-specific working groups also touched on the essential role of ICT in supporting measurement efforts. For example, recognized measurement experts in the asthma group affirmed that metrics for processes of care for asthma are well established. The major challenge now is moving these measures closer toward implementation. One hurdle is that these measures are based on patient reports and chart reviews, rather than on more easily accessible administrative data. Therefore, the asthma group suggested that the focus needs to be on (1) mandating/pressuring providers to collect these data and (2) creating the necessary

---

Box 2-3. Bridges to Excellence Initiative

Bridges to Excellence—a coalition of employers, physicians, health plans, and patients—is a program designed to improve the quality of care by acknowledging and rewarding health care providers that have taken significant steps to build new structural capability and achieve high performance levels to further the *Quality Chasm's* six aims of safety, effectiveness, patient-centeredness, timeliness, efficiency, and equity. Initially, this effort will target three areas—diabetes care, cardiovascular care, and the structure of care management systems—all of which were highlighted during the summit.

One initiative currently under way is the Physician Office Link, which allows physician practices to earn bonuses for implementing structural changes to increase quality, such as investing in ICT and care management tools. These changes include electronic prescribing to reduce medication errors, electronic health records embedded with guideline-based prompts/reminders, disease registries and management programs for patients with chronic conditions, and patient educational resources available in multiple languages. Additionally, a report card for each physician office assessing structural capability in these areas will be issued and made available to the public.

Note: A more detailed description of Bridges to Excellence programs may be found at their website (Bridges to Excellence, 2004).

ICT infrastructure so the data can be collected more easily.

The depression working group identified ICT as the basis for all transformation and for all of their proposed solutions. They acknowledged that, given concerns about privacy and stigma, it will be challenging to incorporate behavioral health information into electronic health records. The working group suggested that behavioral health data should be treated in the same way as all other health information, consistent with the Health Insurance Portability and Accountability Act of 1996 (U.S. DHHS, 2004). The group presented a strategy with the initial 1-year goal of convening a group of 15 communities that would include all of the key stakeholders and defining a shared dataset for behavioral health in primary care. This first year would see pilot collection of these data and conclude with the formulation of recommendations for a national behavioral health data policy. Over the course of 3 years, this effort would be expanded to include a broader base of community agencies and stakeholders. The process for the 3-year goals would mirror that for the 1-year pilot, with an expanded group of participants.

> *"The absence of electronic health records limits the ability to deploy performance measures and gather data. It's a severe limitation. People want to know why we don't approve more performance measures. It's simply unaffordable when you're collecting data by hand. Electronic health records become critically important because they make it possible to gather performance data as a by-product of the care delivery process."*
>
> —Dennis O'Leary, summit participant

Focus on Longitudinal Change in Performance and Patient-Focused Outcomes

Another solution put forward by the strategy session participants was for measurement efforts to focus on longitudinal change in patient health status over time. Implementing this solution would require evolving from the customary collection of process and outcome measures—which tend to focus on provider inputs—to a more multidimensional approach that includes assessing patients' self-reports on their capabilities for self-management and their functional status. Using patient-reported health status to inform the medical encounter, essentially making it part of the "vital signs" taken at any visit, would improve individual patient care, as well as enhance the ability to gauge on a population basis how well care is being delivered for specific conditions and patient subgroups with each condition. A case in point provided during the session was the use of a standardized questionnaire to evaluate heart failure status. This type of feedback could quite easily be obtained from patients while they are sitting in the waiting room, and providers could use this information to customize and improve care. Additionally, data could be plotted over time to track patient-reported progress and/or aggregated to support population-based comparisons.

The heart failure working group also suggested collecting patient-reported health status as a routine part of care. They emphasized the need for adopting multiple approaches to make the collection of information from patients more convenient—such as a computer in the waiting room and web-based entry from home—as well as for organizing the data for clinicians in an easily interpretable format. Such information should be made readily available to the physician/nurse at first contact during the office visit and be automatically incorporated into the patient's electronic health record if entered at home—coupled with an alarm to the health provider if there is a negative change in status. Additionally, patients should be provided with their "scores," and these results should be graphed over time to assist patients in self-management of their condition and allow the provider to examine trends. The group proposed that measures of mental health status also be included and that comorbidities be considered in interpreting quality-of-life scores, as heart failure patients often have multiple chronic illnesses, such as depression and diabetes.

The pain control working group proposed making assessment of pain the "fifth vital sign" and suggested that measures be developed to track and monitor the following: (1) percent of patients being evaluated for pain, (2) interventions conducted, and (3) effectiveness of the interventions (rate of overall decline in pain). These measures would then be incorporated into the Agency for Healthcare Research and Quality's (AHRQ) annual National Health Care Quality Report (AHRQ, 2003) and the National Committee for Quality Assurance's Health Plan Employer Data and Information Set (HEDIS®) report (NCQA, 2004).

The group also proposed taking a patient-centered approach to measuring pain control. Strategies to achieve this goal include (1) providing cancer patients with multiple ways to record their pain outside the clinician encounter, such as over the Internet or by phone, so that results can be reviewed regularly and acted on in a timely way; and (2) establishing measures of family/caregiver experience as part of a performance measures set, for example, adding a question to the death certificate—which is often completed by a caregiver/family member—asking how effective the care team was in treating end-of-life pain.

Agreeing with the strategy session participants, the pain working group recognized the need to evaluate data on the prevalence of pain over time for individual patients. Doing so is particularly important during transitions between settings, such as from hospital to nursing home, when breakdowns in care are most likely to occur. The group suggested that providers adopt a standardized patient flow chart that would be recorded electronically for purposes of quality improvement, performance measurement, and patient education.

Improve Public Reporting by Disseminating Results to Diverse Audiences

This strategy had two prongs: first, to improve public reporting of performance measures by including the patient experience; and second, to package and disseminate this information in a way that is useful and meaningful to different audiences. Underlying assumptions brought forth by the working groups included the need for transparent public reporting and the use of this information to foster quality improvement at multiple levels of the health care delivery system. For example, patients could compare their diabetes outcomes against those of a similar cohort as a stimulus to their self-management, individual clinicians could judge their performance among their peers, and communities could correlate local outcomes with regional and/or national benchmarks.

In response to the first part of this strategy, the condition-specific working groups echoed the need for patient/consumer input in the development and selection of quality measures. The depression working group suggested several strategies to this end: obtaining feedback from objective patient advocates and consumers; conducting focus groups among patients with depression to identify key quality characteristics and outcomes of care; and rallying a collaborative group of stakeholders—patients, physicians, purchasers, and payers—to achieve consensus on performance and satisfaction measures.

The second part of this strategy—reporting measures at different levels of granularity and in a variety of formats to divergent groups—is critical to stimulating consumer demand for quality services and accelerating the uptake of best practices by providers. The asthma working group called for identifying methods to increase consumer use of report cards and for determining how various population subgroups prefer to receive these materials. Intermountain Health Care's Depression in Primary Care Initiative illustrates how performance data can be used and marketed to address the needs of a variety of stakeholder groups (see Box 2-4).

> **Box 2-4. Intermountain Health Care's Depression in Primary Care Initiative**
>
> Intermountain Health Care—an integrated delivery system that includes providers, plans, and hospitals—has implemented a Depression in Primary Care Initiative that provides patients and their families with the tools and organizational supports needed to identify, diagnose, treat, and manage depression. Designed to impact the entire health care system, this quality improvement process employs integrated mental health teams that are made available to primary care practices. In an effort to create a sustainable business case that links financial value to improved clinical outcomes, the program measures and evaluates progress in three areas:
>
> - Clinical outcomes—detection rates, changes recorded over time in mental health measures, and productivity measures
> - Service outcomes—patient, physician, and staff satisfaction surveys, and employer and payer responses to clinical processes
> - Cost outcomes
>   - Payer costs—analysis of claims data
>   - Employer costs—analysis of productivity results
>   - Operational costs—efficiency of care, and productivity of care managers, physicians, and mental health specialists
>
> Data for these three outcome areas are used to engage multiple stakeholders—insurance plans, employers, physicians, mental health specialists, support staff, and patients—and are presented in a "language" that each of these groups understands. An example given at the summit was providing claims data to health plans in a quickly interpretable format. The graph below demonstrates cost savings over a 4-year period for Clinic A, which received the intervention and whose cost trends were stable over time, as compared with the increased costs for a control group (Clinic B) with a similar case mix that did not receive the intervention. These data allowed health plans not only to see potential savings, but also to build a business case to finance and sustain this initiative.
>
> *(Continued on page 35)*

(Continued from page 34)

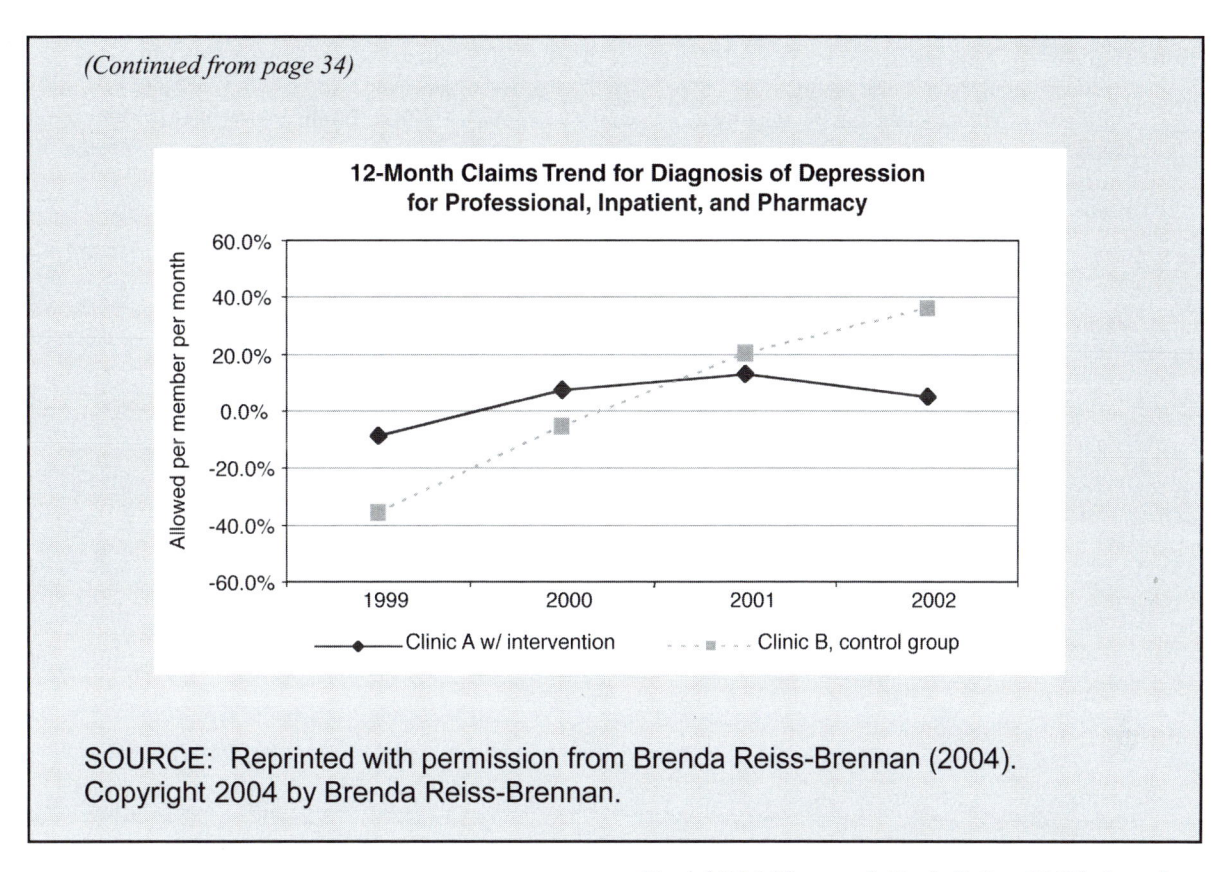

12-Month Claims Trend for Diagnosis of Depression for Professional, Inpatient, and Pharmacy

[Line graph showing Allowed per member per month (ranging from -60.0% to 60.0%) across years 1999-2002. Clinic A w/ intervention line stays relatively flat near 0-15%, while Clinic B control group rises from about -35% in 1999 to about 35% in 2002.]

SOURCE: Reprinted with permission from Brenda Reiss-Brennan (2004). Copyright 2004 by Brenda Reiss-Brennan.

CLOSING STATEMENT

At the summit, measurement was repeatedly identified as the backbone of quality improvement efforts. From the need to measure outcomes to make a business case and link rewards to quality care (see Chapter 6) to the importance of community-based measures and outcomes (see Chapter 7), documenting performance is critical to substantiate the positive effect of interventions—such as care coordination and self-management—and to better direct resources to problem areas.

REFERENCES

AHRQ (Agency for Healthcare Research and Quality). 2003. *National Healthcare Quality Report.* Rockville, MD: AHRQ.

Bridges to Excellence. 2004. *Bridges to Excellence: Rewarding Quality across the Health Care System.* [Online]. Available: http://www.bridgestoexcellence.org/bte/ [accessed April 29, 2004].

Daniel DM, Norman J, Davis C, Lee H, Hindmarsh MF, McCulloch DK, Wagner EH, Sugarman JR. 2004a. Case studies from two collaboratives on diabetes in Washington state. *Joint Commission Journal on Quality and Safety* 30(2):103–108.

Daniel DM, Norman J, Davis C, Lee H, Hindmarsh MF, McCulloch DK, Wagner EH, Sugarman JR. 2004b. A state-level application of the chronic illness breakthrough series: Results from two collaboratives on diabetes in Washington state. *Joint Commission Journal on Quality and Safety* 30(2):69–79.

IOM (Institute of Medicine). 2001. *Crossing the Quality Chasm: A New Health System for the 21st Century.* Washington, DC: National Academy Press.

IOM. 2002. *Leadership by Example: Coordinating Government Roles in Improving Health Care Quality.* Corrigan JM, Eden J, Smith BM, eds. Washington, DC: National Academy Press.

NCQA (National Committee for Quality Assurance). 2004. *NCQA: National Committee for Quality Assurance.* [Online]. Available: http://www.ncqa.org/index.asp [accessed March 24, 2004].

Reiss-Brennan, B. 2004 (January 6). *Quality Chasm Summit*. Presentation at the Institute of Medicine 1st Annual Crossing the Quality Chasm Summit, Washington, DC. Institute of Medicine Committee on Crossing the Quality Chasm.

U.S. DHHS (United States Department of Health and Human Services). 2004. *HHS—Office for Civil Rights—HIPAA*. [Online]. Available: http://www.os.dhhs.gov/ocr/hipaa/ [accessed March 24, 2004].

Chapter 3
Information and Communications Technology

DEFINITION AND OVERARCHING THEMES

The focus of the cross-cutting strategy session on information and communications technology (ICT) was to identify ways that communities can enhance their health care information infrastructure to improve care—including advances in Internet-based communication, electronic health records (EHRs) for small practices, patient registries, and medication order entry systems, among others. To set parameters for this rather broad topic, the following definition of ICT was agreed upon by session participants and served as the starting point for discussion (IOM, 2002, 2003a):

> To use information and communications technology—both within and across organizations—to improve quality and safety; enhance access; and reduce waste, delays, and administrative costs. Attributes of an ICT infrastructure include web-based communication; real-time access to electronic patient information (eventually captured in an EHR system); easy access to reliable science-based information; computer-aided decision support tools, such as medication order entry systems; and the ability to capture patient safety information for use in designing ever-safer delivery systems. Such an infrastructure should include a focus on multiple dimensions, including providers, individual health, and population health.

The importance of ICT in both supporting and sustaining quality improvement efforts was a recurring theme throughout the summit. From providing a platform for the exchange of patient information across multiple providers to helping patients in the self-management of their condition, ICT was identified as an enabling force to accelerate system interventions designed to improve care for individuals with chronic conditions. Specifically, participants in the ICT session proposed strategies directed at both the micro and macro levels, with the ultimate goal of having EHRs in physicians' offices in every community and a transportable health record available to every patient.

KEY STRATEGIES

The session participants proposed three strategies for overcoming barriers to successful integration of ICT into the delivery of care: (1) use standardized systems, (2) provide federal leadership to accelerate the adoption of EHRs, and (3) create a public utility that holds data at the local level.

Use Standardized Systems

There was a resounding call for national data standards during the ICT session, accompanied by an expression of frustration with the current inability to transmit health information across organizational and regional boundaries. Participants voiced a strong sense of urgency to the initiation of change, suggesting that any delay in the adoption of standards would exacerbate or worsen the lack of interoperability that has hindered the spread of best practices and the exchange of patient information among providers. Thus as the number of "stand-alone" EHRs proliferates, it will only become more difficult for those who have tried to move forward despite this barrier to integrate systems in which they have invested such considerable resources into standards-based data storage and communication systems that may or may not be compatible with those existing systems.

Standards are also the building blocks for an ICT infrastructure that enables patient health information to be shared at the point of care (IOM, 2003a). By having this information readily available at the time of care delivery—along with computerized reminders for preventive services—clinicians are better able to provide the right care at the right time to their patients (Balas et al., 2000). The ICT-enhanced program of Madigan Army Medical Center (MAMC) illustrates the critical need for national data standards to provide this type of decision support up front, not after the fact, and to facilitate the diffusion of effective programs, such as MAMC's diabetes initiative (see Box 3-1).

Box 3-1. ICT-Enhanced Program: Barriers and Opportunities

Madigan Army Medical Center (MAMC) is a tertiary care academic medical center with approximately 250 staff and residents who support all Department of Defense direct health care in the Pacific Northwest region. In the community served by MAMC, 76,000 beneficiaries are enrolled in primary care, including 3,000 patients with adult onset diabetes. MAMC also is a purchaser of health care services under the TRICARE program, covering tertiary care for 460,000 beneficiaries in Washington, Oregon, and Alaska.

MAMC has launched an initiative to improve the quality of care for diabetics within its targeted population. This initiative includes an emphasis on "preventive maintenance" and the use of ICT to provide decision support for clinicians and actively engage patients. The centerpiece of the program is an electronic scorecard keyed to evidence-based Diabetes Quality Improvement Program (DQIP) measures and populated automatically from the laboratory, the pharmacy, and other clinical

(Continued on page 39)

(Continued from page 38)

data systems. At the point of care, clinician and patient review the results from the scorecard together and use them to make collaborative decisions about the next steps in the care plan. Below is a sample scorecard, which demonstrates that an annual eye exam and blood pressure and LDL cholesterol testing have been completed; however, hemoglobin A_1c, ACE Inhibitor, aspirin use, and up-to-date foot exam are still outstanding on this sample patient. As a result of this interactive tracking and monitoring of patient outcomes, decreases in emergency department visits and hospital admissions of 40 and 9 percent, respectively, have been realized.

Charts 1 and 2 below present the outcomes of the data discussed above. Brigadier General Michael Dunn, representing the MAMC diabetes initiative, shared with the participants in this session that for the 3,000 diabetics within his controlled primary care population, this tool enabled him to provide a very high standard of evidence-based care. In the TRICARE network, however, he could not easily duplicate this effort, as there are at least 20 incompatible EHRs among his different provider organizations, and none of these systems are able to "talk" to each other.

Diabetes Scorecard on screen at point of care

- ☐ Hemoglobin A1C $\leq$ 7%
- ☒ Annual Dilated Retinal Exam
- ☐ ACE Inhibitor for Microalbuminuria
- ☒ Blood Pressure $\leq$ 130/80
- ☒ LDL Cholesterol $\leq$ 100 or NCEP Target
- ☐ Aspirin Use
- ☐ Up To Date Foot, Vascular, Neuro Checks

Data entered/updated only once, fed from ICDB

(Continued on page 40)

(Continued from page 39)

Chart 1. Diabetes-Related Emergency Room Visits: Baseline vs. Comparison Year

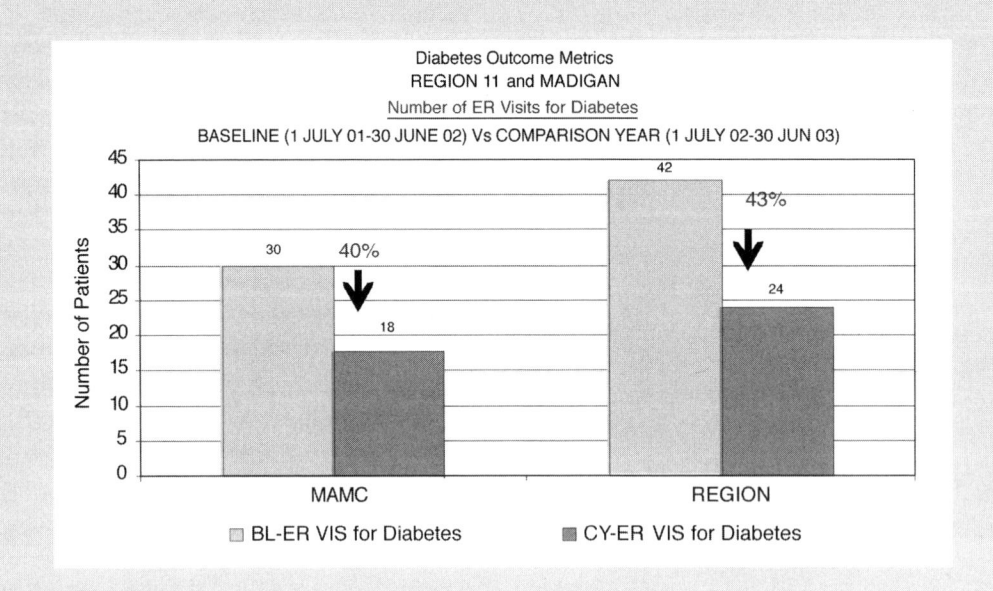

Diabetes Outcome Metrics
REGION 11 and MADIGAN
Number of ER Visits for Diabetes
BASELINE (1 JULY 01-30 JUNE 02) Vs COMPARISON YEAR (1 JULY 02-30 JUN 03)

	MAMC	REGION
BL-ER VIS for Diabetes	30	42
CY-ER VIS for Diabetes	18 (40%)	24 (43%)

Chart 2. Diabetes-Related Admissions: Baseline vs. Comparison Year

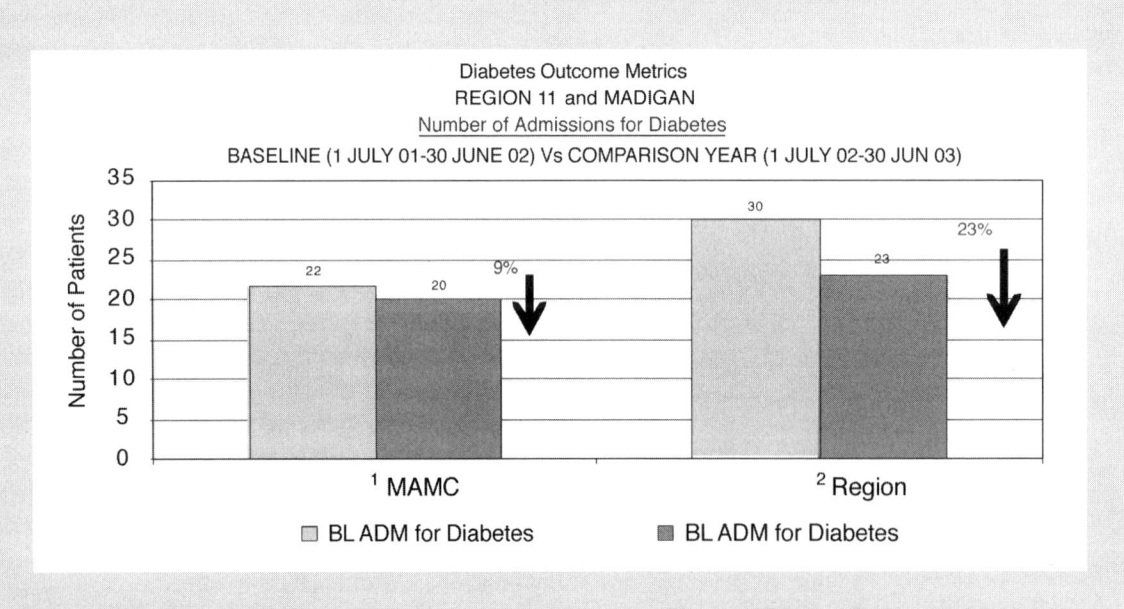

Diabetes Outcome Metrics
REGION 11 and MADIGAN
Number of Admissions for Diabetes
BASELINE (1 JULY 01-30 JUNE 02) Vs COMPARISON YEAR (1 JULY 02-30 JUN 03)

	1 MAMC	2 Region
BL ADM for Diabetes	22	30
BL ADM for Diabetes	20 (9%)	23 (23%)

SOURCE: Reprinted with permission from Michael Dunn (2004). Copyright 2004 by Michael Dunn.

Provide Federal Leadership to Accelerate the Adoption of EHRs

The ICT session emphasized the need for the federal government to provide leadership in four areas: (1) promulgating national data standards for the transfer of electronic health data, (2) setting rules and regulations for the use of EHRs, (3) increasing consumer awareness of the importance of these tools, and (4) financing EHRs.

Promulgating National Data Standards

Like participants in the ICT session, the IOM committee that authored the report *Patient Safety: Achieving a New Standard for Care* called upon the federal government to be a major driver in establishing and disseminating national data standards (IOM, 2003a). Specifically, the committee recommended that Congress provide direction and financial support to the Department of Health and Human Services, the Consolidated Health Informatics Initiative, the National Committee on Vital Health Statistics, AHRQ, and the National Library of Medicine to further this effort. As in the other cross-cutting sessions, there was general consensus that a public–private partnership is essential to accomplish this goal—whether by conducting demonstrations of paying for performance, developing a core set of standardized measures, or instituting flexibility in delivery of care through waiver programs.

Many of the national champions at the summit are actively engaged in joint ventures to improve and promote data standardization. For example, the American Hospital Association was instrumental in establishing the National Alliance for Health Information Technology, a public–private partnership addressing standards for EHRs and medication bar coding. Members of the alliance are from multiple health care sectors and represent hospitals, health systems, medical groups, technology companies/vendors, public and private payers, the pharmaceutical industry, and other standards-setting groups (NAHIT, 2004).

The asthma working group reiterated the need for a multistakeholder approach to resolving the problem of data standardization. They suggested that this approach could be applied practically, for example, first to an electronic personal health summary and then progressing rapidly, but incrementally, toward a uniform EHR. They called specifically for a coalition of health plans, CMS, consumer groups, organized medicine, and other health care providers to facilitate the adoption of a standardized personal health record summary whose format would allow for the transfer of clinical data to any computer system or EHR, as well as a hard-copy report in a readable format for paper transfer.

The heart failure working group proposed that patients be able to carry their health records in some type of easily transportable electronic format, such as a thumb memory stick or "smart card." They suggested this as a way of empowering patients to monitor their status from home and enabling them to transfer their health information back to their case manager electronically. The Continuity of Care Record initiative, about to be put into practice, is one such effort that will bring patients one step closer to a portable personal health record that can easily be transferred electronically (see Box 3-2).

During his keynote speech, Don Berwick called for patients' unfettered access to their health records—"no cost, no barriers, no limitations"—and pointed to the patient-carried record as an attainable first step. Accomplishing this goal, he argued, is an essential precondition to making the patient the source of control, and fulfills the requirements of the third of 10 rules set forth in the Quality Chasm report for redesigning health care processes[1] (IOM, 2001:8).

---

[1] These rules are (1) care based on continuous healing relationships; (2) customization based on patient needs and values; (3) the patient as the source of control; (4) shared knowledge and free flow of information; (5) evidence-based decision making; (6) safety as a systems property; (7) the need for transparency; (8) anticipation of needs; (9) continuous decrease in waste; and (10) cooperation among clinicians.

> **Box 3-2. The Continuity of Care Record**
>
> The Continuity of Care Record (CCR) is an XML document standard that will enable a core set of relevant patient information to be transported easily across health care settings and providers. The rationale behind the development of the CCR was to standardize data—not software or computer systems—so that personal health information can readily be displayed on any computer, thus avoiding proprietary barriers to progress in this area in the past.
>
> The CCR may be viewed by a web browser, a PDF reader, or a word processor. Key components of the CCR include patient health status (diagnoses, allergies, and vital signs), care plan, patient and provider identifiers, and insurance information.
>
> The CCR has the potential to enhance care coordination, particularly during referrals, transfers, and discharges. For example, its use might make it possible to circumvent duplicate laboratory tests, drug interactions, and misdiagnoses attributable to incomplete or missing health records. Additionally, the CCR could serve as a personal health record, helping patients in the self-management of their care.
>
> The CCR is a collaborative effort among ASTM International, the Massachusetts Medical Society, the Health Information Management and Systems Society, the American Academy of Family Physicians, the American Academy of Pediatrics, the American Medical Association, and the Patient Safety Institute. Roll-out of this first interoperability standard is slated for mid-June 2004.
>
> Note: For additional information, contact the ASTM International Technical Committee on Healthcare Informatics (staff manager Dan Smith) at their website (Committee E31 on Healthcare Informatics, 2004).

My own prescription is to give every patient in Flint, Michigan, their medical records, end of story, tomorrow."

—Don Berwick, summit keynote speaker

Setting Rules and Regulations for the Use of EHRs

In May 2003, the Department of Health and Human Services requested that the IOM provide guidance on a set of "basic functionalities"—defined as key care delivery–related capabilities—that an EHR should possess. It was reasoned that consensus around a minimal set of expectations would smooth the progress and accelerate more widespread adoption of EHRs. The IOM committee that undertook this task identified eight core functions for an EHR: (1) health information and data, (2) results management, (3) order entry/management, (4) decision support, (5) electronic communication and connectivity, (6) patient support, (7) administrative support reporting, and (8) population health management (IOM, 2003b). The next step is for these elements to be incorporated into an EHR functional model developed by Health Level 7 (HL7), a leading standards-setting organization (Health Level 7, 2004). Presently, CMS is in the HL7 balloting stage for approval, but given the vast stakeholder interests involved, more debate is likely to ensue around this topic (Personal communication, D. Brailer, Health Technology Center, March 17, 2004).

Increasing Consumer Awareness of the Importance of These Tools

The participants focused on ways in which the government, as well as others, could induce consumer demand for quality services directly linked to the use of ICT. The challenge is to convince consumers that they should be deeply alarmed about the current state of health care quality in the first place. To this end, quality will need to be defined in a way and in terms that are meaningful to consumers as opposed to the current situation, in which consumers seldom seek out performance information on hospitals, providers, or health care organizations becasue they mistrust or do not understand the data (FACCT, 1997; Marshall et al., 2000; Shaller et al., 2003). Strategies discussed during the session included continuing to educate consumers about medical errors, demonstrating ICT solutions that involve consumers in their care, and making quality reporting that arises from this technology available to consumers. In short, the connection between ICT and quality needs to be obvious to consumers, and most important, ICT must be seen as an indispensable tool for improving care.

Financing EHRs

During the summit, extensive attention was given to financial incentives—from both public and private sources—as a mechanism to encourage evidence-based practices and system-level changes that are known to improve the quality of care, particularly the deployment of EHRs. (See Chapter 6 for a detailed overview, as well as the other cross-cutting chapters that weave this concept into their proposed solutions). In this section, as was the case during the ICT sessions, the focus is on how to promote and stimulate the acquisition and use of EHRs by physicians, taking into consideration both the costs and the perceived benefits that impact their adoption. Although time constraints did not permit an extensive discussion of the many factors influencing clinician uptake of ICT, three key elements were discussed by the participants: (1) demonstrating a scientific foundation for the use of ICT, (2) minimizing adverse effects on workflow, and (3) providing a return on investment (Miller and Sim, 2004).

To justify the expense and time commitment required to integrate EHRs into their practice setting, clinicians require empirical evidence that such interventions as computerized physician order entry actually do decrease the potential for adverse drug events, or that electronic prompts reminding them to order screening tests to monitor chronic conditions can help avoid long-term complications (Bates et al., 1999; Casalino et al., 2003; Kaushal et al., 2001). Clinicians must be assured that EHRs will not add to an already heavy workload, and that ICT will ultimately help them deliver safer and more effective care to their patients. Additionally, although the evidence base is growing, financial support for EHRs by Medicare and health plans has been slowed in part by minimal scientific evidence to date that they are efficacious and effective.

Underlying all these obstacles is the need to develop a business case for investing in ICT infrastructure at both the clinician and organization levels. As discussed in Chapter 6, incentives need to be provided to those who will incur the cost of setting up and maintaining these systems, as most of the benefits currently tend to flow to other stakeholders (Hersh, 2002).

Create a Public Utility That Holds Data at the Local Level

Presently, electronic health data are often considered a private resource, benefiting primarily organizations in their internal quality improvement efforts. Participants in the ICT session suggested framing health data as a public good and creating a public utility that would hold the data, making them accessible at the community level. The County of Santa Cruz, California, a summit community, is moving in this direction with its diabetes initiative, currently under way (see Box 3-3).

In the past few years, regional initiatives in Santa Barbara, California, and Indianapolis, Indiana, have established infrastructure for the exchange of health information among physicians, patients, hospitals, and ancillary care facilities. Although both of these efforts are unusual in their origins—both emerged from substantial field research efforts that were adopted by local health system leaders—more than 50 communities and regions are now planning regional health information exchange efforts. While early, these efforts in a diverse range of communities evidence a common response to the broad problem of fragmentation of care across physicians and among health plans and employers, which hampers efficiency and limits patients' control over their care delivery.

These regional projects use a variety of technical solutions, but all are based on three core principles: (1) identified health information is ultimately controlled by the patient; (2) current medical data controls are inadequate, and data loss, theft, and misuse are common vulnerabilities of paper systems; and (3) common infrastructure lowers technical and administrative costs. These initiatives share a vision for improving clinical care and health status that will be realized through broader access to health data at the point of care when the data are needed. Such efforts are being analyzed closely to determine feasibility for widespread use in the United States (Brailer et al., 2003).

CLOSING STATEMENT

Most participants in the summit agreed that few innovations in health care delivery are as promising as ICT, and most acknowledged the substantial obstacles that have prevented these technologies from becoming standards of care. Every community project described by participants identified a set of disease-specific interventions that would be easier, more effective, or less expensive to implement if a functioning ICT infrastructure were in place. The broad dissemination of ICT as a patient care tool is a key step to realizing long-standing goals for consumer well-being, public health, and the health care industry.

Box 3-3. County of Santa Cruz, California, Diabetes Initiatives

Santa Cruz County, California, a blend of urban and rural communities with a population of 260,000, has an estimated prevalence of diabetes of approximately 7 percent, affecting the lives of more than 18,000 people. To address this problem, two competing private medical groups and the Medi-Cal managed care program have joined the public health department in two initiatives—the Regional Diabetes Collaborative and the Santa Cruz Health Improvement Partnership—that bring together front-line professionals from all disciplines and executives to reach consensus on common-ground issues.

To date, a web-based decision support system for comprehensive diabetes care has been developed that integrates claims data, laboratory results, pharmacy data, and information generated during office visits. The database, located on the server in physicians' offices scattered throughout the county, allows them to review the data on line (or on a paper printout if preferred) and compare them against their patients' diabetes care parameters, such as hemoglobin A_1c, blood pressure, and LDL cholesterol levels. Additionally, "action prompts" and an up-to-date list of needed services are generated electronically, serving as a monitoring tool for both the clinician and office support staff.

Currently under development is a uniform format for a "dashboard"—a screen that comes up on the computer showing the patient's diabetes-related indicators—to be used across multiple systems. Thus when patients go from one system to another, their information will be presented and collected in a consistent way, regardless of where they are receiving care. Future plans are to offer this program to community clinics, public health department clinics, and emergency departments in the county, ideally making it a public utility.

Wells Shoemaker, representing the County of Santa Cruz initiatives at the summit, identified four success factors, based on the county's experiences, in incorporating ICT in care processes: (1) providing decision support at the point of care; (2) concentrating on population management, particularly underuse of preventive services; (3) giving feedback and recognition to clinicians who are high performers; and (4) migrating successful strategies to practices that are struggling.

REFERENCES

Balas EA, Weingarten S, Garb CT, Blumenthal D, Boren SA, Brown GD. 2000. Improving preventive care by prompting physicians. *Archives of Internal Medicine* 160(3):301–308.

Bates DW, Teich JM, Lee J, Seger D, Kuperman GJ, Ma'Luf N, Boyle D, Leape L. 1999. The impact of computerized physician order entry on medication error prevention. *Journal of the American Medical Informatics Association* 6 (4):313–321.

Brailer DJ, Augustinos N, Evans LM, Karp S. 2003. *Moving toward Electronic Health Information Exchange: Interim Report on the Santa Barbara County Data Exchange.* Oakland, CA: California HealthCare Foundation.

Casalino L, Gillies RR, Shortell SM, Schmittdiel JA, Bodenheimer T, Robinson JC, Rundall T, Oswald N, Schauffler H, Wang MC. 2003. External incentives, information technology, and organized processes to improve health care quality for patients with chronic diseases. *The Journal of the American Medical Association* 289(4):434–441.

Committee E31 on Healthcare Informatics. *E31.* [Online]. Available: http://www.astm.org/cgi-bin/SoftCart.exe/commit/committee/E31.htm?E+mystore [accessed May 10, 2004].

Dunn, M. 2004 .(January 6). *Madigan Army Medical Center.* Presentation at the Institute of Medicine 1st Annual Crossing the Quality Chasm Summit, Washington, DC. Institute of Medicine Committee on Crossing the Quality Chasm.

FACCT (Foundation for Accountability). 1997. *Reporting Quality Information to Consumers.* Portland, OR: FACCT.

Health Level Seven. *Health Level Seven, Inc..* [Online]. Available: http://www.hl7.org/ [accessed March 25, 2004].

Hersh WR. 2002. Medical informatics: Improving health care through information. *The Journal of the American Medical Association* 288 (16):1955–1958.

IOM (Institute of Medicine). 2001. *Crossing the Quality Chasm: A New Health System for the 21st Century.* Washington, DC: National Academy Press.

IOM. 2002. *Fostering Rapid Advances in Health Care: Learning from System Demonstrations.* Corrigan JM, Greiner AC, Erickson SM, eds. Washington, DC: National Academy Press.

IOM. 2003a. *Patient Safety: Achieving a New Standard for Care.* Aspden P, Corrigan JM, Wolcott J, Erickson SM, eds. Washington, DC: National Academy Press.

IOM. 2003b. *Key Capabilities of an Electronic Health Record System: Letter Report.* eds. Committee on Data Standards for Patient Safety. Washington, DC: National Academy Press.

Kaushal R, Barker KN, Bates DW. 2001. How can information technology improve patient safety and reduce medication errors in children's health care? *Archives of Pediatrics and Adolescent Medicine* 155(9):1002–1007.

Marshall MN, Shekelle PG, Leatherman S, Brook RH. 2000. The public release of performance data: What do we expect to gain? A review of the evidence. *The Journal of the American Medical Association* 283(14):1866–1874.

Miller RH, Sim I. 2004. Physicians' use of electronic medical records: Barriers and solutions. *Health Affairs (Millwood, VA)* 23 (2):116–126.

Shaller D, Sofaer S, Findlay SD, Hibbard JH, Delbanco S. 2003. Perspective: Consumers and quality-driven health care: A call to action. *Health Affairs (Millwood, VA)* 22(2):95–101.

NAHIT (The National Alliance for Health Information Technology). 2004. *Creating a Leadership Legacy.* [Online]. Available: http://www.nahit.org [accessed March 25, 2004].

Chapter 4
Care Coordination

DEFINITION AND OVERARCHING THEMES

The objective of the cross-cutting strategy session on care coordination was to identify ways in which communities can improve how care is coordinated—across settings and clinicians—for people with chronic and complex conditions. It was the universal belief of the participants that the current fragmented process of care delivery should be redesigned to enhance clinical outcomes and reduce expenditures. To frame this topic, the following definition of care coordination was accepted by the group (IOM, 2001, 2003b; Shortell et al., 2000):

> To establish and support a continuous healing relationship, enabled by an integrated clinical environment and characterized by the proactive delivery of evidence-based care and follow-up. Clinical integration is further defined as the extent to which patient care services are coordinated across people, functions, activities, and sites over time so as to maximize the value of services delivered to patients. Coordination encompasses a set of practitioner behaviors and information systems intended to bring together health services, patient needs, and streams of information to facilitate the delivery of care in accordance with the six aims set forth in the *Quality Chasm* report. Such coordination can be facilitated by procedures for engaging community resources, including social and public health services.

At the summit, Martha Whitecotton, representing the voice of the consumer on the opening plenary panel, courageously shared her family's experience navigating the turbulent waters of the health care delivery system with her son, who has major depression. She repeatedly emphasized the importance of care coordination across systems—health care and education—for individuals with depression and extended her message to all chronic health conditions. Regrettably, her family's experience was typical of many of those with chronic illness—one of disjointed care, spotty communication between primary care providers and specialists, and frustration over not knowing where to turn in the community for help. Her son's case involved untimely diagnosis, failure to provide information on the evidence-based guidelines for depression treatment, lack of a centralized care plan shared among providers and the school system, and a myriad of health insurance obstacles. William Bruning, representing the Mid-America Coalition on Health Care Community Initiative on Depression, responded to the recurring themes in Whitecotton's presentation and provided an overview of how the coalition is addressing many of these breakdowns in the system (see Box 4-1).

KEY STRATEGIES

Participants identified four key strategies to address the major barriers to achieving high-quality, well-coordinated care: (1) align financial incentives; (2) provide educational supports; (3) use patient-centered health records supported by information and communications technology; and (4) ensure accountability and define roles for care.

Align Financial Incentives

Aligning financial incentives to reward high-quality care was a resounding theme throughout the summit, but was viewed as particularly compelling by participants in the care coordination session. Currently, the health care financing system is oriented to reward care for acute episodes, administered by a single provider, as opposed to a continuum of care across multiple providers. The disconnect between a system designed for acute care and the needs of more than 125 million people in the United States with chronic conditions is profound (Partnership for Prevention, 2002). The session participants identified important opportunities to address this problem, underscoring the need for a shared vision around:

- An operational construct—consistent with evidence-based medicine—of what good care coordination would be.
- How care coordination would be measured.
- How models of successful reimbursement for care coordination would be disseminated.

To initiate the identification of an operational construct of good care coordination, three elements of such a construct were identified: (1) technical quality or the comprehensiveness of care, (2) measures of efficiency, and (3) a patient-reported set of outcomes. Clearly, interdisciplinary teams of individuals with expertise in chronic diseases, in maximizing functional ability, in supporting family caregivers, in health education, and in social services are needed to specify these elements for chronic disease. Once these elements have been specified, internalized, and accepted by those who provide care, a reliable core set of measures and benchmarks can be established and serve as the basis for reimbursement, with financial incentives for more-effective implementation. This proposal parallels that of the finance group with regard to paying for performance and designing benefit packages around the creative accomplishment of better patient care.

Like the finance group, the care coordination group embraced the concept of budget neutrality. It was collectively acknowledged that effective care coordination could facilitate achieving the mandates of the *Quality Chasm* report to provide care "based on continuous healing relationships," support "decision making [that] is evidence-based," and "anticipate patients' needs, rather than simply reacting to events" (IOM, 2001:8). Care could also be provided in a more cost-effective manner. For example, a heart failure patient who was gaining weight and becoming increasingly symptomatic could be recognized by means of a patient-initiated phone call and

Box 4-1. Mid-America Coalition on Health Care Community Initiative on Depression

The Mid-America Coalition on Health Care Community Initiative on Depression initially began as a cooperative effort with 8 Kansas City employers in 1998 and has grown to encompass 15 employers—now impacting 140,000 lives. To identify the greatest health risks to employees and their families, the Behavioral Risk Factor Surveillance System survey was administered to 45,000 area residents by the Kansas Department of Health and Environment (Centers for Disease Control and Prevention, 2004). Based on the survey results, the founding group strongly endorsed targeting improved quality of care for depression, and thus focused on creating community and clinical support for timely diagnosis and treatment, destigmatization, and identification of the direct and indirect costs attributable to this disease. Some examples of interventions currently under way include the following:

Lack of care coordination

- A depression management toolkit developed jointly by Blue Cross and Blue Shield of Kansas City and New Directions Behavioral Health includes a Continuity of Care Form designed to encourage communications between primary care physicians and mental health professionals. Use of this instrument by providers is monitored by means of chart review.

- A new initiative aimed at changing physician work flow to incorporate screening for depression in cardiology, obstetrics/gynecology, and oncology offices is beginning and will incorporate a feedback loop to primary care providers upon initiation of treatment.

Need for a patient-centered approach to care

- An employee attitudinal survey, administered to 39,000 employees, revealed less stigma associated with depression than might have been assumed. However, the survey also identified a strong perception that there were no resources available for those with the disease within the workplace—even though eight employers had employee assistance programs. These results were used to inform subsequent projects undertaken by the coalition.

Failure to provide information about best practices

- The United Auto Workers–Ford Motor Company project, the Kansas City Quality Improvement Consortium, and the coalition are working on the dissemination of best practices. Evidence-based guidelines developed for depression have been uniformly adopted by all participating health plans. A future community education and awareness effort includes providing information on depression treatment to every employee who is diagnosed with depression and/or prescribed a selective serotonin reuptake inhibitor (SSRI).

- To disseminate information to patients at convenient times for them, intranet modules within each workplace provide links to depression facts and figures, community resources, and mental health benefits available from the employer.

Note: Additional information on the coalition can be found at its website (Mid-America Coalition on Health Care, 2004).

treated, rather than progressing to the point of requiring hospitalization. Thus the participants were not proposing payment for another layer of care, but suggesting a coordinated care approach that would yield savings to support this new structure of care. Three mechanisms were discussed for stimulating change in the current payment system: (1) direct payments for care coordination, (2) pay for performance, and (3) capitation.

To accelerate such changes, Don Berwick in his keynote address called for a dialogue among communities, Medicare, and Medicaid to institute cost-neutral flexibility in the use of funds for the treatment of chronic illnesses. Specific strategies discussed during this cross-cutting session that could be used by national leadership organizations to facilitate and simplify local efforts included granting waivers, collaborating with experts who perform quality measurement and data collection, and linking disparate parts of the system that currently benefit from the lack of coordination.

Provide Educational Supports

The session participants suggested that a major barrier to providing care consistent with the six aims of the *Quality Chasm* report is the difficulty of integrating multiple health providers to develop and communicate a common care plan for patients with chronic conditions. To do so becomes even more challenging as the number of individuals with multiple chronic conditions—now one in five Americans—continues to grow (Wu and Green, 2000). Thus, much attention was paid to the strategy of educational supports, which encompasses the following: (1) multi-disciplinary health professions education; (2) teaching of care coordination principles in academic settings; and (3) development of care teams.

The ability to work in interdisciplinary teams—to "cooperate, collaborate, communicate and integrate care in teams to ensure that care is continuous and reliable"—is a core competency recommended for all clinicians in the IOM report, *Health Professions Education: A Bridge to Quality* (IOM, 2003a:4). Yet concern was expressed by several of the condition-specific working groups that the health care workforce is not adequately trained to meet such demands of the changing practice environment. Overcoming this gap in knowledge requires redesigning both didactic and clinical components of professional training. Indeed, a survey of more than a thousand physicians revealed that two-thirds of respondents felt their training in care coordination and patient education had been inadequate (Anderson, 2003).

The depression working group suggested broadening the scope of training and increasing the knowledge base for that condition in the areas of screening, referral, and treatment. Accomplishing this will require a coordinated effort across the spectrum of mental health providers, including physicians, nurses, social workers, and psychologists. A dual strategy was proposed, beginning with practicing clinicians, managers, and educational leaders, and then progressing through faculty to currently enrolled students. A core set of competencies would need to be developed in these domains of care and then linked to ongoing licensing and certification programs. These competencies would be relevant across various chronic conditions in which depression is a prevalent comorbidity. Implementation of this strategy would begin at the local level in the first year and expand within 3 years to a national-level initiative. For example the depression group proposed:

- Educational credentialing organizations developing a nationally recognized systems-oriented approach to education and training for depression.
- Increased emphasis on these competencies embedded in licensing, certification, and recertification programs.

- Enhanced focus on system-based and practice-based approaches to the evolution of communication and collaboration as a core competency.

The asthma working group highlighted opportunities for expanding such training efforts by targeting office staff and other caregivers, with emphasis on completing and utilizing asthma action plans. For example, the Children's Mercy Hospital/Kansas City Asthma Coalition, a community participating in the summit, provides an excellent example of an office-based training program designed to improve care coordination while engaging patients and their caregivers. The coalition has taken a proactive approach to educating and training physicians to help them properly diagnose and deliver high-quality asthma care. One of its interdisciplinary interventions involves placing certified asthma educators into primary care offices for 8 weeks to provide instruction on evidence-based asthma care, practice role modeling, and stimulate behavior modification. The focus is on teaching clinicians to fully engage patients in the decision-making process and providing timely feedback on performance on key asthma indicators.

Outcomes from this intervention have been positive. A foundation of good asthma care is to emphasize the use of treatments that control/prevent asthma attacks, rather than bronchodilators that relieve symptoms once they have developed. Graph 1 in Box 4-2 demonstrates that from 1999 to 2001, very few controllers were prescribed as compared with relievers.

In 2002, however, after the intervention had been introduced, this ratio shifted favorably. As illustrated by Graph 2 in Box 4-2, quality-of-life scores (with higher numbers indicating better quality of life) were also found to increase postintervention for both patients with asthma and their caregivers (Jones and Portnoy, 2003; Miller et al., 2003).

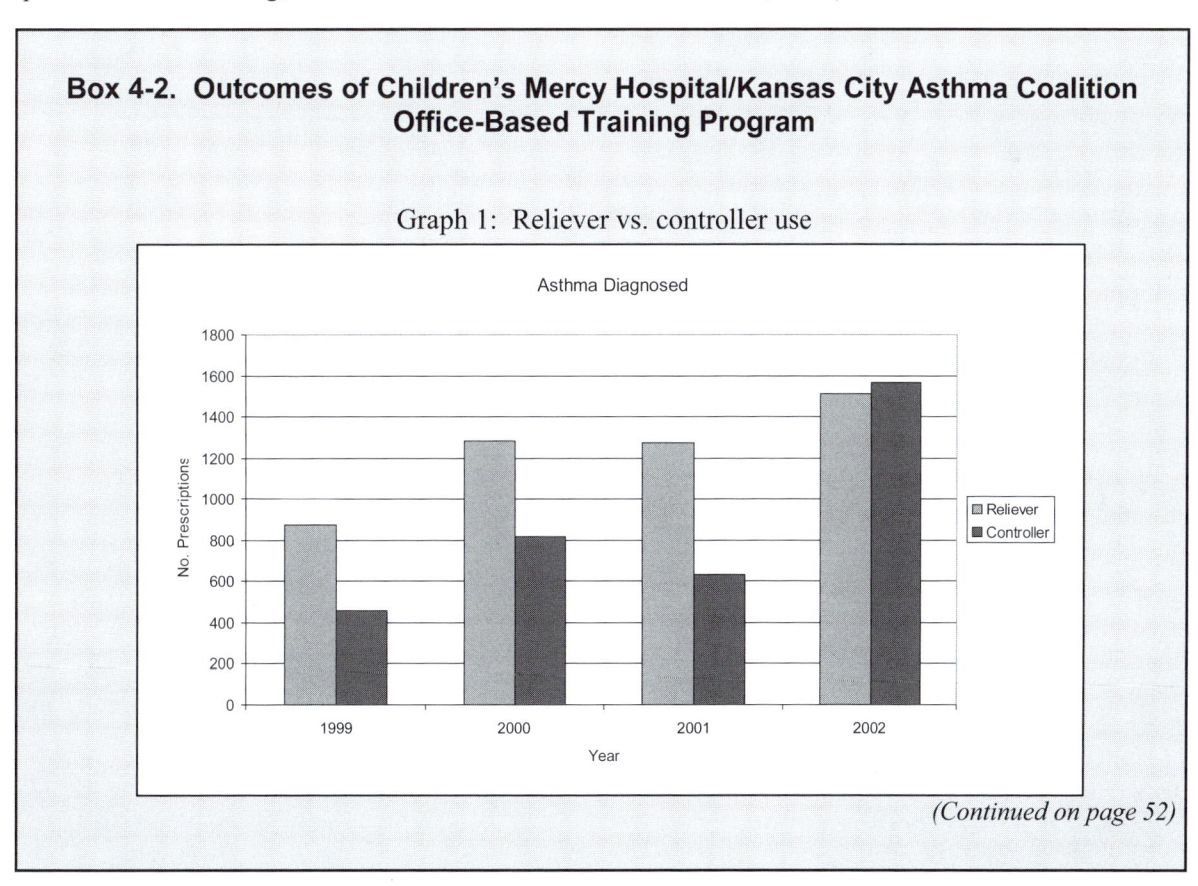

Box 4-2. Outcomes of Children's Mercy Hospital/Kansas City Asthma Coalition Office-Based Training Program

Graph 1: Reliever vs. controller use

(Continued on page 52)

(Continued from page 51)

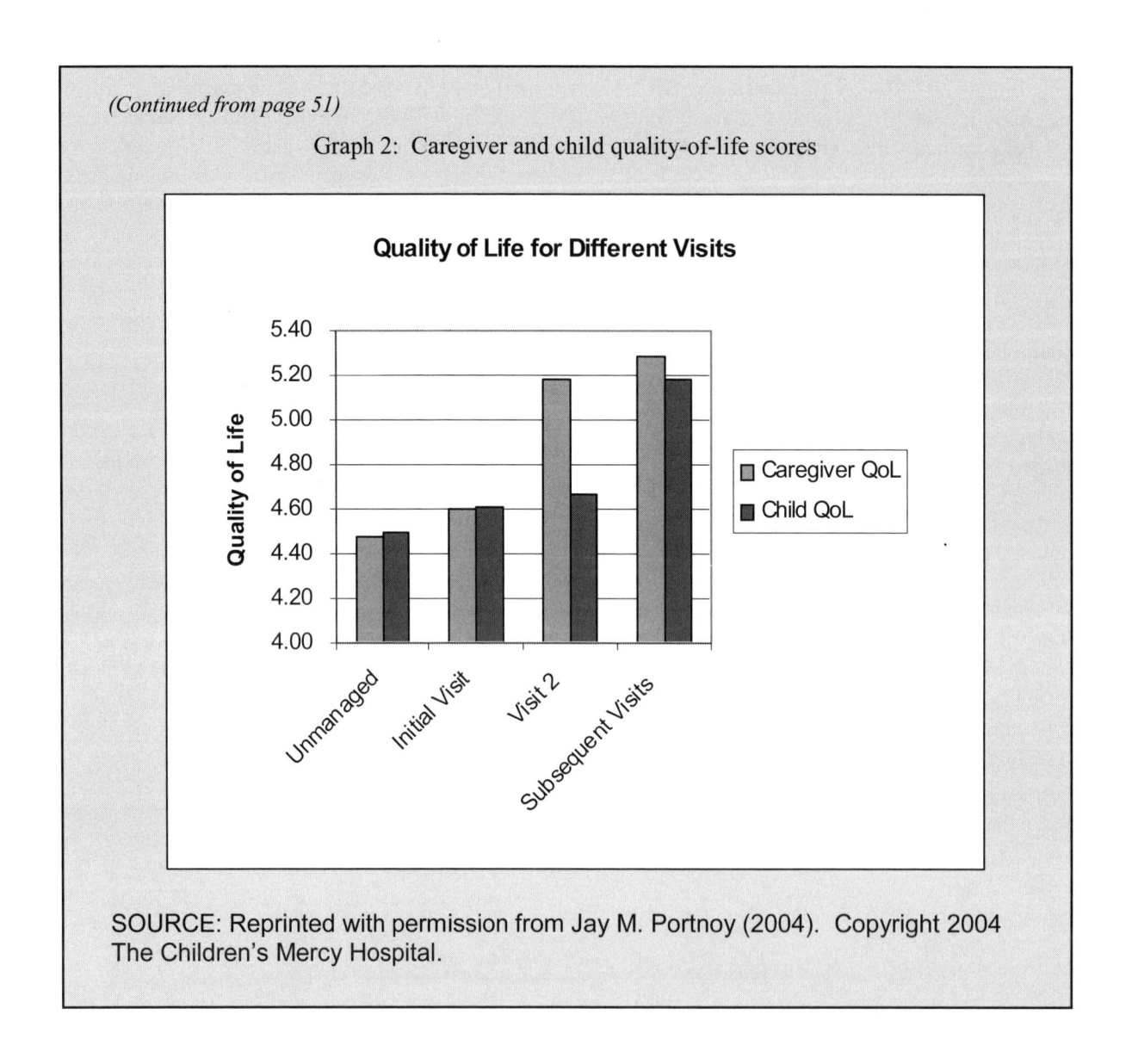

Graph 2: Caregiver and child quality-of-life scores

Quality of Life for Different Visits

Visit	Caregiver QoL	Child QoL
Unmanaged	4.48	4.50
Initial Visit	4.60	4.61
Visit 2	5.18	4.67
Subsequent Visits	5.28	5.18

SOURCE: Reprinted with permission from Jay M. Portnoy (2004). Copyright 2004 The Children's Mercy Hospital.

Richard Brumley, representing the Kaiser Permanente TriCentral Palliative Care Program community, shared with summit participants how that program developed a multidisciplinary care team to provide compassionate, patient-centered care for patients with chronic diseases approaching the end of life. See Box 4-3 for an overview of this program.

"As part of a team we think of all of us as having equal status—physicians, nurses, social workers, volunteers, chaplains, home health aides, the whole gamut. We all work together."

—Richard Brumley, summit participant

Box 4-3. Kaiser Permanente TriCentral Palliative Care Program

The Kaiser Permanente TriCentral Palliative Care Program uses a multidisciplinary approach to coordinate care in the home for patients transitioning from acute to palliative care during the last 12 months of life. After statistics showed that more than 50 percent of Kaiser Permanent TriCentral patients with heart failure, chronic obstructive pulmonary disease, and cancer died in either the medical/surgical unit or the intensive care unit, this program was developed to remedy the mismatch between patient preferences to die peacefully at home and the tendency for the health care system, as currently structured, to steer care at the end of life to the inpatient setting.

In this home-based care program, the patient and the family are considered an integral part of the care team and are supported by an array of professionals, including a physician, nurse, and social worker, while also receiving other psychosocial supports, such as from a chaplain or a volunteer. Making the patient the central focus with a radiating comprehensive care team encouraging active communication among all involved can heighten awareness of patient and family treatment preferences.

The program places a strong emphasis on evidence-based medicine and has developed protocols and care guidelines to reduce variability in practice. For example, it has implemented a checklist of the most important things team members must cover, such as pain management and advanced care planning, to ensure successful management of home-based care. The program has also incorporated continuous quality improvement (QI) into its daily practice. Thus when a problem arises, it is designated as a "QI Indicator" and is monitored monthly, with outcomes being shared within the program.

Results of a recent study, which included a comparison group, demonstrated that program participants had significantly higher satisfaction ratings and fewer emergency department visits, hospital days, skilled nursing facility days, and physician visits. Notably, 88 percent of patients receiving palliative care died at home. Additionally, on average those enrolled in the program experienced a 45 percent decrease in cost as compared with patients who received routine care (Brumley et al., 2003).

Use Patient-Centered Health Records

Recognizing that more than half of people with chronic conditions have three or more different physicians, the participants in this session stressed that an easily accessible, patient-centered health record is critical to ensure communication of treatment plans across providers (The Gallup Organization, 2002). Additionally, as patients are often shuttled to and from multiple care settings—hospitals, nursing homes, and home health—seamless transfer of heath information during these transitions is vital, as this is when patient are most vulnerable to breakdowns in care (Coleman et al., 2003).

Information and communications technology, in the form of electronic health records (EHRs) and patient registries, was proposed as a viable solution to facilitate rapid retrieval and sharing of patient data and address the problems associated with traditional paper health records that inhibit good care coordination, such as charts being misplaced and missing data (Tang et al., 1994). A fundamental concept articulated by many of the working groups was that patients should play a central role in the diffusion and exchange of their health data. To this end, patients should have total access to their records, with some suggesting that they be the ultimate locus of control. Succinctly stated, the overarching message from this session was to provide a common health record, preferably in electronic format, and complete with relevant patient information, to all those involved in care, and to empower patients to be in charge of their records.

In its action plan shared with the plenary session, the diabetes working group proposed specific parameters for EHRs, including standardization of data elements to allow for the flow of information among clinicians and patients. The group also proposed that patients be provided with a portable health record, such as a "smart card" containing their data and/or a web-based repository (see Box 4-4).

Ensure Accountability and Define Roles for Care

Successful management of chronic conditions requires the delivery of a vast array of services, hand-offs to other specialists, and aggressive follow-up. Given this complexity of care, it is essential that the care team's roles be clearly delineated and that administrative support be provided for new functions and responsibilities assumed by staff. In essence, this strategy holds each team member accountable for ensuring that a patient's care is properly managed.

The Chronic Care Model (see Chapter 1) supports this type of delivery system redesign at the micro-system level—the "front line" where small groups interact closely with patients. The model identifies the following elements as essential to the delivery of effective and

---

Box 4-4. Diabetes Working Group: Summary Action Plan

- Conduct a national summit for EHR standardization, hosted by the IOM and the National Health Information Infrastructure
    - Should include data elements for diabetes and other conditions.
    - Should facilitate registries, as well as communication among clinicians and between care providers and patients.
- Provide for portability, availability, and ownership of health records by patients—for example, smart card technology, web-based information repository

efficient care: (1) define roles and allocate tasks among team members; (2) plan interactions between informed, activated patients and a prepared practice team to support care that is evidence-based; (3) ensure regular follow-up by the care team; (4) provide more intense case management for more complex cases; and (5) administer care to patients that is culturally sensitive (Improving Chronic Illness Care, 2004; Quinn, 1992; Wagner et al., 2001).

In addition to defining providers' roles, it was suggested across the working groups that the community's role should be articulated in the overall care plan. The asthma working group encouraged health care practices to partner with community resources to foster two-way communication and sharing of expertise. For example, leaders from churches and social organizations could be targeted to provide peer education for chronic conditions prevalent in their communities in a comfortable, nearby setting. Both the pain control and heart failure working groups called for the development of media campaigns to raise public awareness of their respective conditions.

The Philadelphia Department of Health—recently awarded a Department of Health and Humans Services Steps to a HealthierUS grant (see Box 1-5 in Chapter 1)—described its initiative to coordinate care for children with asthma across multiple systems and link them to resources in the community (Steps to a HealthierUS Initiative, 2004). Box 4-5 provides a description of this program.

CLOSING STATEMENT

The participants in this session outlined several strategies for achieving good care coordination. First, financial incentives need to be in place to reward and encourage care coordination. Implementing this strategy will require conceptualizing and operationalizing what care coordination is so it can be measured and reimbursed accordingly. Second, well-trained interdisciplinary teams of diverse practitioners—physicians, nurses, allied health professionals, social workers, and others—are critical to delivering high-quality, well-orchestrated care. To meet this need, current approaches to clinical training must be redesigned to address the necessary skills. Third, a patient-centered EHR is a viable mechanism for facilitating care coordination. Finally, accountability to the patient is paramount, necessitating clearly defined roles for clinicians, as well as mobilization of community resources.

Box 4-5. Philadelphia Department of Health's Child Asthma Link Line

The Philadelphia Department of Health's Child Asthma Link Line targets children who present to local pediatric emergency departments with an acute exacerbation of asthma. The visit is viewed as a sentinel event and triggers immediate intervention, including a follow-up phone call to the parent or guardian, referral to a specialist, and enrollment in an asthma disease management education program for both caregiver and patient. Educational programs use a train-the-trainer approach, with parents and children who have been through the program serving as mentors to newcomers. Additional interventions include an environmental assessment for asthma triggers, partnering with the school system to ensure that an asthma action plan is in place, and coordination of medical insurance benefits to help families obtain coverage for uninsured children. This multilevel initiative brings all providers together to center care on the child's needs.

REFERENCES

Anderson G. 2003. Chronic care. *Advanced Studies in Medicine* 3(2):110–111. [Online]. Available: http://www.jhasim.com/files/articlefiles/pdf/journal_p110(V3-2)MC_health.pdf [accessed April 30, 2004].

Brumley RD, Enguidanos S, Cherin DA. 2003. Effectiveness of a home-based palliative care program for end-of-life. *Journal of Palliative Medicine* 6(5):715–724.

Centers for Disease Control and Prevention. 2004. *CDC's Behavioral Risk Factor Surveillance System.* [Online]. Available: http://www.cdc.gov/brfss/ [accessed March 23, 2004].

Coleman EA, Boult C, American Geriatrics Society Health Care Systems Committee. 2003. Improving the quality of transitional care for persons with complex care needs. *Journal of the American Geriatrics Society* 51(4):556–557.

Improving Chronic Illness Care. 2004. *ICIC: The Chronic Care Model: Delivery System Design.* [Online]. Available: www.improvingchroniccare.org/change/model/deliv_design.html [accessed February 26, 2004].

IOM (Institute of Medicine). 2001. *Crossing the Quality Chasm: A New Health System for the 21st Century.* Washington, DC: National Academy Press.

IOM. 2003a. *Health Professions Education: A Bridge to Quality.* Greiner AC, Knebel E, eds. Washington, DC: National Academy Press.

IOM. 2003b. *Priority Areas for National Action: Transforming Health Care Quality.* Adams K, Corrigan JM, eds. Washington, DC: National Academy Press.

Jones EM, Portnoy JM. 2003. Modification of provider behavior to achieve improved asthma outcomes. *Current Allergy and Asthma Reports* 3(6):484–490.

Mid-America Coalition on Health Care. 2004. *Mid-America Coalition on Health Care.* [Online]. Available: http://www.machc.org/ [accessed April 30, 2004].

Miller K, Ward-Smith P, Cox K, Jones EM, Portnoy JM. 2003. Development of an asthma disease management program in a children's hospital. *Current Allergy and Asthma Reports* 3(6):491–500.

Partnership for Prevention. 2002. *Better Lives for People with Chronic Conditions.* Baltimore, MD: John Hopkins University, Robert Wood Johnson Foundation.

Portnoy JM. 2004 (January 6). Patient Self Management: Asthma. Presentation at the Institute of Medicine 1st Annual Crossing the Quality Chasm Summit, Washington, DC. Institute of Medicine Committee on Crossing the Quality Chasm.

Quinn JB. 1992. *Intelligent Enterprise: A Knowledge and Service Based Paradigm for Industry.* New York, NY: New York Free Press.

The Gallup Organization. *Serious Chronic Illness Survey.* 2002. The Gallup Organization.

Shortell SM, Gillies RR, Anderson DA. 2000. *Remaking Health Care in America.* 2nd Edition. San Francisco, CA: Jossey-Bass.

Steps to a HealthierUS Initiative. 2004. *Grantees, Steps to a HealthierUS Initiative.* [Online]. Available: http://www.healthierus.gov/steps/grantees.html [accessed March 24, 2004].

Tang P, Fafchamps D, Shortliffe EH. 1994. *Traditional Hospital Records as a Source of Clinical Data in the Outpatient Setting.* Eighteenth Annual Symposium on Computer Applications in Medical Care, Washington, DC. Pp. 575–579.

Wagner EH, Austin BT, Davis C, Hindmarsh M, Schaefer J, Bonomi A. 2001. Improving chronic illness care: Translating evidence into action. *Health Affairs (Millwood, VA)* 20(6):64–78.

Wu SY, Green A. 2000. *Projection of Chronic Illness Prevalence and Cost Inflation.* Santa Monica, CA: RAND Corporation.

Chapter 5
Patient Self-Management Support

DEFINITION AND OVERARCHING THEMES

The overall goal of the cross-cutting session on patient self-management support was to identify strategies that can be used by communities to help patients manage their condition(s) while leading active and productive lives. The focus was on evidence-based self-management programs that include goal setting, problem solving, symptom management, and shared decision making and are applicable for a diverse population, including those with limited health literacy. To establish a common frame of reference, the participants generally accepted the following definitions (IOM, 2003):

> Self-management support is defined as the systematic provision of education and supportive interventions by health care staff to increase patients' skills and confidence in managing their health problems, including regular assessment of progress and problems, goal setting, and problem-solving support. Self-management is defined as the tasks that individuals must undertake to live well with one or more chronic conditions. These tasks include having the confidence to deal with medical management, role management, and emotional management of their conditions.

From the outset, the session participants drew a clear distinction among patient education, support for self-management, and self-management itself. Patient education refers to traditional, largely didactic instruction given to patients, focused mainly on information and technical skills. An example is a diabetes educator lecturing to a group of diabetics and then teaching them how to self-inject insulin or monitor glucose levels. Self-management support consists of the means by which individual practitioners and the broader health care system support patients in the methodical exercise of self-management (Bodenheimer et al., 2002). Self-management encompasses problem-solving skills and patients' collaborative involvement in establishing goals to manage their disease.

KEY STRATEGIES

Participants proposed five key strategies for catalyzing the diffusion of self-management and self-management support: (1) identify and disseminate evidence-based self-management practices; (2) recognize the centrality of self-management to good patient care, and incorporate this recognition into the health care culture (including at the national level); (3) provide incentives for the appropriate use of self-management support integrated into the delivery of health care; (4) develop self-management programs and tools that are applicable to diverse populations; and (5) make better use of all members of the health care team.

Identify and Disseminate Evidence-Based Self-Management Practices

Participants proposed that existing and future best self-management practices be consolidated and disseminated to providers, patients, and their families, perhaps through a centralized clearinghouse. The problem today is that those wishing to implement best self-management practices often cannot find information about them, or distinguish those that are evidence-based from those that are not. Session participants also supported the need for expansion of the existing evidence base on effective self-management practices. There was a call for responsive research that is practical and relatively rapid-cycle so as to provide a sufficient foundation for moving forward.

Participants suggested learning from practical models and, on a parallel track, developing a firmer scientific base. It was emphasized that the scope of this research should extend to all levels of the health care system, from working one-on-one with patients in the practice of self-management, to changing office environments, to revamping entire systems of care. Additionally, best practices must be appropriately tailored for different populations and age groups, particularly children and adolescents.

Two communities represented at the summit—Controlling Asthma in the Richmond Metropolitan Area (CARMA) and the Oregon Heart Failure Project (OHFP)—shared with session participants some of their accomplishments in self-management support and lessons learned in working with patients and their families to assist them in self-managing asthma and heart failure, respectively. Both rely on evidence-based guidelines as the foundation for their programs (see Boxes 5-1 and 5-2).

Box 5-1. Controlling Asthma in the Richmond Metropolitan Area

The Controlling Asthma in the Richmond Metropolitan Area (CARMA) project began in 2001 with the aim of improving asthma management for children from birth through age 18, with particular focus on disadvantaged children with severe, poorly controlled asthma. The goals of the project are to improve the quality of life for children and parents and to decrease emergency room visits and hospitalizations. Funding is provided by the Centers for Disease Control and Prevention as part of a larger agency program, Controlling Asthma in American Cities.

CARMA focuses the efforts of members of a community coalition on offering self-management support to children, their families, teachers, and others so they can better manage asthma and the factors that affect it—such as the environment, diet/nutrition, and physical activity—according to evidence-based guidelines. Collaborative relationships with a variety of service providers, including hospitals, managed care organizations, primary care providers, nursing and case management organizations, pharmacies, schools, preschools (including the Head Start programs), and the American Lung Association, are the foundation for programs incorporating national guidelines developed by the Asthma and Allergy Foundation of America. School programs are based on the You Can Control Asthma and Power Breathing curricula, tailored to accommodate the psychosocial needs of the target population.

Since its inception, CARMA has provided preschool and elementary school programs that have successfully impacted more than 500 children. A newly released manual, *Guidelines for Managing Asthma in Virginia Schools: A Team Approach*, produced by the Virginia Department of Health, Virginia Department of Education, and Virginia Asthma Coalition, offers further support for these programs. PACE (Professional Acknowledgment for Continuing Education) training and academic detailing provide continuing education for primary care providers serving the community. Two managed care organizations collaborate with CARMA to evaluate the effectiveness of intensive case management for Medicaid enrollees with severe asthma.

Note: Additional information about the project can be found at the CARMA website (CARMA, 2004).

> **Box 5-2. The Oregon Heart Failure Project**
>
> Initiated in 2001, the Oregon Heart Failure Project (OHFP) is a statewide study aimed at addressing the persistently high mortality rates among patients who have experienced heart failure and the shortage of cardiologists in certain localities. The project focuses on evidence-based interventions in the ambulatory setting and patient self-management that will improve health outcomes.
>
> OHFP developed out of a partnership between the American College of Cardiology Foundation's (ACCF) Guidelines Applied in Practice (GAP) project and the Oregon Medicare Quality Improvement Organization, with the idea of using Oregon as a testing ground. The project relies on several key features: (1) the implementation of clinical guidelines for heart failure developed by ACCF and the American Heart Association; (2) a heart failure registry for use by physicians to monitor progress; and (3) a toolkit of standardized materials including a clinic visit form, a clinician guide, a patient overview, patient instruction and medication instruction sheets, a patient diary, and information about the patient registry. More extensive materials are also available to physicians to support their participation in OHFP, including a patient-driven action plan, methods for measuring and evaluating outcomes, and guidelines for improving the process of care from a systems perspective. The self-management support "tip sheet" below was developed for physicians and nurse practitioners.
>
> **Increasing Your Patient's Success with Self-Care for Heart Failure**
>
> **Use these questions and tips as a guide for creating a self-care plan with a patient.**
>
> *Listen to your patient*
>
> Find out what your patient believes about living with heart failure. Sample questions:
>
> - What does the diagnosis of heart failure mean to you?
> - What bothers you most about living with heart failure?
> - Do you believe that taking medications and taking care of yourself can improve the quality and length of your life?
> - How confident are you that you can maintain a program of modifying your diet, getting exercise, and recording your daily weight?
> - What interferes with your ability to make changes and stick to them?
> - Does the cost of your medications get in the way of taking them regularly?
> - Do you have family, friends, or a community organization available if you need help?
> - Have you had any bad experiences with medications or treatments that make you reluctant to try new medications or strategies?
>
> *(Continued on page 61)*

PATIENT SELF-MANAGEMENT SUPPORT

> *(Continued from page 60)*
>
> - What are your goals (e.g., "celebrate my 50th wedding anniversary" or "play golf with friends")?
> - Do you think treatment can help you reach your goal?
>
> ***Help the patient set realistic self-care goals***
>
> - Make the recommended treatment plan clear, concrete, simple, and understandable.
> - Focus recommendations on behavior changes such as exercising every day, rather than numerical outcomes such as losing 10 pounds in a month.
> - Guide the patient to focus on one or two small, realistic changes that he or she can begin immediately.
> - Encourage the patient to create a goal that involves positive action (e.g., use lemon juice instead of salt for seasoning).
> - At the end of the visit, ask each patient to describe the actions he or she will begin immediately and why the actions are important.
>
> Note: Information about OHFP and ACCF GAP can be found at the respective websites (American College of Cardiology, 2004a; American College of Cardiology, 2004b; OMPRO, 2004).

Recognize the Centrality of Self-Management to Good Patient Care, and Incorporate This Recognition into the Health Care Culture

Participants suggested that implementing this strategy will require a fundamental shift from the perception of self-management as an "add-on" to care to its becoming an expected and systematic part of patient care. Accomplishing this shift will in turn require transforming physician/provider culture, diffusing these values up to the national level. The asthma group specifically called for changing the culture and finance of health care, and for encouraging health care providers, patients, and communities to embrace self-management as the central aim of good asthma care.

It was generally agreed that the reactive, visit-based design of the current health care system—rather than simply clinician attitudes—is the major barrier to the widespread adoption of self-management principles. For example, the standard 10- to 15-minute office visit is not conducive to patient-centered care or to more labor-intensive interactions, such as collaborative goal setting and problem solving/action planning. Furthermore, payment mechanisms are not designed to reward these types of exchanges or follow-up support for self-management.

In addition to supply-side issues that impact the uptake of self-management by clinicians, demand-side issues related to patient and family expectations should also be considered. Establishing a consumer culture and creating demand for evidence-based self-management services were suggested by both the asthma and diabetes working groups, including social marketing techniques to activate patients in seeking self-management programs and following self-management suggestions.

Jack Ebeler, President and CEO of the Alliance of Community Health Plans, shared with summit participants information about a collaborative formed among health plans that are developing system supports to promote patient engagement and self-management. The alliance's Advancing Better Care Project is described in Box 5-3.

Box 5-3. Advancing Better Care Project

The Advancing Better Care project is a collaborative effort by member organizations of the Alliance of Community Health Plans in the broad area of patient engagement and activation. The project responds to the priority area of self-management/health literacy identified by the IOM (2003), as participating organizations will be developing and improving tools and system supports that make self-management, self-care, and shared decision making tenable. Currently, nine health plans are participating in the collaborative, with a range of projects under way. The following are two of the projects focused on collaborative goal setting and self-management:

- Kaiser Permanente (Oakland, California) is pursuing an initiative to develop and improve its members' self-care skills by facilitating shared medical decision making among members and providers. A major focus is self-management of chronic disease. The initiative encompasses five overarching strategies: (1) embedding self-management support into population management, (2) promoting self-management support in the clinical encounter, (3) strengthening medication adherence, (4) turning didactic patient education into self-management education, and (5) offering alternatives to classroom-based self-management education.
- Group Health Cooperative (Seattle, Washington) is pursuing an initiative to improve its members' health through a patient on-line health record feature on its member website—MyGroupHealth. The patient on-line health record is a privacy- and security-protected view into patients' individual health records, housed in Group Health's clinical information system. MyGroupHealth allows patients to refill and renew prescriptions, make and view appointments, view laboratory and other test results, and email their health care providers via the Internet. Through the use of this system, patient and physician now write the formerly physician-centric health record together.

Note: Additional information on other projects in the Advancing Better Care collaborative can be found at the project's website (Alliance of Community Health Plans, 2004).

Provide Incentives for the Appropriate Use of Self-Management Support Integrated into the Delivery of Health Care

Participants suggested that the assimilation of self-management practices will continue to be delayed unless these practices are fully integrated into the core components of health care delivery. Historically, interventions that promote self-management have not been reimbursed, partly because of the lack of a strong business case for short-term return on investment (see Chapter 6). Additionally, it is difficult to imagine progress in self-management support without parallel progress in care coordination, as discussed in Chapter 4, particularly with regard to the importance of interdisciplinary teams and a system that reimburses the bundling of harmonized services. Although evidence is mounting that chronic disease self-management programs are effective in changing health behaviors, improving health status, and decreasing health service utilization, participants emphasized that research in this area must continue to expand and be steadily infused into the mainstream payment structure of both public and private purchasers of health care (Gibson et al., 2000; Lorig et al., 1999, 2001; Norris et al., 2001).

Develop Self-Management Programs and Tools Applicable to Diverse Populations

Rather than a one-size-fits-all approach, this strategy involves developing self-management support and self-management programs that are appropriate in terms of culture, language, age, literacy, and community. Developing such a program involves more than translation and/or simplification; rather, the program and associated supports must be flexible enough to be individualized around patient preferences, including age, gender, and lifestyle. There was considerable discussion on the topic of health literacy, focused not only on reading comprehension, but more important on the ability to assimilate and process medical information (IOM, 2004). It was suggested that, while traditional self-management programs have been delivered on a one-to-one or small-group basis, newer technologies, such as computers and automated telephone messaging systems, might be used in the future (Piette et al., 2000; Schillinger et al., 2002).

Completing a patient-generated "action plan" is a key feature of a self-management program. This tool assists in developing short-term goals (1–2 weeks) to help patients initiate changes and achieve success in managing their condition effectively. The key to good action planning is for the actions to be undertaken to be generated by the patient, not the provider. First, the patient indicates what he or she would like to do and what is achievable given the family and social environment. Then collaboratively with the provider, the patient refines the action plan to make it behaviorally specific. Finally, the provider asks how certain the patient is that he or she will complete the plan on a scale of 0 (being totally uncertain) to 10 (being totally certain). If the patient gives an answer of 7 or above, self-efficacy theory predicts that the plan will be accomplished, and no further work is needed. If the answer is below 7, the patient is asked what the problems might be, and problem solving ensues. Box 5-4 presents a case scenario for developing a self-management action plan with a patient.

Make Better Use of All Members of the Health Care Team

All members of the health care team should understand and carry out their roles in offering self-management support or directly providing interventions (Glasgow and Eakin, 2000; Glasgow et al., 2003). For example:

- The receptionist might mail out and collect self-management assessments or refer all chronic disease patients to classes.
- A team of health professionals might prepare a series of customized handouts at different reading levels on a variety of self-management issues, which would be stored

> **Box 5-4. Case Scenario for Developing a Self-Management Action Plan**
>
> Provider: We have discussed several things you might want to do to help with your high blood pressure. What do you think would be realistic for you to do in the next week or two?
>
> Patient: Maybe I could exercise.
>
> Provider: That would be great. Exactly what will you do and how often?
>
> Patient: I guess I will walk for 15 minutes.
>
> Provider: Generally, we like to see people exercising 3 to 5 days a week. How many days each week will you walk 15 minutes?
>
> Patient: I can do this at least 4 days.
>
> Provider: Great! Can you tell me when in the day you will do this?
>
> Patient: I can do it before I eat lunch on my lunch hour.
>
> Provider: Sounds like you have a plan. How certain are you that you will walk for 15 minutes 4 days a week during your lunch hour, with 10 being totally certain and 0 being totally uncertain.
>
> Patient: Well, now that I think about, it 5 or 6.
>
> Provider: What do you think will be the problem?
>
> Patient: It is sometimes really hot at noon, and I don't like going outside.
>
> Provider: Boy, I understand that—can you think of some alternatives?
>
> Patient: Yeah, on days that are hot, I will walk after dinner.
>
> Provider: Now how sure are you—remember 0 to 10.
>
> Patient: Oh, now I am an 8.
>
> Provider: Terrific—I will be really interested in how you are getting on.
>
> SOURCE: Lorig (1999). Copyright 2004 by Stanford University.

in the computer and printed out by any staff member as the need might arise.
- The physician might see some patients in group visits, offering a combination of self-management support and clinical care.
- The nurse or social worker might provide information on self-management programs or action planning and follow-up support after the patient has met with the provider.

Similar to the emphasis in the care coordination session on learning how to interact cooperatively on multidisciplinary teams (see Chapter 4), the importance of teaching self-management principles in both the academic and clinical settings was stressed during this session. Health care workers should not only have specific training in clearly defined competencies appropriate to their profession, but also practice and train together as a team with specified roles and performance expectations. However, physicians and most other health professionals do not routinely receive formal training in self-management techniques during their professional education. As a result, they usually are unfamiliar with the attributes of these interventions and tend to be ill equipped to provide them.

Self-management support is well established as a fundamental component of nursing education, which can serve as a resource for moving forward in this area. A case in point is a recent a study funded by the National Institute of Nursing Research that presents a model of care addressing self-management support for the elderly with heart failure. This model provides chronically ill patients and their families with the knowledge and care management skills to help avoid declines in health and offset future hospitalizations (Naylor et al., 2004).

It is important to view self-management support in tandem with family-management support, being cognizant of the contributions of caregivers. For example, referrals might be provided to websites offering helpful tips on bathing, incontinence, behavior problems, and preparing for the future. Finally, health care professionals would benefit from collaborating with consumer groups, which have played a major role in patient advocacy and support.

CLOSING STATEMENT

In summary, self-management and self-management support are increasingly being recognized as part of evidenced-based best practices in health care. This is especially true for people with chronic disease, with self-management being recognized as central in the Chronic Care Model (Glasgow et al., 2002). However, the present health care system is ill prepared to integrate self-management into mainstream patient care. Changes are needed at many levels, from financing for self-management support/interventions to training of health care professionals. While all these changes are not within the purview of any one person or organization, such changes can take place. The participants in this session expressed their strong belief that self-management and self-management support are not only desirable but necessary to bridge the quality chasm.

REFERENCES

Alliance of Community Health Plans. 2004. *Alliance of Community Health Plans.* [Online]. Available: http://www.achp.org [accessed April 30, 2004].

American College of Cardiology. 2004a. *Guidelines Applied in Practice (GAP) Program.* [Online]. Available: http://www.acc.org/gap/gap.htm [accessed April 28, 2004].

American College of Cardiology. 2004b. *American College of Cardiology, Oregon Chapter.* [Online]. Available: http://www.oregoncardiology.org/default.html [accessed April 30, 2004].

Bodenheimer T, Lorig KR, Holman H, Grumbach K. 2002. Patient self-management of chronic disease in primary care. *The Journal of the American Medical Association* 288(19):2469–2475.

CARMA (Controlling Asthma in the Richmond Metropolitan Area). *CARMA—Controlling Asthma in the Richmond Metropolitan Area.* [Online]. Available: http://www.carmakids.org [accessed April 30, 2004].

Gibson PG, Coughlan J, Wilson AJ, Abramson M, Bauman A, Hensley MJ, Walters EH. 2004. Self-management education and regular practitioner review for adults with asthma. The Cochrane Library (3):

Glasgow RE, Davis CL, Funnell MM, Beck A. 2003. Implementing practical interventions to support chronic illness self-management. *Joint Commission Journal on Quality and Safety* 29 (11):563–574.

Glasgow RE, Eakin EG. 2000. Medical office-based interventions. In: Snoek F, Skinner C, eds. *Psychology in Diabetes Care* 6:141–168.

Glasgow RE, Funnell MM, Bonomi AE, Davis C, Beckham V, Wagner EH. 2002. Self-management aspects of the improving chronic illness care breakthrough series: Implementation with diabetes and heart failure teams. *Annals of Behavioral Medicine: A Publication of the Society of Behavioral Medicine* 24(2):80–87.

IOM (Institute of Medicine). 2003. *Priority Areas for National Action: Transforming Health Care Quality.* Adams K, Corrigan JM, eds. Washington, DC: National Academy Press.

IOM. 2004. *Health Literacy: A Prescription to End Confusion.* Nielsen-Bohlman L, Panzer AM, Kindig DA, eds. Washington, DC: National Academy Press.

Lorig KR. 1999. *The Chronic Disease Self-Management Workshop Leaders Manual.* Stanford, CA: Stanford University.

Lorig KR, Ritter P, Stewart AL, Sobel DS, Brown BW Jr, Bandura A, Gonzalez VM, Laurent DD, Holman HR. 2001. Chronic disease self-management program: 2-year health status and health care utilization outcomes. *Medical Care* 39(11):1217–1223.

Lorig KR, Sobel DS, Stewart AL, Brown BW Jr, Bandura A, Ritter P, Gonzalez VM, Laurent DD, Holman HR. 1999a. Evidence suggesting that a chronic disease self-management program can improve health status while reducing hospitalization: A randomized trial. *Medical Care* 37(1):5–14.

Naylor MD, Brooten DA, Campbell RL, Maislin G, McCauley KM, Schwartz JS. 2004. Transitional care of older adults hospitalized with heart failure: A randomized, controlled trial. *Journal of the American Geriatrics Society* 52(5):675–684.

Norris SL, Engelgau MM, Narayan KM. 2001. Effectiveness of self-management training in type 2 diabetes: A systematic review of randomized controlled trials. *Diabetes Care* 24(3):561–587.

OMPRO. 2004. *Welcome to OMPRO, a Healthcare Quality Resource.* [Online]. Available: http://www.ompro.org/about_ompro/about_index.htm [accessed March 18, 2004].

Piette JD, Weinberger M, McPhee SJ. 2000. The effect of automated calls with telephone nurse follow-up on patient-centered outcomes of diabetes care: A randomized, controlled trial. *Medical Care* 38(2):218–230.

Schillinger D, Grumbach K, Piette J, Wang F, Osmond D, Daher C, Palacios J, Sullivan GD, Bindman AB. 2002. Association of health literacy with diabetes outcomes. *The Journal of the American Medical Association* 288(4):475–482.

Chapter 6
Finance

DEFINITION AND OVERARCHING THEMES

The goal of the cross-cutting session on finance was to identify strategies that can be used by communities to change the way care is paid for by both the public and private sectors, with the aim of encouraging and rewarding higher-value care delivery. Finance and payment reforms building on demonstrations with the potential to lead to ongoing systemwide changes were highlighted, as well as methods communities might use to develop a business case for a given intervention from a variety of perspectives.

The following definition of finance that supports quality improvement—whose origins trace to the *Quality Chasm* report—was accepted by participants in this session and served as the framework for the discussions that followed:

> Payment incentives should be aligned with quality improvement. Fair payment should be provided for good clinical management of patients, so that providers neither gain nor lose financially for taking care of the sickest patients and most complex cases. Providers should have an opportunity to share in the benefits of quality improvement. Incentives should be aligned with the implementation of care processes based on best practices and the achievement of better patient outcomes, as well as other desired actions, such as investment in information and communications technology infrastructure. Finally, finance in this context may also include defining a business case for a given intervention from a variety of perspectives, including the physician group, hospital, or community at large.

The objectives for the health care finance system articulated by participants in this session were to create a system that helps prevent the onset of disease and comorbidities; impedes the progression of chronic illness; and pays for effective, evidence-based health care. The participants also underscored that any changes to the finance system should be budget neutral—meaning that the issue is not the absence of sufficient resources. To the contrary, many participants noted that, if anything, the current system is characterized by substantial waste, and the needed changes involve redirecting and redistributing revenue streams rather than just spending more money. As a result, it must be accepted that there will be winners and losers. The challenge identified by the group was to overcome the considerable incentives to maintain the status quo among those who might be negatively impacted. Participants suggested that the key will be to align payments with incentives for providing high-quality care.

This sentiment was also echoed in Don Berwick's keynote speech when he called for payment reform—not more money, but different ways to pay—as a critical strategy for improving the quality of health care for all Americans. Throughout his address, he provided numerous examples of overuse of procedures that do not help, or even harm, patients; underuse of procedures that are proven to be beneficial to patients; and misuse or errors of execution of care (Chassin and Galvin, 1998). These examples included, respectively, excessive use of intensive care and invasive care at the end of life (Wennberg et al., 2004); failure to adhere to evidence-based care protocols for diagnosing, treating, and monitoring depression, as illustrated by Martha Whitecotton's presentation (see Chapter 4) (Wang et al., 2000); and the ill effects of medication errors experienced by 7 of every 100 patients admitted to America's hospitals (Bates et al., 1995).

Berwick also cited the work of John Wennberg at Dartmouth College—a pioneer in the study of variation in the delivery of care—and others to demonstrate that inconsistencies in care persist throughout the country despite first being called to our attention more than 30 years ago (Wennberg and Gittelsohn, 1973). For example, in a study using Medicare data, even after controlling for confounding variables, a 400 percent variation was found nationwide, by hospital service area, in the likelihood that a person with heart failure would be admitted to the hospital (Fisher et al., 2000). Another study identified the potential for generating savings to Medicare of almost 30 percent of total costs if all regions provided care as efficiently as do those in the top quartile, with some indications that more efficient areas provide higher-quality care (Fisher et al., 2003a,b). In response, Berwick proposed ridding the existing health care system of waste and addressing variations in care, rather than funneling more money into the system (which currently accounts for more than 15 percent of gross domestic product) (Levit et al., 2004). He urged finding better ways to pay for chronic care, move payment toward better alignment with high quality, encourage best practices, and increase cooperation among providers (Berwick, 2004).

> *"The United States spends 40 percent more than any other western democracy on health care per capita...for which our outcomes of care are generally no better than, and in many well-documented cases worse than, care in these other countries. We spend more and we get less."*
>
> —Don Berwick, summit keynote speaker

An important caveat expressed during the session was that finance strategies, such as those discussed at the summit, developed to do more on a prepayment basis focus on individuals who are already part of the health care system and have some type of insurance coverage, excluding the uninsured. The IOM has issued several reports calling for universal health insurance coverage (IOM, 2002a, 2003a, 2004). While this issue was not a specific focus of the summit, many participants expressed the view that action must be taken immediately to provide all Americans with insurance coverage.

KEY STRATEGIES

The session participants identified four strategies for addressing the primary barriers facing the finance system: (1) implement performance-based payment models; (2) employ evidence-based benefit design; (3) provide payment for proven quality support services; and (4) engage consumers with information and incentives.

Implement Performance-Based Payment Models

This key strategy was described by session participants as paying clinicians or provider groups (physician organizations, hospitals, and health plans) differentially based on the quality and efficiency of the care they deliver. Inherent in this model is the ability to measure performance and outcomes, which requires agreement on the evidence supporting the measures used, including those for quality support services such as group visits, patient education, and care management. To achieve this goal would require changing the current base payment system and providing incentives for both providers and patients to change behavior.

Although the participants shared a sense of urgency regarding the implementation of this strategy, they acknowledged that the broad system changes needed might best be accomplished through a series of transitional (but not small) steps, as opposed to a one-step overhaul of the entire current system. They also identified the following impediments to redesigning existing payment models to reimburse only effective care:

- The CPT® (current procedure terminology) code encounter model rewards clinicians on the basis of volume (AMA, 2004). A shift to some other payment model, such as providing aggregate payment in the form of performance-based capitation by chronic condition—could result in some providers seeing a decline in revenues (predictably to be met with resistance) if components of evidence-based chronic care such as those described in the Chronic Care Model are not in place (Wagner et al., 2001; see Chapter 1 for a description of the Chronic Care Model).
- The accurate and reliable metrics and data infrastructure needed to link quality and efficiency to payment models are lacking.

There was strong agreement that the foundation of valid pay-for-performance efforts is having standardized performance measures. Session participants noted that federal agencies, such as the Centers for Medicare and Medicaid Services (CMS), must take a leadership role in requiring national-level performance reporting on a core set of measures. Participants agreed with the recommendation of the IOM report *Leadership by Example: Coordinating Government Roles in Improving Health Care Quality* that while the role of the federal government is crucial, such an effort would best be advanced through public–private partnerships (IOM, 2002b). The condition-specific working groups also stressed the need for a succinct set of measures on which to focus assessment of quality improvements efforts (see Chapter 8).

Requesting help from CMS, national champion Pacific Business Group on Health (PBGH) committed to supporting local and national initiatives to pay for performance for whole communities. Arnold Milstein, M.D., Medical Director at PBGH, summed up the dilemma of the current payment system with the following statement during the commitment portion of the summit: "I was struck by Don Berwick's remarks yesterday, that Appleton Wisconsin's has the lowest decile per beneficiary costs for Medicare and that the major health plan serving that area had the highest HEDIS® scores in the country in 2002 [American Hospital Publishing, Inc, 1999; personal communication, G. Pawlson, NCQA, March 22, 2004]. This is a community that I'm sure is in no way rewarded for that kind of spectacular performance on two very important dimensions of quality" (NCQA, 1997).

As recommended in the IOM's *Quality Chasm* and *Priority Areas for National Action* reports (IOM, 2001, 2003b) and illuminated during this session, a starting point to accelerate the adoption of performance-based payment models might be to focus on a set of priority conditions, such as the five targeted for this summit (asthma, depression, diabetes, heart failure, and pain control in advanced cancer). Ideally, payment would be made on a condition-specific basis for what is known to be effective processes of care; an example is a compound metric encompassing the core aspects of diabetes care—HbA_1c monitoring, blood pressure monitoring, biennial lipid testing, and annual eye and foot screening. Such an approach, currently under way at HealthPartners, Inc. in Minneapolis (Personal communication, G. Isham, HealthPartners, Inc., February 9, 2004), requires treating the patient holistically and fully recognizing multiple comorbidities, including a decline in functional ability or an increase in sensory deprivation, that may not be directly linked with any one disease. Thus there would be a natural evolution toward paying less for visits and procedures and covering more system-level interventions, such as care coordination, with the eventual goal of an evidence-based benefit package. This approach is discussed in the next section as another possible solution to restructuring the health care finance system.

Kim Horn, president and chief executive officer of Priority Health and a team member of the Grand Rapids Medical Education and Research Center community, provided an example of a pay-for-performance initiative during the finance session. See Box 6-1.

Box 6-1. Priority Health's Physician Incentive Program

Priority Health is a not-for-profit, community-based health plan with approximately 450,000 members serving the western portion of the state of Michigan. Seven years ago, Priority Health initiated a Physician Incentive Program, which gives monetary rewards to primary care providers for delivering superior-quality care and for achieving high levels of patient satisfaction—as measured against national standards and benchmarks. Three of the priority areas highlighted at the summit—diabetes, asthma, and depression—are part of this program, which also includes screening for tobacco use and a host of preventive health care measures. The program is driven by the clinical evidence base and grounded in the principle of transparency, facilitated by the use of information and communications technology. For example, on-line resources assist patients in finding a physician with "three apples"—a known provider of high-quality care. There is also a website where physicians and patients can retrieve information on good care for diabetes, for example, as well as for other conditions.

Priority Health will spend almost $5 million in 2004 on this program, and the number of physicians who qualify for payment has tripled since the program's inception in 1997. Overall, average scores on performance measures have increased by approximately 5 points, comparable to national trends. Most notable, however, is that Priority Health has been successful in significantly decreasing the variation in practice patterns among its clinicians.

> *As we've gone about our payment practices, we've learned three principles: (1) Keep it simple. (2) Bundle payment for services whenever possible. (3) Align incentives so people are focused on the same things, whether you're a hospital, a physician, or a patient."*
>
> —Kim Horn, summit participant

Additionally, Karen Ignani, president of America's Health Insurance Plans (AHIP), committed to sharing her organization's experiences with pay-for-performance initiatives in which AHIP members are engaged—some in collaboration with employers, purchasers, and consumers. Said Ignani, "We're tracking it, we have a great deal of information, we will report it every step of the way, so if you have questions we'd be happy to be a gateway for that."

The importance of promoting pay-for-performance systems was reinforced by the condition-specific working groups, which identified payment reform as a key strategy for achieving high-quality care. For example, the depression working group proposed a "transformational aim" of redesigning the finance system to pay for equitable, effective, and efficient performance based on evidence-based guidelines. That group also echoed the notion of budget neutrality, identifying it as an overriding criterion. Box 6-2 lists the pay-for-performance strategies discussed by this group.

The depression working group also outlined strategies at both the local and national levels for aligning financial incentives to support an approach that integrates primary and specialty care, employers, and payers for the assessment and treatment of depression. One such strategy was to conduct local experiments on pay-for-performance models of evidence-based care, for example, paying for a bundled set of visits, team collaboration, and screening for depression in comorbid conditions. Another was to encourage local health insurers/payers to have explicit policies, coupled with outreach to providers, delineating how depression care will be reimbursed. Data from these local pilots would then be used to develop a national payment model.

The working group also stressed that Congress should remediate the current inequities in mental health care copayments under Medicare. Along with the above changes in finance, issues of financing access to care were highlighted. The group adopted the philosophy of "no wrong door," which means that those who suffer from depression should have high-quality access,

---

Box 6-2. Depression Working Group's Pay-for-Performance Strategies

- Reimbursing new modalities for delivering care, such as telephone- and web-based clinical systems
- Covering depression screening for all members upon enrollment, as well as periodic follow-up
- Assigning one agent who is responsible for intervening if care is not coordinated effectively across multiple providers
- Integrating employee assistance programs with mental health benefit administration
- Incorporating depression screening, longitudinal monitoring, and treatment into the management of chronic conditions

referral, and treatment regardless of where they present for care within the health care system.

The diabetes working group focused on strategies that could be used to make a business case for payers to support patient self-management and care coordination for those with diabetes. There was general consensus on the need for additional studies or demonstrations to further substantiate the return on investment of these interventions in the long run. Strategies put forth by this group included paying for process improvement and outcome performance; paying for currently uncovered services, such as group visits, nutritional supports, and care coordination; and creating incentives for support for patient self-management. Additionally, this group highlighted the importance of consumer demand, suggesting that a menu of self-management options might be covered rather than a "one-size-fits-all" approach, with the option selected being based on the nature and severity of the disease and individual patient choice. Finally, the diabetes group proposed that innovative finance mechanisms could generate a resource pool from savings that would accrue over time, which would be reinvested in diabetes care—used, for example, to build on information and communications technology infrastructure. The heart failure and pain control working groups also supported channeling savings from pay-for-performance initiatives back to improvements in information and communications technology to ensure that outcomes are tracked and monitored.

Although not specifically addressed as a separate cross-cutting question by the pain control group, compensating or marketing higher-quality care was identified as an essential element in the development of seamless and reliable care plans for the prevention and relief of cancer pain. Strategies put forth included payers demanding continuity of care by mandating consistent interventions, and reimbursing at higher levels if patients' self-reports of pain average 3 or less on a scale of 1–10 over the preceding month. The pain group also suggested a demonstration project, spearheaded by Medicaid, to document the effectiveness of care coordination, with the resulting data being used to help institute a change in current federal reimbursement policies.

Employ Evidence-Based Benefit Design

The integration of evidence-based medicine into benefit design was identified as holding promise for matching resources with more effective care. For example, evidence-based benefit design might include covering bundles of high-value services that are known to work clinically for many of the chronic conditions featured at the summit. Participants emphasized that the design of benefits as a means to change consumer behavior must be solidly grounded in evidence. Thus when such evidence exists, reimbursement would be tied to interventions that have proven to be effective, and there would be a corresponding move away from paying for services that have been shown not to work or may even might be harmful. For example noncoverage of high-dose chemotherapy plus autologous bone marrow transplants for breast cancer today is appropriately based on the evidence, as five major randomized clinical trials have documented no improvement in survival rates as compared with the less-costly standard-dose chemotherapy regimen (Mello and Brennan, 2001); in the early 1990s, however, there was enormous consumer pressure for coverage of this treatment when there was little evidence for its relative efficacy. There will certainly be more instances in which the evidence base lags behind demand for a specific intervention, and policy decisions regarding coverage will need to be made on a case-by-case basis. Nonetheless, the goal should be to have as many design decisions as possible be anchored in evidence.

Undoubtedly, implementation of this strategy would require considerable behavioral change at both the provider and patient levels. Participants suggested that additional research is needed to determine how to construct these incentives so as to achieve ideal outcomes without causing unintended consequences, such as patients forgoing preventive care as the result of a copayment.

Francois de Brantes, program leader for Health Care Initiatives at General Electric—a national champion participant at the summit—offered the following perspective with regard to purchasers' roles in benefit design:

> We ought to as purchasers, both large and small, reiterate our core functions, which means to have benefit designs that are going to in some way increase the likelihood that consumers will be sensitive to both the cost and quality of health care services that they consume. But in addition, we also must have some incentives around better self-management, which doesn't exist today and I think is something we need to address robustly. Many of us have, but it's getting it to that next tier for the majority of purchasers.

The asthma working group also embraced the concept of an evidence-based benefits package, as reflected in their report to the plenary session at the summit. They coupled this approach with community collaboration as a mechanism for accelerating system-level change for asthma care. The group suggested defining the appropriate mix of finance solutions—emphasizing not only health insurance, but also schools, community health foundations, and state health department funding—to deliver a package of evidence-based chronic disease management and community services, including care coordination, self-management support, and education. This might best be accomplished through a process of community activation involving the creation and maintenance of coalitions. These coalitions should include key community stakeholders, especially individuals and families with asthma, and have agreed-upon short- and long-term goals. The Pediatric/Adult Asthma Coalition of New Jersey is a good example of such a coalition (see Chapter 7).

Provide Payment for Proven Quality Support Services

Services such as care coordination and patient self-management support enhance the delivery of quality care but are often not covered benefits outside of integrated delivery systems. Additionally, those services when performed by hospital nurses are embedded in housekeeping costs. Thus the work is invisible, and performance and outcomes are not monitored. This state of affairs has consequences for worker morale as well as for patient care.

Support services that foster higher-quality care are difficult to measure and are rarely rewarded. Payment for such interventions will require a shift from the current piecemeal approach of financing encounters associated with a single provider to paying for elements that are linked to systems of care involving a team of diverse practitioners. (This concept is addressed more fully in Chapters 4 and 5.)

Engage Consumers with Information and Incentives

This strategy addresses empowering consumers to modify their behavior using monetary incentives and/or providing them with information to make better health care decisions on the basis of quality. In stark contrast with the increasing trend to shift costs to consumers, this strategy is anchored in having costs borne by consumers, but with the specific intent of encouraging better access to the right care at the right time. Suggestions from participants to this end included tiered premiums to mirror modifiable health behaviors, such as smoking, and changes in benefit design to make consumers aware of the value of the providers they select. An issued raised with regard to implementing this type of mechanism is the need for additional evidence to ensure that incentive arrangements do not have the unintended consequence of impeding patient access to needed care. As noted by Karen Ignani of AHIP, "I think what we found is that tiering in the pharmaceutical arena has given us an insight into how to align incentives. The key will be what gets rewarded, how it gets determined, how we get to consensus."

The asthma, diabetes, and heart failure working groups affirmed the importance of providing consumer-based information and incentives to influence patients to engage in self-management activities, such as attending group classes and self-monitoring glucose levels from home. It was stressed that consumers should share in any cost savings that might result. Two groups (asthma and heart failure) identified premium rebates as a possible strategy for patients who make use of available supports.

John Miall, Director of Risk Management for the city of Ashville, North Carolina, presented a heartening case study illustrating how his community effectively used consumer incentives to provide high-quality, patient-centered diabetes care. Box 6-3 describes the Ashville Project of the Mission-St. Joseph's Health System.

Box 6-3. The Asheville Project

The city of Asheville is a small community in the mountains of western North Carolina. As a major employer in the area, the city government provides health care benefits to approximately 1,000 employees and 2,500 dependent family members. In an effort to improve diabetes care for its employees, in 1997 the City of Asheville launched the Asheville Project—a collaborative partnership with Mission-St. Joseph's Hospitals, the North Carolina Association of Pharmacists, and the University of North Carolina.

First, a curriculum was developed, with input from a multidisciplinary team including local physicians, diabetes educators, and pharmacists. Based on a pharmaceutical care model, patients receive "hands-on" care that includes a monthly visit to a specially trained pharmacist. During these visits, patients receive counseling and continuing education on diabetes management and on monitoring of glucose levels by downloading of hand-held glucometers—given free of charge. In addition to assessing medication use, adherence, side effects, interactions, and achievement of therapeutic goals, pharmacists check blood pressure, perform foot exams, and help patients set goals during these visits. Additionally, as an incentive to patients to participate, copayments were waived for disease-related medications and all diabetic supplies, including syringes, and test strips were provided free of charge as long as participants remained compliant with the contract they agreed to at the start of the program.

It was found early on that this system, created as a community effort, resulted in earlier and more appropriate referrals to physician offices rather than to more costly emergency room visits and hospitalizations. At the end of the first year, medical care costs had decreased by $2,573 per diabetic (from a 1996 average of $6,127 to a 1997 average of $3,554), primarily as a result of reductions in emergency room visits and hospitalizations. Although costs per diabetic have climbed since then, they remain well below the projected expenditures each year, based on the Consumer Price Index rate of inflation for medical care. In 2001, the last year for which data are available, there was a 36 percent savings per diabetic—actual costs of $4,651, compared with a projection of $7,248. A 50 percent reduction in sick leave utilization has also been documented.

> *"The point I'm here to advocate is if you're serious about reconnecting with health and committing the resources to make people well, we have to begin to think seriously about what we want to do differently with our dollars than just paying for the sick."*
>
> —*John Miall, summit participant*

CLOSING STATEMENT

Providing incentives and rewarding high-quality care were themes woven throughout all the cross-cutting sessions. The message from the summit was clear: there is an urgent need to embark on some actionable items now, recognizing that fundamental restructuring of the health care finance system may require more time.

REFERENCES

AMA (American Medical Association). 2004. *AMA (CPT) CPT Process—How a Code Becomes a Code*. [Online]. Available: http://www.ama-assn.org/ama/pub/category/3882.html [accessed April 30, 2004].

American Hospital Publishing, Inc. 1999. The quality of medical care in the United States: A report on the Medicare program. In: Wennberg JE, Cooper MM, eds. *The Dartmouth Atlas of Health Care*. Chicago, IL: American Hospital Publishing, Inc.

Bates DW, Cullen DJ, Laird N, Petersen LA, Small SD, Servi D, Laffel G, Sweitzer BJ, Shea BF, Hallisey R. 1995. Incidence of adverse drug events and potential adverse drug events: Implications for prevention. *The Journal of the American Medical Association* 274(1):29–34.

Berwick DM. 2004. *Crossing the Quality Chasm: Health Care for the 21st Century*. Powerpoint Presentation.

Chassin MR, Galvin RW. 1998. The urgent need to improve health care quality: Institute of Medicine national roundtable on health care quality. *The Journal of the American Medical Association* 280(11):1000–1005.

Fisher ES, Wennberg DE, Stukel TA, Gottlieb DJ, Lucas FL, Pinder EL. 2003a. The implications of regional variations in Medicare spending. Part 2: Health outcomes and satisfaction with care. *Annals of Internal Medicine* 138(4):288–298.

Fisher ES, Wennberg DE, Stukel TA, Gottlieb DJ, Lucas FL, Pinder EL. 2003b. The implications of regional variations in Medicare spending. Part 1: The content, quality, and accessibility of care. *Annals of Internal Medicine* 138(4):273–287.

Fisher ES, Wennberg JE, Stukel TA, Skinner JS, Sharp SM, Freeman JL, Gittelsohn AM. 2000. Associations among hospital capacity, utilization, and mortality of US Medicare beneficiaries, controlling for sociodemographic factors. *Health Services Research* 34(6):1351–1362.

IOM (Institute of Medicine). 2001. *Crossing the Quality Chasm: A New Health System for the 21st Century*. Washington, DC: National Academy Press.

IOM. 2002a. *Fostering Rapid Advances in Health Care: Learning from System Demonstrations*. Corrigan JM, Greiner AC, Erickson SM, eds. Washington, DC: National Academy Press.

IOM. 2002b. *Leadership by Example: Coordinating Government Roles in Improving Health Care Quality*. Corrigan JM, Eden J, Smith BM, eds. Washington, DC: National Academy Press.

IOM. 2003a. *The Future of the Public's Health in the 21st Century*. Committee on Assuring the Health of the Public in the 21st Century, eds. Washington, DC: National Academy Press.

IOM. 2003b. *Priority Areas for National Action: Transforming Health Care Quality*. Adams K, Corrigan JM, eds. Washington, DC: National Academy Press.

IOM. 2004. *Insuring Health—Insuring America's Health: Principles and Recommendation.* Committee on the Consequences of Uninsurance, eds. Washington, DC: National Academy Press.

Levit K, Smith C, Cowan C, Sensenig A, Catlin A, Health Accounts Team. 2004. Health spending rebound continues in 2002. *Health Affairs (Millwood, VA)* 23(1):147–159.

Mello MM, Brennan TA. 2001. The controversy over high-dose chemotherapy with autologous bone marrow transplant for breast cancer. *Health Affairs (Millwood, VA)* 20(5):101–117.

NCQA (National Committee for Quality Assurance). 1997. *HEDIS 3.0: What's In It and Why It Matters.* Washington, DC: NCQA.

Wagner EH, Austin BT, Davis C, Hindmarsh M, Schaefer J, Bonomi A. 2001. Improving chronic illness care: Translating evidence into action. *Health Affairs (Millwood, VA)* 20(6):64–78.

Wang PS, Berglund P, Kessler RC. 2000. Recent care of common mental disorders in the United States: Prevalence and conformance with evidence-based recommendations. *Journal of General Internal Medicine: Official Journal of the Society for Research and Education in Primary Care Internal Medicine* 15(5):284–292.

Wennberg JE, Gittelsohn AM. 1973. Small area variations in health care delivery. *Science* 182 (117):1102–1108.

Wennberg JE, Fisher ES, Stukel TA, Skinner JS, Sharp SM, Bronner KK. 2004. Use of hospitals, physician visits, and hospice care during last six months of life among cohorts loyal to highly respected hospitals in the United States. *British Medical Journal* 328(7440):607–612.

Chapter 7
Coalition Building

DEFINITION AND OVERARCHING THEMES

The topics for the cross-cutting sessions discussed in the preceding chapters were selected to assist participants in implementing the applications of the priority areas described in the *Quality Chasm* report (IOM, 2001:96):

- Synthesize the evidence base and delineate practice guidelines.
- Organize and coordinate care around patient needs.
- Provide a common base for the development of information and communications technology.
- Reduce suboptimization of payment.
- Simplify quality measurement, evaluation of performance, and feedback.

In addition to those topics, a session on coalition building was added in response to feedback received during preliminary inquiries with summit community participants. Since coalitions were viewed as an effective structure for catalyzing change, additional knowledge and skills for developing mechanisms for community engagement were a priority for community participants. Thus the goal of this session was to identify strategies that can be used by communities to integrate and support the work of diverse coalition stakeholders and enhance attainment of their common goal of improving the quality and efficiency of care. In addition, attention was given to public and private partnerships and ways to obtain human and financial resources, as well as expertise.

The following definition of community coalition building was adopted by the working group and helped guide the ensuing discussions (IOM, 2002; Sofaer, 2003):

> Coalition building aims to build an organizational structure that integrates and supports the work of multiple, diverse stakeholders—often at both the local and national levels—on a focused and shared goal, in this case improving care quality and efficiency at the community level. Such coalitions, sometimes referred to as partnerships or collaborations, may foster visibility and information exchange; serve as planners, coordinators, or implementers of joint activities; mobilize broader support for an initiative; or promote policy changes. Coalitions that span the public and private sectors have been encouraged.

KEY STRATEGIES

Participants in the session on coalition building focused on three key strategies for developing and sustaining effective coalitions: (1) identify those who should to be involved in the coalition, (2) obtain agreement on a common objective, (3) determine how the achievement of this objective can be measured. At the summit, four community coalitions shared their strategies and lessons learned in engaging many diverse groups around a mutual goal: the Greater Flint Health Coalition (GFHC), the Mid-America Coalition on Health Care Community Initiative on Depression (MACHC), the Pediatric/Adult Asthma Coalition of New Jersey (PACNJ), and the Rochester Health Commission (RHC). The MACHC initiative is described in Box 4-1 in Chapter 4; the other three initiatives are described in this chapter.

Identify Those Who Should Be Involved

The participants concurred that one of the most important steps in the process of activating a coalition is getting the right people to the table. In the recruitment phase of coalition building, care needs to be taken to ensure a proper balance among stakeholders—at both the community and organizational levels. Although there is no set number of people that should participate, emphasis should be placed on casting a wide net to ensure that multiple perspectives are represented and to harness a range of skills and resources (Sofaer, 2003). Often, this involves bringing together groups that have competing interests, which can prove challenging. RHC (see Box 7-1) illustrates the evolution of a coalition influenced by stakeholder relations.

Participants also discussed leadership within a community coalition and desirable characteristics for individuals assuming this role. They cautioned against either appointing a strong expert as a leader, who might limit dialogue, or relying solely on the energies of a charismatic leader, whose departure could result in the coalition's demise. Rather, the notion of "servant leadership" was embraced—a facilitator who is capable of bringing together a group of people with varied agendas, slowly developing trust, and then building consensus on what must be done to achieve a mutually desired outcome (Greenleaf, 1983). It was also pointed out that this leader must be culturally competent, not only with regard to race and ethnicity, but also in balancing the strategies necessary for community organization at the grassroots level with those required to build interagency groups or business coalitions.

> **Box 7-1. Rochester Health Commission**
>
> The Rochester Health Commission (RHC), established in 1995, is a nonprofit, community-based organization with representation from a broad array of stakeholder groups, including consumers, business leaders, health care providers, and insurers. RHC was designed to be (1) a source of independent, objective health care information; (2) an advocate; and (3) a convener.
>
> An early initiative undertaken by RHC involved public reporting of information on health plan and provider performance. This initiative provoked great turmoil, particularly when it was extended to hospitals. The commission then received a grant under the State of New York Healthcare Reform Act that sustained it for the next year and a half until it held the Summit on Rochester Healthcare in 2000. That summit produced a new finance structure for RHC, with operational expenses being derived from health insurance premiums. Additionally, the summit launched the Rochester Health Forum (RHF) as an arm of the commission to serve as a vehicle for community input and consensus building. The RHF helped redefine the commission's role, which now focuses on facilitating local interventions to improve the delivery of quality care.
>
> To identify priorities, RHC used the "one-text" negotiation process, through which ten initiatives to embark upon were identified (Fisher and Ury, 1991; Program on Negotiations at the Harvard Law School, 2004). Examples are implementation of communitywide clinical guidelines for care, interventions focused on reducing medical errors, and strategies to address shortages of health care workers. Two further initiatives were subsequently added: improving support for end-of-life and palliative care, and implementing communitywide hospital orders, linked to the national Leapfrog Group (The Leapfrog Group, 2004). The former initiative was featured at the summit for its work dedicated to improving pain management in cancer, as well as in other conditions requiring pain control, which spans a range of care settings from physicians' offices to nursing homes and hospices (Farley et al., 2003).

Obtain Agreement on a Common Objective

Once a coalition has been assembled, the next critical step is to identify a common objective that supercedes differences in interests or perspectives—to determine early in the process what the salient issues are for each participant and then negotiate a win/win solution addressing those issues. Maintaining transparency and revealing biases and conflicts of interest up front are paramount, since individuals by nature are inclined to act out of self-interest, and organizational interests often surface strongly in coalitions. The rallying point should be the creation of community-focused goals that the coalition can tackle collectively.

Session participants raised concern that the consensus-building process often results in action being taken on the "lowest common denominator," rather than on a "stretch" goal. They suggested the need to avert such behavior, which tends to push sensitive but worthy issues off limits. Typically, this is best done at the outset, when mutual trust is beginning to be established. Rather than settle for less challenging goals as a way to achieve consensus, a track record of one or two successes should first be established, and having thus built trust, the coalition can move on to higher goals.

PACNJ provides an example of how a coalition can quickly be solidified and take action if it joins forces around a common objective. See Box 7-2 for a description of that group's initiative.

While some coalitions evolve a long-term vision over time, the working group on pain control in advanced cancer articulated a mission statement

---

Box 7-2. Pediatric/Adult Asthma Coalition of New Jersey

The Pediatric/Adult Asthma Coalition of New Jersey (PACNJ) was formed by a group of volunteers who decided to band together and marshal resources around the common goal of improving asthma care in their community. What brought this objective into focus was Camp Super Kids, a 1-week residential asthma camp for children sponsored by the American Lung Association of New Jersey. Although the children would leave the camp with their asthma under control, organizers found that 30 percent of the children each year were "return campers" and had not retained the skills they had been taught to self-manage their condition.

To address this problem, the American Lung Association of New Jersey and the New Jersey Thoracic Society convened a meeting of interested individuals across the state who were working on implementing the guidelines of the National Heart, Lung, and Blood Institute. From an initial group of 50 people, PACNJ has grown to include 150 members. Remarkably, this effort evolved without any seed money or external mandate to assemble.

The coalition consists of a steering committee whose members serve as cochairs on six task forces: school, child care provider, physician, community, managed care, and environmental. This multifaceted approach was adopted to ensure that all the forces influencing high-quality asthma care would be addressed in a cohesive fashion. A window of opportunity presented itself to the coalition when the State of New Jersey passed a law requiring that asthma action plans be on file for all children carrying inhalers and that school nurses and personnel receive asthma education—all within a 180-day time frame. PACNJ quickly mobilized and launched its first project—a statewide satellite broadcast targeting asthma management in the school setting. Funding from the U.S. Centers for Disease Control and Prevention through the New Jersey Department of Health and Senior Services and from the United States Environmental Protection Agency, Region 2, sustained the effort. Since then, the coalition has expanded its scope to include adults and is looking at ways of incorporating information and communications technology to facilitate compliance with asthma action plans. Additionally, the group is exploring a research endeavor with the University of Medicine and Dentistry of New Jersey to measure the effects of public law on health outcomes (The Pediatric/Adult Asthma Coalition of New Jersey, 2003).

during the summit. The group identified as its key objective to "raise the bar on public awareness and clinical performance," making it unacceptable to tolerate bad pain management. With this as its central issue, the group identified two ways to activate the community: (1) coordinate a public information campaign, led by the American Pain Association (APA)—an action item to which the APA committed at the summit; and (2) ask national professional groups and associations to formally adopt and implement the working group's mission statement. Box 7-3 presents that statement, along with concrete measures defined by the group that would be used to measure achievement of this objective (see the next section).

Box 7-3. Working Group on Pain Control in Advanced Cancer: Mission Statement and Goals

Mission Statement

Every person living with cancer can count on, and every clinician can promise, that the patient can live to the end of life without having to endure unacceptable cancer pain.

Definition of Success by 2006

- 100 percent of cancer patients report that their pain was regularly measured, and they were routinely asked whether that pain was acceptable.

- Greater than 95 percent of cancer patients report that their pain was less than 5 on a scale of 0 to 10.

Or

- Greater than 95 percent of cancer patients report that their pain was within a level acceptable to them.

Determine How the Achievement of This Objective Can Be Measured

Participants stressed the importance of coalitions measuring both quantitatively and qualitatively the impact they are having on their communities. To this end coalitions must establish objectives and agree on which measures are necessary to document progress (as was done by the working group on pain control in advanced cancer). Such metrics must be meaningful for diverse members of the community and for an array of stakeholders and yet be straightforward and limited in number. There should be a focus on processes and outcomes that impact change in the real world and assess the degree of penetration the coalition has achieved within a defined community. The role of measurement is not only to document progress. Measures that are concrete, actionable, and supported both by scientific and community consensus become a powerful expression of shared accountability. This shared accountability, in turn, reinforces community cohesion and guides the rational distribution of coalition resources to needed areas. In addition, documented and credible measures of success attract additional support and resources. GFHC illustrates the evolution of a coalition over time and the incorporation of measures to demonstrate the group's contribution to the community (see Box 7-4).

The heart failure working group suggested that community activation is an important strategy for overcoming barriers to the delivery of high-quality care for this chronic disease. They called for community-based performance reports by 2004 and community-based performance measures by 2007. Box 7-5 outlines strategies proposed by this working group to heighten awareness of the current gaps in heart failure care within the community, and thereby motivate initiatives to achieve the needed improvements. These strategies included holding dialogues at the grassroots level with a diverse set of local groups to learn what resources the community needs to play a dominant role in improving heart failure care, conducting local demonstration projects to implement these ideas, influencing local leadership to elevate the problem and create the will for the improvement to come from within the community, developing local media campaigns and sharing heart failure patients' stories, and engaging business coalitions to support improvement initiatives.

Box 7-4. Greater Flint Health Coalition

The Greater Flint Health Coalition (GFHC) was formed in 1992 by several community leaders to examine issues affecting Genesee County's health status. This initial core group of advocates launched three pilot projects: increasing smoking cessation, decreasing cesarean births, and increasing diabetes awareness.

In 1996, GFHC reorganized, becoming a broad-based organization with funding from the insurance, provider, and purchaser sectors. This transition helped solidify the collaborative nature of the coalition, positioning it to address a wide array of health care–related issues. Since then, GFHC has expanded its outreach to encompass 16 initiatives, and its membership has grown to include providers, purchasers, consumers, committed citizens, government representatives, and faith-based organizations.

An example of a GFHC initiative currently under way is the Mid-Michigan Guidelines Applied to Practice-Heart Failure program (GAP-HF), which was featured at the summit. This program is designed to increase inpatient compliance with American College of Cardiology/American Heart Association guidelines and to promote the seamless transfer of patients from the hospital to their primary care physician. Hospitals participating in the program are provided with a number of resources, such as an intervention toolkit complete with standing orders, nursing critical pathways, and a discharge contract. Additionally, clinicians and administrators have access to a physician–nurse team trained in guideline implementation, and each participating institution is given a report card documenting performance on standardized heart failure quality indicators.

By working collaboratively with multiple stakeholders, GFHC has been able to significantly improve the health care of its constituents. For example, outcomes from the coalition's Acute Myocardial Infarction/Guidelines Applied in Practice project, directed at improving adherence to evidence-based guidelines for acute myocardial infarction, demonstrated a 22 percent increase in counseling for smoking cessation, a 15 percent increase in appropriate prescribing of cholesterol-lowering drugs, and a 24 percent increase in prescribing of ACE inhibitors—interventions all proven to be effective in the treatment and management of heart disease (Greater Flint Health Coalition, 2003; Mehta et al., 2004).

> **Box 7-5. Working Group on Heart Failure: Local Strategies to Implement Change**
>
> - Hold community dialogues
>   - Start next week! Can be as small as a family/focus group of patients and caregivers.
>   - Implement ideas quickly.
>   - Develop local demonstration projects.
> - Influence local leadership to elevate the problem and sustain focus through a local infrastructure.
> - Develop local media campaigns.
> - Highlight patient experiences.
> - Engage business coalitions.

CLOSING STATEMENT

In summary, focused group actions (as opposed to individual actions) linked to relationships among organizations, such as are found in coalitions, are useful approaches for solving complex system-level problems. In forming and sustaining a coalition, it is critical to identify and balance diverse stakeholder groups. Coalitions must commit to a long-range vision—buttressed by early successes and evolving over time to suit the tasks taken on as the group matures. Establishing objectives and agreement on measures for assessing progress makes it possible to document progress and develop shared accountability among coalition members.

REFERENCES

Farley DO, Haims MC, Keyser DJ, Olmsted SS, Curry SV, Sorbero M. 2003. *Regional Health Quality Improvement Coalitions: Lessons across the Life Cycle.* Santa Monica, CA: RAND Corporation.

Fisher R, Ury W. 1991. *Getting to Yes: Negotiating Agreement without Giving In.* Patton B, ed. New York, NY: Penguin.

Greater Flint Health Coalition. 2003. *ACC 52nd Annual Scientific Session Poster Presentation.* PowerPoint Presentation.

Greenleaf RK. 1983. *Servant Leadership: A Journey into the Nature of Legitimate Power and Greatness.* Mahwah, NJ: Paulist Press.

IOM (Institute of Medicine). 2001. *Crossing the Quality Chasm: A New Health System for the 21st Century.* Washington, DC: National Academy Press.

IOM. 2002. *Fostering Rapid Advances in Health Care: Learning from System Demonstrations.* Corrigan JM, Greiner AC, Erickson SM, eds. Washington, DC: National Academy Press.

Mehta RH, Montoye CK, Faul J, Nagle DJ, Kure J, Raj E, Fattal P, Sharrif S, Amlani M, Changezi HU. 2004. Enhancing quality of care for acute myocardial infarction: Shifting the focus of improvement from key indicators to process of care and tool use. *Journal of the American College of Cardiology* 43(12):2166–2173.

Program on Negotiations at the Harvard Law School. 2004. *PON: Harvard Negotiation Project.* [Online]. Available: http://www.pon.harvard.edu/research/projects/hnp.php3 [accessed March 24, 2004].

Sofaer S. 2003. *Working Together, Moving Ahead.* New York, NY: School of Public Affairs, Baruch College.

The Leapfrog Group. 2004. *The Leapfrog Group.* [Online]. Available: http://www.leapfroggroup.org/ [accessed March 24, 2004].

The Pediatric/Adult Asthma Coalition of New Jersey. 2003. *Your Pathway to Asthma Control: Fact Sheet.* Online. Available at http://www.pacnj.org/docs/Stepwise.PDF [accessed Jan 6, 2004].

Chapter 8
Condition-Specific Action Plans

The 15 communities that participated in the summit were actively involved in developing action plans to redesign care in one of the five priority areas of: asthma, depression, diabetes, heart failure, and pain control in advanced cancer. Prior to the summit, they completed preparatory work so that the working groups addressing each area could be as productive as possible (see Chapter 1 for a description this preparatory work).

At the summit, participants were assigned to condition-specific breakout groups. Care was taken to ensure a proper balance among local and national-level stakeholder groups and to include individuals with proficiency in the cross-cutting areas discussed in Chapters 2–7, as well as nationally recognized experts in each condition. Subgroups were assigned specially tailored discussion questions (see Appendix J), and a facilitation process was used to generate broad ideas that were later narrowed and refined into more detailed strategies. The working groups were instructed that ideally, they should identify a couple of pragmatic strategies—the "art of the possible"—and one "transformational" strategy that could be considered more radical and groundbreaking than the others.

It is important to note that the working groups acknowledged that in many of the priority areas featured at the summit, health care disparities persist for minority/underserved populations within a community. Although this specific issue was not the focus of the summit, its importance was stressed. The IOM has issued several reports on this topic, including *Unequal Treatment: Confronting Racial and Ethnic Disparities in Health Care* and a six-volume compendium on the uninsured (IOM, 2001b, 2002a,b,c, 2003a,b, 2004).

Following are brief synopsizes of the strategies identified by the working groups as most salient to their respective conditions (see Table 8-1). Audience feedback on the working groups' proposals is summarized at the end of each section.

ASTHMA

Impact

Asthma affects more than 20 million Americans, including 6.3 million children and adolescents. It is the sixth most common chronic condition in the United States, resulting each year in more than 4,400 deaths. Economic costs of the disease total $14 billion, $4.6 billion of which is due to lost productivity. Asthma is also the leading cause of school absenteeism due to a chronic illness. The strain on the health care system is immense. Yearly, asthma leads to 9.3 million physician visits, more than 400,000 hospitalizations, and more than 1.8 million emergency room visits (ALA, 2002).

The nation's pediatric and minority populations bear the brunt of this disease; a disproportionate number of acute asthma attacks, deaths, hospitalizations, and emergency department visits are seen among children and racial minorities (ALA, 2002). In 2001, the highest prevalence rates of asthma were among those aged 5–17, with a rate of 98.1 cases per 1,000 children. Among African American patients, the prevalence of asthma was 22.7 percent higher than that among whites.

Key Strategies for High-Quality Asthma Care

The asthma working group identified the following strategies for overcoming current barriers to high-quality care for this disease:

- Measurement and transparency
- Information and communications technology
- Finance and community collaboration
- Patient/family control

Table 8-1. Key Strategies Identified by Condition-Specific Working Groups

Strategy	Asthma	Depression	Diabetes	Heart Failure	Pain Control
Finance	✓	✓	✓	✓	
Information and Communications Technology	✓	✓	✓		
Patient/Family Control	✓		✓	✓	
Community Collaboration	✓			✓	
Measurement	✓				
Training and Education		✓			
Clinical Engagement				✓	
Public Awareness					✓
Restructuring of Clinical Service Provision					✓
Coordinated Leadership					✓

Measurement and Transparency. The working group suggested that national organizations and appropriate subspecialty providers promote mandatory reporting of a defined set of valid performance measures for asthma care—including measures of self-management—within 3 years. The group emphasized that validated measures now exist; the challenge is routine incorporation of the data required to generate such measures into the information systems of care. The group also emphasized the importance of enhancing population-based surveillance of asthma to complement clinical measures.

Information and Communications Technology. A coalition of health plans, the Centers for Medicare and Medicaid Services (CMS), consumer groups, and other health providers should facilitate the adoption of an easily accessible personal record summary, such as the Continuity of Care Record described in Box 3-2 in Chapter 3. The format of the record would allow clinical data to be transferred to any computer system, as well as allow for a printed report in a readable format for paper transfer. Additionally, the group proposed that patients have full access to their health records and that decision support be incorporated into those records for both clinicians and patients.

Finance and Community Collaboration. This dual strategy calls for defining an appropriate mix of finance solutions—focused not only on health insurance, but also on such alternatives as schools, community health foundations, and state health departments—to effectively deliver a package of evidence-based chronic disease management and community services for asthma. These resources would be linked to communitywide aims established through a process of community activation, such as a multistakeholder coalition. Additionally, progress and outcomes would be monitored through a transparent system of continuous measurement and evaluation based on communitywide surveillance and stakeholder feedback.

Patient/Family Control. This strategy requires a total transformation of the culture of health care, characterized by a universal emphasis on and acknowledgment of the importance of self-management. The group proposed both a national approach—mainly through standards and measures—and a local approach based on engaging consumers and consumer organizations, as well as working with clinicians and others to create programs and tools that will allow patients and families to take control. Access to on-line records and tools is extremely important to achieving this goal.

Audience Feedback

The audience requested further clarification concerning the relationship between coalition structures and financing. The intent of the asthma working group was that coalitions be responsible for establishing aims that would then ultimately drive dollars; at the same time, the group acknowledged that community coalitions often do not have the authority or expertise to formally allocate resources and monitor their use. The group emphasized that community-based asthma efforts should draw on all available resources, such as housing authorities, schools, and employers—not just health insurance—looking at different streams of funding that would be appropriate to each.

A separate concern was raised about whether self-management could foster a culture of self (patient or family)-blame. The asthma group acknowledged the importance of safeguarding against this eventuality, and shared the perspective from the literature that effective self-care (see Chapter 5) creates partnerships based on respect and collaborative goal setting, rather than transfer of sole authority and blame to the patient.

Finally, the audience stressed the importance of environmental determinants of health, particularly for asthma. It was suggested that these factors must be an integral component of any asthma action plan.

DEPRESSION

Impact

Major depression is a disorder characterized by depressed mood, loss of interest or pleasure, and other symptoms that may include changes in sleep and appetite and thoughts of suicide. The disorder differs both quantitatively and qualitatively from normal sadness and bereavement (APA, 1994). Approximately one in seven men and one in four women will have an episode of major depression at some point during their lives (Blazer et al., 1994). In a given year, 18.8 million American adults—9.5 percent of the adult population—suffer from a depressive disorder or depression (NCQA, 2003).

Major depression is associated with enormous clinical and societal burdens in the United States. Depressed patients suffer from levels of disability similar to or greater than those associated with a host of other chronic medical conditions (Wells et al., 1989). The 2000 Global Burden of Disease Study estimates that major depression contributes more than any other single medical condition to disability in the United States (WHO, 2000). The economic costs of depression to the nation are $43.7 billion annually: $23.8 billion in indirect costs, such as mortality and work loss, and $19.9 billion in direct costs. In 1995, the annual economic cost of depression was $600 per depressed worker; one-third of this cost was for treatment, and 72 percent was related to absenteeism and lost productivity (NCQA, 2003). Despite these substantial costs, national health expenditures for depression are low relative to the disorder's associated disability (Druss et al., 2002).

Key Strategies for High-Quality Depression Care

The depression working group identified the following strategies for overcoming current barriers to high-quality care for this condition:

- Finance
- Information and communications technology
- Training and education

Finance. The working group called for transforming the way depression care is currently financed—both privately and publicly—to support payment for performance of evidence-based screening and treatment. Mental health is particularly fragmented in this regard, with private-sector funding being primarily employer based and public-sector funding spanning multiple agencies, such as Medicare, Medicaid, and state and local programs. Coupled with the need to redesign reimbursement are issues of access and the availability of "no wrong door"; that is, those who suffer from depression should have high-quality access, referral, and treatment regardless of where they present for care within the spectrum of health services.

Specific strategies at the national level proposed by the working group for year one included the following:

- Congress fixing the inequities in mental health care copayments under Medicare.
- The National Quality Forum and national coalitions establishing metrics for effective and efficient care.
- CMS implementing the recommendations for depression care management from the report of the President's New Freedom Commission on Mental Health (New Freedom Commission on Mental Health, 2003).
- CMS incorporating evidence-based depression care into disease management demonstrations.

Within 3 years, lessons learned from implementation of the above strategies should inform a national policy and practice model, as well as be used to update evidence-based practice and metrics to build a business case for quality.

At the local level in year one, the working group proposed (1) conducting experiments to test a pay-for-performance model of evidence-based care, for example, paying for a bundled set of visits or team collaboration; and (2) encouraging health insurers/payers to have explicit policies and educational efforts regarding which providers get paid for depression care and how. By year three at the local level, data from these pilots should be used to develop a national payment model, and there should be a move toward national guidelines for screening and follow-up.

Information and Communications Technology. The group identified information and communications technology as a cross-cutting requirement for all of its proposed strategies. One of the fundamental challenges is that the way behavioral health information is treated must be the same as for all other health information, and consistent with the Health Insurance Portability and Accountability Act (U.S. DHHS, 2004).

The initial 1-year goal proposed by the group is for the Substance Abuse and Mental Health Services Administration, the Agency for Healthcare Research and Quality, the Health Resources and Services Administration, CMS, and others to convene the 15 communities participating in the summit so as to include all the key stakeholders and define a shared dataset for behavioral and primary care services. This first year would see pilot collection of these data and conclude with recommendations for a national data policy. Over the course of 3 years, the initiative would be expanded to include a broader base of community agencies and stakeholders. The process for the 3-year effort would mirror that for the 1-year pilot, but with an expanded group of participants.

Training and Education. A central goal defined by the working group was broadening the scope of training, expertise, and knowledge with regard to the screening, referral, and treatment of the disease. A dual strategy was proposed, beginning in year one with existing providers, as well as those in the training phase. This workforce initiative would be linked to ongoing licensing and certification programs. A set of core competencies would be developed; it was speculated that these competencies could be relevant across each of the five priority areas addressed at the summit. After the first year, the 3-year goal would be to expand the initiative to the national level.

Audience Feedback

The importance of primary care practitioners and specialists screening for depression in patients with chronic conditions such as diabetes and heart failure was emphasized. Additionally, given the prevalence of depression, it was suggested that screening be expanded into the community, using community-based agencies or other entities for initial detection and follow-up. The working group had focused on interventions at the provider level—health care practitioners and behavioral health specialists—but agreed that moving toward a more encompassing public health model would be a desirable though challenging option.

Privacy issues were also debated, with two opposing viewpoints being presented. On one side was the belief that behavioral health information should have the same protection as other health care data—the philosophy of the depression working group. This approach would foster integration of such information into electronic health records and other health information systems. Others, however, were adamant about the need for special protection for behavioral health data, such as double passwords. Regardless, it was agreed that patients ultimately should have control over which of their behavioral health information is shared or withheld.

Closing comments from the audience served to heighten awareness of significant gaps in the evidence base for appropriate screening and treatment of children and adolescents with depression. These shortfalls were acknowledged by the working group, and the need for further research directed at this age group was underscored.

DIABETES

Impact

Diabetes ranks as the sixth leading cause of death in the United States, affecting 18 million people and contributing to more than 213,000 deaths in 2000 (ADA, 2004). Diabetes is associated with many long-term, serious medical complications, including heart disease, stroke, hypertension, blindness, kidney disease, neurological disease, and increased risk of lower-limb amputation. In 2002, the economic costs attributed to diabetes-related illness totaled $132 billion. Of this total, $92 billion was direct costs, such as personal health care spending and hospital care, and $40 billion was indirect costs, including disability, premature mortality, and work-loss days. Controlling for differences in age, sex, and race/ethnicity, medical expenditures for diabetics were approximately 2.4 times higher than those that would have been incurred by the same group in the absence of diabetes (Hogan et al., 2003).

Unfortunately, diabetes is a growing problem. In the 1990s, its prevalence increased by 33 percent. This increase occurred across all groups—gender, racial, educational, economic, and age—though racial/ethnic disparities exist. Compared with Caucasians and Asian/Pacific Islanders, diabetic-related deaths are three times more frequent in African Americans, 2.5 times in American Indians/Alaska Natives, and 1.5 times in Hispanics (CDC, 2000).

Key Strategies for High-Quality Diabetes Care

The diabetes working group identified the following strategies for overcoming current barriers to high-quality care for diabetes:

- Team approach to comprehensive care
- Greater application of information and communications technology
- Research on patient-centered wants and needs
- Finance

Team Approach to Comprehensive Care. Multidisciplinary teams are critical to achieving high-quality, comprehensive diabetes care. The working group encouraged the development of systems and alignment of incentives to support this approach to care, while moving away from an exclusive focus on the one-on-one office visit.

Greater Application of Information and Communications Technology. The working group proposed that patients should own a portable electronic health record, made possible by either "smart card" technology or web-based information repositories. To move closer to this goal, the group suggested that a national summit be convened by the IOM and the National Health Information Infrastructure (NHII) to address electronic health record standardization. Topics to be considered include (1) data elements for diabetes and other conditions; and (2) means to facilitate registries, as well as communication among clinicians and between health care providers and patients.

Research on Patient-Centered Wants and Needs. Additional research is needed to illuminate the patients' perspectives on the care they wish to receive and on the tools they need to manage their diabetes effectively.

Finance. Payment systems should focus primarily on process improvement and outcome performance. The working group suggested paying for currently uncovered services such as group visits, nutritional support, and care coordination, and creating incentives to support patients in the self-management of their care. Innovative financial mechanisms could generate a resource pool from savings over time for reinvestment in diabetes care, such as information and communications technology infrastructure.

Audience Feedback

Of all diseases, diabetes is probably the one for which the best consensus exists on a core set of performance measures. The audience stressed the need for more widespread implementation of programs that pay for performance on the basis of these measures—programs that hinge on demonstrating a return on investment, particularly to purchasers and employers. Reformatting the compensation system to reward team-based care and addressing multiple comorbidities among diabetics, such as high blood pressure and depression, are lingering challenges.

HEART FAILURE

Impact

Heart failure has become an epidemic:

- It currently affects 4.9 million Americans, with an additional 550,000 cases being diagnosed annually.
- Fully 80 percent of men and 70 percent of women under age 65 diagnosed with heart failure are expected to die within 8 years.
- From 1979 to 2000, heart failure–related deaths increased by 148 percent.
- Heart failure is particularly pervasive among the elderly. After age 65, its incidence approaches 1 percent of the entire population, and this figure rises precipitously in those aged 75 and older.
- Several events portend further increases in the prevalence of heart failure. Recent improvements in the treatment and survival of acute myocardial infarction have resulted in a larger number of patients with impaired cardiac function. Simultaneously, the aging of the population will result in greater numbers of patients with heart failure.
- In 2003, the National Heart, Lung, and Blood Institute estimated the total costs of heart failure at $24.3 billion. Heart failure is the most frequently occurring Medicare diagnosis-related group (DRG), accounting for $3.6 billion ($5,471 per hospital discharge) in payments to hospitals for Medicare beneficiaries in 1998 (AHA, 2003).

These sobering figures underscore the importance of revolutionizing heart failure care to realize its potential level of quality.

Key Strategies for High-Quality Heart Failure Care

The heart failure working group identified strategies at three levels for overcoming current barriers to high-quality care:

- At the community level, community awareness and activation—creating demand for high-quality heart failure care at the local level.
- At the patient level, creating a patient-centered health environment that includes patient-carried health information.
- At the provider-level, clinical engagement, including aligning financial incentives and creating a business case for quality, and creating methods to make it easier for clinicians to provide good care.

The working group suggested that transforming heart failure care necessitates a certain tension—simultaneously creating anxiety over the status quo while committing to measurable improvement in the quality of care. This tension would provide the impetus for change. Additionally, the group envisioned patients playing a pivotal role in managing their care, as well as in assessing and reporting their health status. Finally, the group underscored the importance of overall prevention, although full development of this component was beyond the scope of the summit discussions.

Community Activation. Multiple strategies at the local level were proposed to immediately begin raising awareness and creating a community-level sense of urgency for better heart failure care. These strategies included (1) holding dialogues to educate communities and, most important, learn from them what they need in order to take a more dominant role in improving care; (2) implementing the feedback gathered from communities quickly through local demonstration projects; (3) influencing local leadership to elevate the problem and sustain focus through a local infrastructure; (4) instigating and supporting local media campaigns; (5) engaging business coalitions to advocate for better care so afflicted individuals can be more financially productive; (6) mobilizing caregivers to be more creative and opportunistic in meeting the demands of those for whom they care; and (7) highlighting the experiences of patients who have heart failure to generate community commitment to the urgency and value of improving heart failure care. In addition, efforts should be initiated to audit local communities with regard to their current state of and commitment to high-quality heart failure care.

The working group also discussed possibilities for linking the Oregon Heart Failure Project (see Box 5-2 in Chapter 5) and the Greater Flint Health Coalition's Guidelines Applied to Practice program (see Box 7-4 in Chapter 7), addressing outpatient and inpatient care, respectively.

Patient-Carried Health Information. The ability to exchange patient health information electronically across multiple systems is essential. The working group suggested that the federal government should take a leadership role in accelerating the adoption of national data standards. The group supported the concept that patients should have full control over their health records and the ability to "hand carry" this information among providers. Critical elements of this hand-carried record include the patient's previous diagnostic evaluations; current doses of evidence-based therapies and records of previous experiences with poorly tolerated treatments; current self-management practices—for example, records of ideal and serial weights, along with strategies for responding to deviations in weight; and serial health status assessments. By providing patients with such records, many of the substantial barriers to coordination of care could readily be overcome. The group suggested that this effort should begin now and be further expanded by 2007.

Aligning Financial Incentives. At the hospital and system levels, an immediate effort to pay for performance is essential as a means to hasten the implementation of well-established best practices. The working group acknowledged that unique patient and community features require a flexible approach to rendering care. If current reimbursement approaches were redesigned to pay for performance—including adhering to established processes of care, minimizing hospitalizations, and optimizing patients' health status—providers could have greater flexibility in providing care without the risk of incurring a financial penalty.

Enabling Clinicians. The current frenetic pace of clinical practice demands consideration of new models that make it easier to increase the efficiency and effectiveness of heart failure care. Potential strategies and resources to this end at the national level include:

- The American College of Cardiology supporting registry efforts that adhere to its Guidelines Applied to Practice program (American College of Cardiology, 2004).
- The American Heart Association continuing its work in guideline development and dissemination (AHA, 2004).
- Linking community information to the American Heart Association's heart profiler, a web-based resource providing treatment options and links to evidence-

based heart failure care in a user-friendly format (AHA, 2004).
- Monitoring and tracking performance standards promulgated by the Physician Consortium for Performance Improvement, convened by the American Medical Association (AMA, 2004).
- Expanding recognition programs of the National Committee for Quality Assurance that feature clinicians who provide high-quality care relative to certain benchmarks (NCQA, 2004).

The working group also proposed mobilizing state public health systems with experience in developing registries and tracking cases over time. Additionally, efforts to link heart failure care to care for other conditions, such as depression and diabetes, ought to be initiated so the totality of patients' comorbidities can be addressed as efficiently as possible. Finally, the working group suggested that to support the community activation approaches noted above, guidelines and performance measures for communities should be developed by 2007.

Audience Feedback

Audience feedback on heart failure care focused mainly on the use of disease registries. The drawbacks of having separate registries for each chronic disease were noted, which feasibly could multiply to hundreds of conditions and become unmanageable. Instead, a registry-like application or database could be conveniently populated by whatever mechanism was currently being used to document care. For example, if an electronic health record were being used, the ability to export some registry-like function would be built into its design, so as to avoid duplicate data entry and decrease administrative overhead. Thus, there was an explicit call for data standards that would include as a criterion the ability for the data to be useful and serviceable for disease registries.

PAIN CONTROL IN ADVANCED CANCER

Impact

Virtually all patients approaching the end of life with cancer can live reasonably comfortably without disabling side effects. Achievement of this goal, however, requires employing current clinical guidelines. The American Pain Society, the Agency for Healthcare Research and Quality, the World Health Organization, and the National Comprehensive Cancer Network all provide guidelines to assist with decision making in pain management (IOM, 2001a). Identification of the cause and type of pain, repeated use of standardized assessment tools to assess pain severity and response to treatment, evaluation of the effect of pain interventions on mental alertness, and flexibility in revising treatment regimens are the mainstays of effective care.

Unfortunately, continuing misconceptions about dependence and addiction, the risks of oversedation, and regulatory problems with opiates have contributed to inadequate implementation of these clinical guidelines. Educating providers about the use of opiates and other medications restricted by policies of the Drug Enforcement Agency is essential to resolve problems of inadequate dosing and reluctance to prescribe (IOM, 2001a). The results of a 1999 study on the effectiveness of physician adherence to pain management guidelines highlight the importance of this point. After oncologists employed a multilevel treatment algorithm based on the Agency for Healthcare Policy and Research Guidelines for Cancer Pain Management, significant reductions in patients' usual pain intensity occurred (Du Pen et al., 1999).

Key Strategies for High-Quality Pain Control in Advanced Cancer Care

The pain control working group identified the following strategies for overcoming current barriers to high-quality care in this area:

- Raising public awareness
- Restructuring clinical service provision
- Creating strong, coordinated leadership

The working group emphasized the importance of articulating the following vision of what could be achieved within a few years if society really wanted "no unacceptable pain" to be the norm:

> Every person living with cancer pain can count on, and every clinician can promise, that the patient can live to the end of life without having to endure unacceptable cancer pain.

The working group's definition of success was that within 3 years, 100 percent of cancer patients would report that their pain was being regularly measured and that they were being routinely asked whether that pain was acceptable. Additionally, greater than 95 percent of cancer patients would report that their pain was less than 5 on a scale of 0–10, or in deference to differences in patient choices, greater than 95 percent of cancer patients would report that their pain was within a level acceptable to them. These three criteria were meant to be examples; a set of such measures would need to be developed and rapidly implemented.

Public Awareness. There is a fundamental problem with inaccurate and inadequate information concerning pain control that contributes to misunderstanding among both patients and clinicians. Pain control cuts across many conditions, and although it is "owned by many" has the dilemma of being "owned by none" with regard to a lack of clarity around leadership—both clinical and organizational. To address this pressing issue, the American Pain Association committed at the summit to coordinating the development of a public awareness campaign. The availability of publicly reported, standardized, valid performance measures would be an essential support for this initiative.

Restructuring of Clinical Service Provision. The working group suggested the following strategies for redesigning the way pain control is provided to cancer patients, focused on enhanced continuity, rapid response, and availability of expertise:

- Round-the-clock accessibility of technical support and health record information for patients, their families/caregivers, and clinicians
- Correct prescribing practices—including for opioids—without retribution
- Incorporation of evidence-based prescribing practices into maintenance of certification and accreditation for clinicians

Strong, Coordinated Leadership. The working group stressed that a lack of coordination and shared mission creates a more substantial barrier to success in this area than does any lack of research insights or proven model programs. Despite the many passionate advocates dedicated to the effective assessment and management of pain, this endeavor is without the clear, coordinated leadership needed to realize the vision put forth by the working group. To address this issue, therefore, the Agency for Healthcare Research and Quality offered to serve as the convening body to bring together key players such as the American Pain Foundation, the National Cancer Institute, CMS, the National Business Group on Health, and the Department of Veterans Affairs. Together these groups would forge a consensus on a timetable and responsibilities for carrying the effort forward.

Audience Feedback

An audience member suggested developing a detailed charge for the above group that would be spearheading national efforts around pain control. It was suggested that the tasks to be accomplished by the group—whether developing a stronger evidence base or dealing with clinicians' fears of having their licenses revoked as a result of prescribing opioids—be prioritized.

REFERENCES

ADA (American Diabetes Association). 2004. *ADA: Basic Diabetes Information.* [Online]. Available: http://www.diabetes.org/diabetes-statistics/national-diabetes-fact-sheet.jsp [accessed April 30, 2004].

AHA (American Heart Association). 2003. *Heart Disease and Stroke Statistics: 2003 Update.* [Online]. Available: http://www.americanheart.org/presenter.jhtml?identifier=1200026 [accessed May 1, 2003].

AHA. 2004. *American Heart Association.* [Online]. Available: http://www.americanheart.org [accessed April 28, 2004].

ALA (American Lung Association). 2002. *Trends in Asthma Morbidity and Mortality, 2002.* Online. Available: http://www.lungusa.org/atf/cf/%7B7A8D42C2-FCCA-4604-8ADE-7F5D5E762256%7D/ASTHMA1.PDF [accessed Jan. 6, 2004].

AMA (American Medical Association). 2004. *AMA (CQI) Physician Consortium for Performance Improvement.* [Online]. Available: http://www.ama-assn.org/ama/pub/category/2946.html [accessed April 28, 2004].

American College of Cardiology. 2004. *Guidelines Applied in Practice (GAP) Program.* [Online]. Available: http://www.acc.org/gap/gap.htm [accessed April 28, 2004].

APA (American Psychiatric Association). 1994. *Diagnostic and Statistical Manual of Mental Disorders.* 4th Edition. Washington, DC: American Psychiatric Association

Blazer DG, Kessler RC, McGonagle KA, Swartz MS. 1994. The prevalence and distribution of major depression in a national community sample: The National Comorbidity Survey. *The American Journal of Psychiatry* 151(7):979–986.

CDC (Centers for Disease Control and Prevention). 2000. *Unrealized Prevention Opportunities: Reducing the Health and Economic Burden of Chronic Disease.* Atlanta, GA: CDC.

Druss BG, Marcus SC, Olfson M, Pincus HA. 2002. The most expensive medical conditions in America: This nationwide study fund that the most disabling conditions are not necessarily the ones we spend the most to treat. *Health Affairs (Millwood, VA)* 21(4):105–111.

Du Pen SL, Du Pen AR, Polissar N, Hansberry J, Kraybill BM, Stillman M, Panke J, Everly R, Syrjala K. 1999. Implementing guidelines for cancer pain management: Results of a randomized controlled clinical trial. *Journal of Clinical Oncology: Official Journal of the American Society of Clinical Oncology* 17(1):361–370.

Hogan P, Dall T, Nikolov P. 2003. Economic costs of diabetes in the U.S. in 2002. *Diabetes Care* 26(3):917–932.

IOM (Institute of Medicine). 2001a. *Improving Palliative Care for Cancer.* Washington, DC: National Academy Press.

IOM. 2001b. *Insuring Health—Coverage Matters: Insurance and Health Care.* Committee on the Consequences of Uninsurance, eds. Washington, DC: National Academy Press.

IOM. 2002a. *Insuring Health—Care without Coverage: Too Little, Too Late.* Committee on the Consequences of Uninsurance, eds. Washington, DC: National Academy Press.

IOM. 2002b. *Insuring Health—Health Insurance is a Family Matter.* Committee on the Consequences of Uninsurance, eds. Washington, DC: National Academy Press.

IOM. 2002c. *Unequal Treatment: Confronting Racial and Ethnic Disparities in Health Care.* Smedley BS, Stith AY, Nelson BD, eds. Washington, DC: National Academy Press.

IOM. 2003a. *Insuring Health—A Shared Destiny: Community Effects of Ununsurance.* Committee on the Consequences of Uninsurance, eds. Washington, DC: National Academy Press.

IOM. 2003b. *Insuring Health—Hidden Costs, Value Lost: Uninsurance in America.* Committee on the Consequences of Uninsurance, eds. Washington, DC: National Academy Press.

IOM. 2004. *Insuring Health—Insuring America's Health: Principles and Recommendation.* Committee on the Consequences of Uninsurance, eds. Washington, DC: National Academy Press.

NCQA (National Committee for Quality Assurance). 2003. *Antidepressant Medication Management: State of Health Care Quality 2002.* [Online]. Available: http://www.ncqa.org/sohc2002/SOHC_2002_AMM.html [accessed April 10, 2003].

NCQA. 2004. *Heart/Stroke Recognition Program.* [Online]. Available: http://www.ncqa.org/hsrp/ [accessed April 28, 2004].

New Freedom Commission on Mental Health. 2003. *Final Report—Achieving the Promise: Transforming Mental Health Care in America.* Pub. No. SMA-03-3832. Rockville, MD: U.S. DHHS.

U.S. DHHS (United States Department of Health and Human Services). 2004. *HHS—Office for Civil Rights—HIPAA.* [Online]. Available: http://www.os.dhhs.gov/ocr/hipaa/ [accessed March 24, 2004].

Wells KB, Stewart A, Hays RD, Burnam MA, Rogers W, Daniels M, Berry S, Greenfield S, Ware J. 1989. The functioning and well-being of depressed patients: Results from the Medical Outcomes Study. *The Journal of the American Medical Association* 262(7):914–919.

WHO (World Health Organization). 2000. *Global Burden of Disease 2000 Version 1 Estimates.* [Online]. Available: http://www3.who.int/whosis/menu [accessed May 29, 2002].

Chapter 9
Next Steps

This final chapter captures the insights of key stakeholder groups represented on a Reactor Panel convened to respond to the overarching themes that emerged during the summit. It also integrates comments of participants and the public present in the audience and listening to the proceedings on the web. The chapter ends by returning the focus to communities, emphasizing the importance of collaboration across stakeholder groups at both the local and national levels. Amplifying this point, commitments made by many of the national champions participating in the summit (see Chapter 1) are presented, thus setting the stage for next steps in implementing the many strategies put forth by the summit participants for making real progress in crossing the quality chasm in health care.

SYNOPSIS OF REACTOR PANEL AND AUDIENCE FEEDBACK

After a day and a half of intense work informed by panel discussions, audience interaction, and breakout groups, the Reactor Panel was convened. It included four summit participants and a moderator, who broadly represented consumers, health care systems, purchasers, employers, and community coalitions. The panel's charge was to frankly assess the strategies put forth during the summit—drawing on their unique perspectives—and to identify areas of strength as well as weakness. Following is a synthesis of the main points made during the panel discussion and the subsequent audience feedback.

The Patient as "True North"

The summit began with a consumer focus, as Martha Whitecotton shared her family's struggles with the health care system in obtaining high-quality care for her son with major depression (see Chapter 4). The summit ended on this same note, placing the patient's experience at the center.

Sylvia Drew Ivie from The Help Everyone Clinic in Los Angeles, representing consumers on the panel, provided a reality check drawn from her experience advocating for the poor, who often present with multiple health challenges and are dealing with a myriad of psychosocial issues. She poignantly asked whether the system changes proposed at the summit would actually help improve the quality of care for the patients and families she serves, and offered this as a test for determining the overall effectiveness of the interventions undertaken.

Concern was raised during the audience feedback that the major social and environmental determinants of health had not been fully considered during the summit. Although the summit was convened to address redesign of the care delivery system, public health issues were emphasized as critically important to improving overall health status. However, time constraints did not permit full exploration of these intricately related factors. Additionally, the audience stressed the importance of treating patients holistically and not artificially segmenting them into single disease categories, as most clinicians are treating patients with multiple chronic conditions (Partnership for Prevention, 2002). Caution was directed at the condition-specific working groups to avoid falling into this trap, and it was emphasized that the strategies from these sessions must be integrated.

Integration of Preventive Care

The audience repeatedly emphasized prevention as an essential component of managing chronic disease. Ongoing preventive strategies were cited as necessary to the treatment and provision of high-quality care for patients with chronic conditions—a case in point being blood pressure control, lipid management, and diet and exercise for patients with heart failure. George Isham from HealthPartners, Inc. in Minneapolis, representing health systems on the panel, suggested that attention be focused on three major behaviors that drive illness in this country—tobacco, exercise, and nutrition. He then offered a two-pronged approach: first, incorporate these three areas into the management of diseases and conditions for which they are significant risk factors; and second, look beyond the face-to-face visit and explore alternative sites for the provision of care, while adopting new technologies to extend care beyond its traditional boundaries.

Change in Roles for Public and Private Purchasers

The panel members underscored the importance of galvanizing both public and private purchasers to reorganize and redesign how health care is currently financed. There was general agreement that additional revenue streams from the public sector would not be forthcoming; thus any strategies put forth must be budget neutral, with resources being redistributed to pay for forms of care traditionally not reimbursed. Strong leadership will be required to decide how to reallocate these resources. Helen Darling from the Washington Business Group on Health, representing purchasers on the panel, suggested that payment be tied to evidence-based practices, seeing this as an opportunity to redirect funds from services known not to be effective to those demonstrated to improve care.

An audience member asked the panel what strategies might be implemented now in the absence of comprehensive finance reform. Examples of system-level approaches that have progressed despite the lack of such a major transformation include implementation of automated health records, integration of evidence-based guidelines into clinical practice settings, and the use of multidisciplinary care teams. However, finance reform was cited as essential to provide momentum for these interventions, now scattered across the country as demonstrated by the communities represented at the summit. It was suggested that small-scale demonstration projects and multilevel collaborations across health systems, states, communities, and others could promote the diffusion of best practices and innovations.

Quality Improvement and Measurement

To implement the changes to the health care finance system recommended by summit participants, transparency and accountability at the results level were stressed as crucial. The panel echoed the point discussed in Chapter 8 that if more emphasis were placed on outcomes, such as patients being healthier and more satisfied with their care, more flexibility might be afforded to cover alternative treatment modalities, such as telephone or e-mail follow-up with patients, as long as they produced better results. Likewise, the panel reiterated the need for outcome measures for all levels of the health care system—patient, clinician, group practice, health plan, home health, nursing home, and hospital.

Roles of National Organizations and Communities

As demonstrated by the 15 communities participating in the summit, health care consumers are often well served by local strategies that bring together many different players through collaborative efforts. Al Charbonneau from the Rochester Health Commission, representing communities on the panel, made an appeal for leadership at the national level to support the ongoing work in these communities and others across the nation. Public–private partnerships could accelerate progress in all the cross-cutting areas addressed at the summit for helping the care team better meet the needs of patients—measurement, information and communications technology, care coordination, patient self-management support, finance, and community coalition building. Many of these communities have made great strides in improving the quality of care for their constituents; however, they require national-level support to overcome many of the barriers discussed at the summit and sustain their laudable efforts.

COMMITMENTS OF NATIONAL CHAMPIONS

Despite the gallant efforts of individuals, communities, and national leadership, a deplorable quality chasm persists between the abundance of evidence-based interventions established by clinical research and the routine practice of medicine in the United States. Recognizing that no individual or organization can overcome all the barriers to providing high-quality care discussed at the summit, participants identified collaboration across the private and public sectors as a critical success factor for change. In response, 24 representatives from national champions participating in the summit publicly declared their commitment to furthering community efforts. They channeled their support in response to key strategies identified at the summit for effecting the needed changes: instituting finance reform to reward evidence-based care, including care coordination and patient self-management; simplifying measurement to facilitate assessing and providing continuous feedback on quality of care; improving information and communications technology infrastructure and interoperability; and marshaling community resources for collaboration and coalition building.

There are many champions of health care redesign around the nation. Some play on a national stage in the scope of their work, while some are regional and others are located in communities. The national champions whose commitments are presented below are among the key players at the national level. Some of them, as well as others not listed, make an impact at the international level as well. It is hoped that others will join this list, and we emphasize that any omissions are unintentional.

Agency for Healthcare Research and Quality (AHRQ)
Carolyn Clancy
www.ahrq.gov

AHRQ is a component of the U.S. Department of Health and Human Services (DHHS) whose mission is to improve the quality, safety, effectiveness, and efficiency of health care. In December 2003, AHRQ released the first annual National Healthcare Quality and Disparities Reports (www.qualitytools.ahrq.gov/qualityreport), providing the first comprehensive picture of the state of quality for the population at large and for racial, ethnic, and other subgroups. The reports provide a roadmap for communities to follow in addressing the quality challenge. Although these are national reports, similar reports could be produced at the community or provider level, and indeed their production would be consistent with the goal of harmonizing measurement and reporting efforts. AHRQ also maintains a clearinghouse of practical, ready-to-use tools for measuring and improving the quality of health care (www.qualitytools.ahrq.gov). In the coming months, AHRQ will be releasing a series of evidence-based reports synthesizing scientific knowledge pertaining to each of the 20 priority areas identified by the IOM (IOM, 2003) and, when possible, pointing to best practices in care delivery. AHRQ will also work with other agencies in DHHS and private-sector foundations to support an evaluation of the improvement efforts of the IOM summit communities.

Alliance of Community Health Plans (ACHP)
Jack Ebeler
www.achp.org

The Alliance of Community Health Plans (ACHP) represents 12 leading health plans and provider organizations. ACHP is sponsoring an initiative called Advancing Better Care that includes eight projects. Of these eight, three provide patients and clinicians with on-line access to electronic health records. Two are focused on communitywide efforts to measure performance at the provider group level (one in Minnesota, the other in Massachusetts). The remaining three projects involve on-line health risk assessments with referrals, a "know your numbers" campaign initially targeting heart disease and expanding to other chronic illnesses, and a tool to engage women more actively in managing their own health needs and those of their family. The knowledge and experience gained from the Advancing Better Care initiative should be highly useful to all of the summit communities, as well as to the broader health care community. ACHP is making descriptive information, measurement tools, and evaluative material available on its website (www.achp.org).

American Board of Internal Medicine (ABIM)
ABIM Foundation
Christine Cassel
www.abim.org

Internal medicine is the largest medical specialty. ABIM is a member of the American Board of Medical Specialties, which represents all 24 of the recognized board-certified specialties. Over the last few years, many specialty boards have started to require maintenance of certification of their diplomats, but in 2002 more than 24 boards agreed that all certificates would now be "time-limited," requiring that all board-certified physicians maintain certification continuously over the life of their practice. The certification process will require not only tests of cognitive knowledge, but also practice performance assessment and improvement.

In support of this transition, ABIM has started developing practice assessment and improvement modules (PIMs), which include measures of technical performance and surveys of patient perceptions. PIMs have already been developed for three of the five priority areas that were the focus of the summit—congestive heart failure, diabetes, and asthma—and modules for depression and pain management are under development. In collaboration with the American Academy of Family Practice and the American Academy of Pediatrics, ABIM is now launching the Improving Performance in Practice project. This project will work with innovative provider practices in various communities to pilot test and refine the PIMs. ABIM is prepared to develop a teleconference for the IOM summit communities to discuss the Improving Performance in Practice project and identify ways in which innovative practices from these communities might participate in this effort. The intent is to allow the summit communities to benefit from the knowledge, technical resources, and momentum associated with this program.

American Cancer Society (ACS)
LaMar McGinnis
www.cancer.org

ACS is the largest volunteer health organization in the world. It is nationwide and community based with 14 divisions, 3,400 units, more than 2 million volunteers, and 6,555 staff. Relative to the summit, ACS makes the following commitments:

- ACS supports the recommendations of the pain control group within the scope of its organizational objectives and the capacity of its budget. The organization is committed to improving the quality of life for cancer patients, with improved pain control one of the primary goals.
- ACS supports evidence-based practice through the use of regularly updated, evidence-based quality guidelines. In collaboration with the National Comprehensive Cancer Network (NCCN), ACS has translated NCCN's continuously updated physician practice guidelines for patient utility (available in English and Spanish) and made them available through the ACS website (www.cancer.org) and call center (1-800-ACS-2345). These patient guidelines have been widely distributed (50,000+) and assist patients in understanding and evaluating treatment options, thus making patients advocates for their own quality care.
- In collaboration with the American College of Surgeons Commission on Cancer (CoC), ACS is developing standardized performance measures for quality cancer management. ACS sponsors, within the CoC hospital approved cancer program (1,500 hospitals), reportable criteria and measures for quality pain control. Further, ACS sponsors the CoC National Cancer Database (NCDB), containing long-term analytic data on more than 10 million cancer patients.
- ACS is considering sponsorship of a national public media campaign on a patient's right to pain relief, consistent with the NCCN practice guidelines. This project is subject to budgetary limitations.
- ACS has developed a pain advocacy toolkit now being piloted in 15 states. Pain control advocacy is carried out at the state and national levels.
- A sizable portion of the ACS research budget is devoted to cancer pain research.
- The ACS Behavioral Research Center is presently conducting longitudinal and cross-sectional research on quality of life among 100,000 cancer survivors.

American Heart Association
Augustus Grant
www.americanheart.org

The American Heart Association is a national voluntary health agency whose mission is to reduce disability and death from cardiovascular disease and stroke. Working collaboratively with the American College of Cardiology, the association is committed to the availability of up-to-date practice guidelines (www.acc.org/clinical/statements.htm). Through its Guidelines Applied in Practice program, the association maps guidelines to "teachable moments" when patients and physicians will be most receptive to applying specific aspects of the guidelines. The association also maintains patient information portals, such as the Heart

Profiler, which provides patients with information on their disease and helps them identify the types of questions they should ask their physician. The American Heart Association is working with the American Medical Association on the development of standardized physician-level performance measures for heart disease and on a recognition program for physicians who practice in office settings. It is also collaborating with the American Diabetes Association and the American Cancer Society to develop and implement measures related to smoking, diet, and exercise, patient behaviors that influence the course of many chronic conditions.

American Hospital Association (AHA)
Don Nielsen
www.aha.org

AHA's quality agenda is directly aligned with the six aims of the *Quality Chasm* report. In 2002, AHA and two other hospital associations—the Federation of American Hospitals and the Association of Academic Medical Centers—undertook the National Voluntary Hospital Reporting Initiative in collaboration with the Centers for Medicare and Medicaid Services (CMS), the Joint Commission on Accreditation of Healthcare Organizations (JCAHO), the American Medical Association, the National Quality Forum, and others. The initiative includes public reporting on acute myocardial infarction, community-acquired pneumonia, and congestive heart failure. In the future, other clinical measures addressing the 20 priority areas identified by the IOM (IOM, 2003) will be added. In the near future, the initiative will also pilot test a new instrument on patient experience of care developed by AHRQ and CMS.

AHA is also addressing some of the cross-cutting issues discussed at the summit. To encourage and maximize the return on investment in information and communications technology, AHA was instrumental in establishing the National Alliance for Health Information Technology, a public–private partnership focused on standards for electronic health records and medication bar coding. In 2004, projects addressing patient-centered health care delivery and patient self-management of chronic conditions will be initiated. Lastly, AHA's research arm, the Hospital Research and Education Trust, would welcome working with the summit communities to develop coalitions for health care improvement.

America's Health Insurance Plans (AHIP)
Karen Ignagni
www.ahip.com

AHIP's member organizations provide health care coverage to about 200 million people. Its health plans operate in every state, and AHIP will be pleased to serve as a gateway for communities to come together with health plans. AHIP is also prepared to arrange for community representatives to enter into a dialogue with the chief medical officers of the health plans, perhaps as a part of its executive leadership program. AHIP is involved in numerous collaboratives around the country on diabetes, asthma, women's health, depression, domestic violence, and other health issues (see www.ahip.com), and is prepared to share detailed information on these efforts with the IOM summit communities. Member health plans are working to design and implement pay-for-performance programs, and AHIP is tracking and making information available on these efforts so others can learn from them. On the policy front, AHIP's board of directors wants to make this the year for improving quality and access, and one effort in this area will be to encourage greater investment in applied research aimed at translating clinical knowledge into practice. Lastly, AHIP concurs with and will support the efforts of the many national champions who are working toward the adoption of a uniform strategy for measuring and reporting on performance.

Blue Cross and Blue Shield Association (BCBSA)
Allan Korn
www.bcbs.com

The member health plans of BCBSA insure nearly 91 million people in the United States, and can be of help in many ways in addressing the country's health care challenges. First, the Blues are an enormous resource with respect to data on the health needs of communities and information about the resources available to meet those needs. They also have information on successful efforts by various BCBS plans to improve health, such as the efforts of the Blues plan in Kansas City to improve asthma management, and would be glad to share that information. Second, the BCBS plans have established communication channels with their business communities, health professionals, pharmacies, and others and can share this resource on behalf of efforts to improve health in communities. Lastly, BCBSA will work collaboratively with others to ensure that there are nationally endorsed guidelines for clinical practice that can be used to report provider performance. BCBSA views this is a very powerful way to help patients navigate a highly complex health care environment.

Centers for Medicare and Medicaid Services (CMS)
Steve Jencks
www.medicare.gov

CMS is committed to working with communities, national partners, and the National Quality Forum on the development of standardized performance measure sets for the five priority areas addressed at the summit and for many other conditions as well. CMS and JCAHO have agreed to use the same measures for hospitals, and hope that this sets a precedent for collaborative efforts in other areas. CMS is also committed to publishing performance data on health plans, hospitals, nursing homes, group practices, and other providers (see www.Medicare.gov). A secure data warehouse has been created for data on quality, including both Medicare and non-Medicare data.

CMS hopes that the summit communities will continue to put substantial pressure on the national champions and the IOM to keep working together, and CMS will host and participate in future meetings. The quality improvement organizations (QIOs) will be working even harder in the future to engage in community collaborations, and communities are encouraged to contact the QIO in their state (http://www.medqic.org/content/qio/qio.jsp?pageID=4). There is also a website created for QIOs and providers of services to Medicare beneficiaries that contains literature, tools, and other information by clinical setting and priority topics (www.medqic.org).

CMS will soon be sponsoring two new demonstration projects that may prove helpful to the summit communities. The first is a pay-for-performance demonstration in office settings that will provide strong incentives for providers to invest in electronic health records to capture and report the necessary performance data. The second is a population-based disease management demonstration.

General Electric Company (GE)
Francois de Brantes
www.ge.com/healthcare

Health care purchasers, both large and small, influence the health care marketplace through two mechanisms—the design of health insurance benefits and the selection of health plans. In addition, many purchasers, through their participation in the Leapfrog Group and the Bridges to Excellence program, are involved in efforts to directly reward physicians and hospitals for better performance.

As a large purchaser and active participant in the broader purchaser community, GE makes several commitments. First, GE will pursue the design of benefit packages that encourage consumers to be sensitive to both the quality and cost of health care services and to engage in better self-management. Second, it is imperative that all employers support the use of standardized performance measures, specifically ones approved by the National Quality Forum, in efforts to link payment to performance. Third, GE will contract with health plans that do the best job of rewarding better performance by physicians and hospitals. In support of this third point, GE encourages AHIP and BCBSA to focus on the design of new provider compensation systems that reward value, and encourages the National Business Group on Health to promote the use of best practices by benefits consultants and health plans to diffuse market change.

Grantmakers in Health (GH)
Lauren LeRoy
www.gih.org

GH is an educational resource to foundations that fund in health. It identifies important issues, clarifies the role of philanthropy in addressing these issues, and provides information and connections to grant makers to help them use their resources wisely.

GH makes two commitments. The first is to forge connections between foundations and community coalitions. Foundations may be able to provide financial support to a community, but they can also do more. They can serve as conveners to bring together stakeholders in a community and help them work across sectors, make connections between communities and other grantees that may be able to share expertise and provide technical assistance, raise public awareness and inform policy makers, and help with leadership development and dissemination of community work.

GH's second commitment is to stimulate broader foundation interest and involvement in the key issues identified at the summit by using these issues as organizing principles or cross-cutting themes for national meetings. For example, GH's annual meeting in February 2004 will focus on system redesign, and some of these issues will be integrated into that program.

Institute for Healthcare Improvement (IHI)
Donald Berwick
www.ihi.org

IHI can provide the summit communities with access to knowledge and opportunities to work together. For tools and approaches to improving quality, communities are encouraged to consult the IHI websites (www.qualityhealthcare.org and www.ihi.org). IHI will also set up a managed list serve where communities can talk to each other, share experiences, and work together to solve problems. Communities are also invited to attend IHI's national meeting in December 2004. Since this is just 3 months after the national meeting of Improving Chronic Illness Care, sidebar meetings of the summit communities will be arranged at both of these events. If IHI is able to mobilize the necessary resources, it will organize a formal community collaborative.

Institute of Medicine (IOM)
Janet Corrigan
www.iom.edu

IOM is committed to continuing its quality initiative. During the last 6 years, about a dozen reports have been produced in the *Quality Chasm* Series. Over the next 3 years, IOM will focus its attention on producing several reports that address key environmental levers— payment processes, performance improvement programs, and benefits design. The first report, which is congressionally mandated, will provide guidance on linking Medicare fee-for-service and capitated payment systems to performance. The IOM committee for this study will identify specific performance measures to be used and evaluate alternative approaches for adjusting payments based on performance. The second report is also congressionally mandated, and will focus on strengthening Medicare's performance improvement processes, most notably the QIOs. The third report in this series will be on quality-based benefit design. In summary, IOM is committed to addressing each of the major environmental forces identified by the summit participants.

Joint Commission on Accreditation of Healthcare Organizations (JCAHO)
Dennis O'Leary
www.jcaho.org

JCAHO accredits more than 16,000 organizations across all major settings of care in the United States and around the world. Its stock in trade is its accreditation standards and performance measurement capabilities. JCAHO, in collaboration with others, has promulgated pain management standards, as well as measures for heart failure, diabetes, and pediatric asthma. Collaborative efforts with the National Committee for Quality Assurance (NCQA) and the American Medical Association to develop pain management measures are continuing, as are efforts to work with the psychiatric hospital community to develop measures for depression and other mental health conditions. JCAHO is committed to working with key players on the ongoing development and maintenance of measure sets and the adaptation of these measures to various practice settings and communities to accommodate changing accountabilities. Beginning in July 2004, JCAHO will publicly report all of the performance measurement data it collects.

More must be done, however, to support the efforts of communities to achieve the IOM's quality goals. The nation lacks key elements of a quality infrastructure. First, there are no clearly defined, measurable national quality goals, and no agreed-upon authority that could proclaim such goals. In 1998, the President's Commission on Consumer Protection and Quality recommended that a National Quality Council be established; Congress's failure to act on that recommendation was a missed opportunity. Second, there is no national strategic plan for the development of a health information infrastructure.[1] The lack of electronic health records clearly limits the ability to measure and improve quality. Third, there is no process for the prioritized identification of condition-specific measure sets to systematically address quality goals. One way to identify the work that needs to be done is to develop a matrix with the IOM's six quality aims on one axis and priority conditions on the other, and to populate the resulting matrix with appropriate measures to create relevant measure sets. Lastly, we need carefully thought-out pay-for-performance models that will both reward desired behaviors and provide incentives for performance improvement. This work must be accomplished over the next 3 to 5 years to give the necessary support to community initiatives and, it may be hoped, enable thousands more such efforts to blossom.

MacColl Institute for Healthcare Innovation at Group Health Cooperative (MIHI)
Brian Austin
www.improvingchroniccare.org

For 6 years, MIHI has served as the national program office for The Robert Wood Johnson Foundation's program on Improving Chronic Illness Care. The institute has established a website (www.improvingchroniccare.org) that serves as a repository for information on the Chronic Care Model, including tools and best practices. MIHI also serves nationally as a resource for those interested in improved care for chronic illness, and encourages anyone seeking to identify individuals who have addressed or are currently working on similar challenges to contact the institute. Lastly, the institute sponsors a national meeting each year, and this year's meeting, to be held in September 2004, will focus on community-based innovations. Each of the summit communities is invited to participate in this meeting. Information about the conference is available on the above website.

---

[1] Note: Following the Summit, on May 6, 2004, David J. Brailer was appointed as the first Health Information Technology Coordinator for the DHHS (http://www.hhs.gov/news/speech/2004/040506.html).

National Association of Community Health Centers
Daniel Hawkins
www.nachc.com

Community health centers are the family doctor for nearly 15 million Americans in more than 3,500 communities across the country. Virtually all of these people are low-income, and more than one-third are uninsured. During the last few years, more than 500 health centers have participated in "health disparities collaboratives" supported by the Health Resources and Services Administration. Health centers, consistent with their founding purpose as both agents of care and agents of change in their communities, are ready and willing to serve as "foot soldiers" in the campaign to improve health care quality, and to work with other community and national stakeholders to achieve that goal.

National Business Group on Health
Helen Darling
www.businessgrouphealth.org

The National Business Group on Health will work with IOM and other national partners to accelerate the dissemination of effective methods for achieving major improvements in the quality of health care. The group will continue, as in the last 2 years, to aggressively promote (1) transparency in health care among purchasers, national legislators, and executive and regulatory agencies; and (2) fundamental payment and finance reform tied to high-quality performance and evidence-based practice.

The National Business Group on Health will also create a special website that highlights outstanding examples of business groups working with other stakeholders to advance quality and bridge the quality chasm. This effort will begin immediately with posting of the exemplary work done in Kansas City, highlighted at the summit, involving leadership by group member Sprint.

National Cancer Institute (NCI)
Molla Sloane Donaldson
www.nci.nih.gov

NCI has several efforts under way to improve cancer care, and specifically pain management. First, NCI has issued a request for proposals aimed at overcoming system, provider, and patient barriers to effective palliative care. Communities interested in applying for one of these grants should consult http://grants.nih.gov/grants/guide/rfa-files/RFA-CA-05-013.html. The NCI Outcomes Research Branch (http://outcomes.cancer.gov/) has a particular focus on patient-reported outcomes, such as health-related quality of life, patient experience and satisfaction with care, and economic burden. A complete portfolio of NCI funding opportunities in the palliative care arena can be found at http://www.cancer.gov/researchandfunding/announcements/symptommanagement.

Second, as a part of NCI's Quality of Care Initiative, numerous public- and private-sector collaborative efforts are under way to improve the quality of cancer care, including work on assessing and improving palliative care for patients with cancer. Work has begun on a public–private project aimed at redesigning cancer care, spanning the cancer continuum from suspicion to end of life. Finally, in terms of quality measurement, NCI and its federal partners AHRQ, CMS, and the Centers for Disease Control and Prevention are supporting the National Quality Forum in identifying a set of consensus measures of cancer quality (http://outcomes.cancer.gov/translation/canqual/). That effort includes both tumor-specific and cross-cutting measures.

National Center for Healthcare Leadership (NCHL)
Marie Sinioris
www.nchl.org

NCHL, founded 2 years ago, is dedicated to the development of health care leaders who will be capable of implementing the summit's aggressive agenda for health system change. NCHL is identifying the core competencies leaders must possess to carry out that agenda, sponsoring educational programs, and conducting evaluation research to ensure that these competencies will be obtained. A national database on leadership best practices and critical success factors will soon be available on the NCHL website. The center welcomes the opportunity to work directly with the summit communities on cultural change and leadership development.

National Committee for Quality Assurance (NCQA)
L. Gregory Pawlson
www.ncqa.org

NCQA makes three commitments: (1) continuing its work with multiple stakeholder groups to populate the full spectrum of performance measures related to the six aims of the *Quality Chasm* report, striving to reduce duplication and redundancy; (2) working with the 15 summit communities in a number of areas related to measurement, from helping to choose appropriate measures to implementing measures for a specific project; and (3) adapting current NCQA evaluation programs to focus more on cross-cutting areas, such as consumer–patient education and support, care management, and means of enhancing provider performance. Additionally, NCQA has developed several tools and resources that are available to communities:

- Quality Compass®, a database derived from the population of nearly 90 million Americans enrolled in health plans, compiled over the last 9 years, which includes patient surveys and clinical performance measures related to depression, asthma, diabetes, heart disease, and some other chronic illnesses.
- Quality Dividend Calculator, an on-line tool that allows purchasers and others to see how improvements in quality of care for the major chronic diseases can enhance productivity and reduce absenteeism in the workplace.
- Quality Profiles®, a compendium of best-practice examples providing tips on how to implement quality improvement projects in about 12 different disease areas, as well as some cross-cutting areas.
- Practice Systems Assessment Survey, an assessment tool patterned after the Chronic Care Model, that measures the degree to which physician practices incorporate such systems as registries, reminders, and feedback, as well as the use of nurses and other health professionals in extended roles.

Pacific Business Group on Health (PBGH)
Arnold Milstein
www.pbgh.org

One of the many wise observations in the *Quality Chasm* report is the importance of focusing on a few strategic interventions to improve health system performance. As a participant in the leadership of both the Leapfrog Group and the Disclosure Project, I commit to three strategic interventions. The first is to accelerate national consensus on the public reporting of measures of quality, efficiency, and care redesign at multiple levels, including individual physician office teams, hospitals, larger health care organizations, and communities. The second is to coordinate local and national provider-focused initiatives on pay for performance, including private-sector coordination with CMS. The third, to ambitious aims; specifically of no less than a "30/30" gain within 10 years: a 30 percentage point offset of projected per capita U.S. health care spending and a 30 percent average improvement in standardized measures of quality.

Substance Abuse and Mental Health Services Administration (SAMHSA)
Ronald Manderschied
www.samhsa.gov

In 2003, the President's Commission on Mental Health issued a report that addressed transforming the mental health system in ways consistent with the agenda for change set forth in the *Quality Chasm* report, thus affording a real opportunity for collaboration. To this end, SAMHSA has provided support to IOM for convening a workshop and producing a report on how best to apply the conceptual framework and principles of the *Quality Chasm* report to the area of mental health and substance abuse. This ongoing IOM project provides an excellent vehicle for continuation of the summit's work in the area of depression. In the near future, SAMSHA will also be announcing the creation of a new center on policy in mental health and primary care. Lastly, SAMSHA is prepared to commit financial resources to convening the summit communities and helping them address key issues such as quality measurement, and invites others to join in this activity.

The Robert Wood Johnson Foundation (RWJF)
Tracy Orleans
www.rwjf.org

RWJF sponsored the summit as a way to further the agenda set forth in the *Quality Chasm* report, and what was accomplished far exceeded its expectations. The foundation is committed to following up on the summit in some very specific ways. First, RWJF supports 15 national programs focused on improving chronic illness care or promoting healthy behaviors. Within 2 weeks, the foundation will provide IOM with a list of these programs, the contact individuals, and the types of assistance they can provide. Second, RWJF will make available a list of its grantees in the summit communities that are working on relevant issues and can serve as valuable allies. Third, the foundation is committed to working with IOM to continue the kind of unique gathering that occurred at the summit, and specifically to continuing the convening of the national champions. Finally, RWJF is investing in a number of projects directed at the harmonization and standardization of quality measures for outpatient chronic care and will keep IOM abreast of these efforts.

URAC
Liza Greenberg
www.urac.org

URAC is a national accreditation organization that has developed standards for functions within health care systems, including disease management, utilization management, and case management, as well as for health plans, preferred provider organizations, and health websites. Over the next 2 years, URAC will be revising its accreditation standards to bring them into closer alignment with the six aims specified in the *Quality Chasm* report. As part of this process, efforts will be made to identify ways in which the accreditation process can encourage collaborative efforts across all stakeholders, such as those that the summit communities are trying to involve.

CLOSING STATEMENT

The 1st Annual Crossing the Quality Chasm Summit was the beginning of what we may hope will become an ongoing dialogue among local and national individuals, communities, and organizations committed to improving the quality of health care in America. Many of the strategies proposed by the participants are actionable now, and can be hastened by cross-fertilization and cooperation among the diverse stakeholders represented at the summit. These include:

- Aligning financial incentives to encourage and reward evidence-based care—including care coordination and patient self-management support.

- Establishing a core set of valid and reliable standardized measures for the five priority areas featured at the summit—subsequently expanded to the other 15 priority areas.
- Giving patients access to electronic copies or versions of their health record.
- Creating national data standards to facilitate the electronic transfer of health information across multiple providers and health care settings.

The action plans that emerged from the summit will need to be further refined and modified for different settings, but the message is clear that change is possible—as illustrated by the work already being done in the communities featured at the summit. The outcomes from the summit can serve as a guide for tackling some of the major barriers to the diffusion of these best practices. The IOM hopes to convene future summits focused on implementaitn of the vision of the *Quality Chasm*, and looks forward to hearing about the progress of the community participants.

REFERENCES

IOM (Institute of Medicine). 2003. *Priority Areas for National Action: Transforming Health Care Quality.* Adams K, Corrigan JM, eds. Washington, DC: National Academy Press.

Partnership for Prevention. 2002. *Better Lives for People with Chronic Conditions.* Baltimore, MD: John Hopkins University, Robert Wood Johnson Foundation.

Appendix A
Biographical Sketches of Committee Members

Reed V. Tuckson, M.D., Chair. Dr. Tuckson joined UnitedHealth Group in November 2000 as Senior Vice President of Consumer Health and Medical Care Advancement, a position in which he is responsible for working with all of the company's business units to improve the quality and efficiency of health services. Prior to joining UnitedHealth Group, he served as Senior Vice President, Professional Standards, for the American Medical Association. Former President of the Charles R. Drew University of Medicine and Science in Los Angeles from 1991 to 1997, Dr. Tuckson also served as Senior Vice President for Programs of the March of Dimes Birth Defects Foundation from 1990 to 1991. From 1986 to 1990, he was Commissioner of Public Health for the District of Columbia. Dr. Tuckson currently is a member of several health care–related and academic organizations, including the Institute of Medicine. A graduate of Howard University and the Georgetown University School of Medicine, Dr. Tuckson trained as an intern, resident, and fellow in general internal medicine at the Hospital of the University of Pennsylvania. A Robert Wood Johnson Clinical Scholar of the University of Pennsylvania, he also studied health care administration and policy at the Wharton School of Business.

Ron J. Anderson, M.D. Dr. Anderson has been President and Chief Executive Officer of Parkland Health and Hospital System since 1982. He is also a director of Parkland Foundation and Texans Care for Children, and is Chief Executive Officer and a member of the board of directors of Parkland Community Health Plan. Dr. Anderson is also President and Chairman of the Texas Hospital Association, and a member of the board of directors of the National Association of Public Hospitals and the National Public Health and Hospital Institute. In 1997 he was elected to the Institute of Medicine. He has authored or coauthored more than 200 articles on medicine, ethics, and health policy. Dr. Anderson received his medical degree from the University of Oklahoma and his pharmacy degree from Southwestern Oklahoma State University, where he was selected as a distinguished alumnus in 1987.

Regina M. Benjamin, M.D., M.B.A. Dr. Benjamin is founder and Chief Executive Officer of the Bayou La Batre Rural Health Clinic in Bayou La Batre, Alabama. She is also Associate Dean for Rural Health at the University of South Alabama College of Medicine in Mobile, where she administers the Alabama Area Health Education Center program and previously administered the telemedicine program. She currently serves as President of the Medical Association, State of Alabama. In 1998 Dr. Benjamin was the U.S. recipient of the Nelson Mandela Award for Health and Human Rights. In 1995, she was the first physician under age 40 and the first African American woman to be elected to the American Medical Association's (AMA) board of trustees. She has also served as President of the AMA Education and Research Foundation, and is a member of the AMA's Council on Ethical and Judicial Affairs. Dr. Benjamin attended Xavier University in New Orleans and was a member of the second class of Morehouse School of Medicine. She received her medical degree from the University of Alabama, Birmingham, and completed her residency in family practice at the Medical Center of Central Georgia. She also received a masters in business administration from Tulane University.

Linda Burnes Bolton, R.N., Dr.P.H. Dr. Burnes Bolton is Vice President and Chief Nursing Officer of Cedars-Sinai Health System and Research Institute, Los Angeles, California. She also holds graduate faculty appointments at the University of California, Los Angeles; University of California, San Francisco; and California State University, Los Angeles. Her primary research focus is women's health, health policy, and organizational development. As a member of the Cedars-Sinai Research Institute, she leads interdisciplinary research teams addressing health services and nursing research. Dr. Burnes Bolton is codeveloper of the National Black Nurses Association Community Collaboration Model. This model has been tested and is currently used in more than 100 communities throughout the United States and as a framework for improving community health. Dr. Burnes Bolton holds a bachelor of science degree in nursing from Arizona State University, masters degrees in nursing and public health, and a doctorate in public health from the University of California, Los Angeles. She is a fellow of the American Academy of Nursing.

Bruce E. Bradley, M.B.A. Mr. Bradley is Director, Health Plan Strategy and Public Policy for General Motors (GM) Health Care Initiatives. He is responsible for health care–related strategy and public policy, with a focus on quality measurement and improvement, consumer engagement, and cost-effectiveness. Mr. Bradley joined GM in June 1996 after 5 years as Corporate Manager of Managed Care for GTE Corporation. In addition to his health care management experience at GTE, he spent nearly 20 years in health plan and health maintenance organization (HMO) management. He was cofounder of the HMO Group (now the Alliance of Community Health Plans), a national corporation of 15 nonprofit, independent group-practice HMOs, and the HMO Group Insurance Co., Ltd. Mr. Bradley has gained recognition for his work in achieving health plan quality improvement and for his efforts in developing the Health Plan Employer Data and Information Set (HEDIS)® measurements and processes. He is a board member of the National Quality Forum, Treasurer of the board of the Foundation for Accountability, a past board member of The Academy for Health Services Research and Policy, and a founding member and past Chair of the Leapfrog Group board. Mr. Bradley holds a bachelors degree in psychology from Yale University and a masters degree in business and health care administration from the Wharton School at the University of Pennsylvania.

Allen S. Daniels, LISW, Ed.D. Dr. Daniels is Chief Executive Officer for Alliance Behavioral Care—a regional managed behavioral health care organization—and serves as Executive Director for University Psychiatric Services, a multidisciplinary behavioral group practice.

BIOGRAPHICAL SKETCHES OF SUMMIT COMMITTEE MEMBERS

Both of these organizations are affiliated with the Department of Psychiatry at the University of Cincinnati. Dr. Daniels is Professor of Clinical Psychiatry at the University of Cincinnati, College of Medicine. He has published extensively in the area of managed care and group-practice operations, quality improvement and clinical outcomes, and academic health care. Dr. Daniels is Chair of the American Managed Behavioral Healthcare Association. He is a graduate of the University of Chicago School of Social Services Administration and the University of Cincinnati.

Lillee Smith Gelinas, R.N., M.S.N. Ms. Gelinas is Vice President and Chief Nursing Officer at VHA Inc.—an alliance of more than 2,200 health care organizations. She supports efforts aimed at systemwide performance improvement to enhance members' economic strength through better patient care, operations, and supply change management. She works extensively with both health care organizations and VHA's 18 local offices to close the quality gap through VHA's focused agenda. In 1986 Ms. Gelinas spearheaded the formation of the VHA Nursing Initiative, which addresses the education, networking, and business needs of VHA's nursing leaders. Ms. Gelinas is a nationally recognized speaker on clinical, health care management, and nursing issues, and has published numerous articles on these subjects. She earned her bachelors degree in nursing from the University of Southern Louisiana in Lafayette and a masters degree in nursing, with honors, from the University of Pennsylvania, where she also studied at the Wharton School of Business. She is a member of the Joint Commission on Accreditation of Healthcare Organizations' National Nursing Council and cochaired the 2003 National Quality Forum project to establish performance measures for nursing care. In addition, she is a member of the board of directors for Exempla Healthcare, Denver, Colorado.

Charles J. Homer, M.D., M.P.H. Dr. Homer is President and Chief Executive Officer of the National Initiative for Children's Healthcare Quality (NICHQ), a research and educational organization whose sole focus is improving the quality of health services for children. In addition to his role at NICHQ, Dr. Homer is Chair of the American Academy of Pediatrics Steering Committee on Quality Improvement and Management. He is also Associate Professor of Pediatrics and of Public Health at Harvard University. He was a member of the third U.S. Preventive Services Task Force from 1999 to 2002. Dr. Homer formerly directed fellowship training programs in pediatric primary care and health services research at Children's Hospital in Boston, where he also established the Clinical Effectiveness program, focused on health services research and training. Dr. Homer received his undergraduate degree from Yale University and his medical degree from the University of Pennsylvania. He also obtained a masters in public health from the University of North Carolina.

David C. Kibbe, M.D., M.B.A. Dr. Kibbe is Director of Health Information Technology for the American Academy of Family Physicians (AAFP), the membership organization that represents over 95,000 U.S. family doctors. In this position, he is responsible for formulating AAFP's strategic direction and policy affecting a broad range of information and communications technology initiatives, including those related to the Health Insurance Portability and Accountability Act (HIPAA), electronic health records, computer security, practice management systems, and quality measurement. Dr. Kibbe serves as Medical Director and Board Chairman for Canopy Systems, a software firm that provides web-based case management software to many of the country's largest academic health centers and the U.S. Navy hospital system. He has authored numerous peer-reviewed articles and several book chapters on e-health, computer security, and HIPAA, and is coauthor of the AMA's *Field Guide to HIPAA Implementation*. He is a frequent speaker on HIPAA privacy and security compliance for clinical audiences around the country. Dr. Kibbe received his bachelors degree from Harvard University, his medical degree from Case-Western Reserve University School of Medicine, and a masters in business administration from the University of Texas at Austin.

Mary Anne Koda-Kimble, Pharm.D. Dr. Koda-Kimble is Dean of the School of Pharmacy at the University of California, San Francisco (UCSF), where she teaches and has cared for patients at the university's Diabetes Center. She holds the Thomas J. Long Endowed Professorship in Chain Pharmacy Practice and previously served as Chairwoman of the Department of Clinical Pharmacy. Dr. Koda-Kimble received her Pharm.D. from UCSF and joined its faculty in 1970, helping to develop an innovative clinical pharmacy curriculum. She is a member of the United States Pharmacopoeia Board of Trustees and is Vice Chair of the board of directors of the American Council of Pharmaceutical Education. Dr. Koda-Kimble is a past President of the American Association of Colleges of Pharmacy and has served on the California State Board of Pharmacy, the Food and Drug Administration's Nonprescription Drugs Advisory Committee, and many other boards and task forces of national professional associations. She is frequently invited to address national and international groups and has authored many publications, the best known of which is *Applied Therapeutics*, a text widely used by health professional students and practitioners throughout the world.

Peter V. Lee, J.D. Mr. Lee is the President and Chief Executive Officer of the Pacific Business Group on Health (PBGH), where he oversees the organization's efforts to improve access to high-quality health care, moderate costs, and work collaboratively with other groups to achieve these goals. PBGH plays a leadership role in an array of health care quality initiatives that include providing consumers with standardized comparative quality information and developing methods for assessing and communicating the quality of care delivered by health plans, medical groups, and hospitals. Mr. Lee is a member of the boards of the National Committee on Quality Assurance and the National Business Coalition on Health, and is Cochair of the Consumer/Purchaser Disclosure Project, a national effort to promote better transparency of health care providers' performance. He has served on numerous national and statewide bodies; testifies and speaks regularly on health care quality issues; and has authored a number of studies on health care issues, including reports on health care quality information and patient advocacy programs. Prior to joining PBGH, Mr. Lee was Executive Director of the Center for Health Care Rights; he was also an attorney in private practice and worked on health care issues in Washington, D.C., where he was the Director of Programs for the National AIDS Network. He received his law degree from the University of Southern California and his undergraduate degree from the University of California, Berkeley.

Kate R. Lorig, R.N., Dr.P.H. Dr. Lorig is a Professor of Medicine and Director of the Patient Education Research Center at Stanford University School of Medicine. She is a leading expert on the development and evaluation of community-based, peer-led patient education programs, with emphasis on those programs that serve older people. For the past 20 years, Dr. Lorig has worked on testing the applicability of self-efficacy theory to health education programs. In addition, she and her colleagues have developed, validated, and published more than 40 patient education outcome instruments. Dr. Lorig's work has resulted in more than 60 peer-reviewed articles, 7 books, numerous book chapters, and many articles in the popular press. She received a bachelors degree in nursing from Boston University; a masters in nursing from the University of California, San Francisco; and a masters and doctorate in public health education from the University of California, Berkeley.

BIOGRAPHICAL SKETCHES OF SUMMIT COMMITTEE MEMBERS

Joanne Lynn, M.D. Dr. Lynn is a geriatrician who has taken on the challenge of improving end-of-life care. She is currently Director of the Washington Home Center for Palliative Care Studies, a collaboration among the Washington Home—a long-term care and hospice provider—RAND Health, and the Institute for Healthcare Improvement. She is also President of Americans for Better Care of the Dying, a nonprofit public-interest organization that promotes public understanding and coalitions across organizations to improve end-of-life care. Dr. Lynn was Project Director for the President's Commission for the Study of Ethical Problems in Medicine and Biomedical and Behavioral Research and principal writer of that commission's book, *Deciding to Forego Life-Sustaining Treatment: A Report on the Ethical, Medical and Legal Issues in Treatment Decisions*. A member of the National Academy of Sciences, she was elected to the Institute of Medicine in 1996. She has served on numerous Institute of Medicine committees, including the Committee on Care at the End of Life, the Committee to Study the Social and Ethical Impact of Biomedicine, and the Committee on Identifying Priority Areas for Quality Improvement. Dr. Lynn received her medical degree from Boston University. Additionally, she holds masters degrees in philosophy and social policy from The George Washington University and in clinical evaluative sciences from Dartmouth College.

David M. Nathan, M.D. Dr. Nathan is Director of the General Clinical Research Center and of the Diabetes Center at Massachusetts General Hospital and a Professor of Medicine at Harvard Medical School. Having produced more than 200 articles in the medical literature, he is an internationally recognized expert on diabetes and its complications. Dr. Nathan focuses on the development of innovative therapies for treating type 1 and type 2 diabetes and preventing their long-term complications. He was a pioneer in the development of intensive therapies for diabetes and was one of the architects of the landmark Diabetes Control and Complications Trial. Dr. Nathan currently is Cochair of the Epidemiology of Diabetes Interventions and Complications Study in Type 1 Diabetes and Chairman of the Diabetes Prevention Program, a National Institutes of Health-sponsored multicenter trial focused on prevention of type 2 diabetes. He received his bachelors degree from Amherst College and his medical degree from Mount Sinai School of Medicine.

Cheryl M. Scott, M.H.A. Ms. Scott is President and Chief Executive Officer of Group Health Cooperative (GHC), based in Seattle. GHC is the nation's second-largest consumer-governed, nonprofit health care system. Prior to assuming her present position in 1997, Ms. Scott served as GHC's Regional Vice President and Executive Vice President/Chief Operating Officer. She is currently Associate Clinical Professor in the graduate program in Health Services Administration at the University of Washington. At the national level, she chairs the Alliance of Community Health Plans and serves on the boards of the American Association of Health Plans and the Health Technology Center. Locally, Ms. Scott chairs the external advisory committee for the University of Washington's Health Administration Program. She received a bachelors degree in communications and a masters degree in health administration from the University of Washington.

John A. Spertus, M.D., M.P.H. Dr. Spertus is a cardiologist and Professor of Medicine in the Department of Internal Medicine, Section of Cardiology, at the University of Missouri, Kansas City. He is also Director of Cardiovascular Education and Outcomes Research at the Mid America Heart Institute. Dr. Spertus developed the Seattle Angina Questionnaire and the Kansas City Cardiomyopathy Questionnaire, which have been translated into more than 20 languages and are emerging as the gold standards for quantifying patients' health status in coronary artery disease and heart failure. Dr. Spertus has served on numerous national committees, including his role as cochair of the AMA/

American College of Cardiology (ACC)/ American Heart Association (AHA) Consortium task force developing outpatient performance measures for the Centers for Medicare and Medicaid Services', Doctors' Office Quality project in the areas of hypertension, coronary disease, and heart failure. He serves on the AHA/ACC Joint Task Force on Performance Measures; is a member of AHA's Outcomes Research Interdisciplinary Working Group and the National Heart, Lung, and Blood Institute's Expert Panel on Outcomes Research; and cofounded the Annual AHA/ACC Scientific Forum on Quality of Care and Outcomes Research. He also founded the Cardiovascular Outcomes Research Consortium and CV Outcomes, a nonprofit 501(c)(3) corporation dedicated to the advancement of health care quality and outcomes research in cardiovascular disease. Dr. Spertus received his medical degree from the University of California, San Francisco, and his masters in public health from the University of Washington School of Public Health and Community Medicine.

I. Steven Udvarhelyi, M.D. Dr. Udvarhelyi is Senior Vice President and Chief Medical Officer for Independence Blue Cross and its affiliated companies Keystone Health Plan East and AmeriHealth. In this role, he has overall responsibility for medical management programs and policies and is chief medical spokesperson for the company. In addition, he serves as executive sponsor for the Corporate Data Warehouse initiative. Dr. Udvarhelyi has more than 10 years of experience in the managed care industry. Prior to his current position, he worked for Prudential Health Care as National Medical Director, and later as Vice President of Operations for Prudential's four health plans in Florida. He has also served on the faculty of Harvard Medical School. Dr. Udvarhelyi is on the board of directors of the National Committee for Quality Assurance and the National Council of Physician Executives, and is also Chairman of the American Association of Health Plans Committee on Quality Care. He is a board-certified internist who completed his residency in internal medicine at the University of Minnesota and completed a fellowship in general medicine at Brigham and Women's Hospital in Boston. Dr. Udvarhelyi is a graduate of Harvard University and The Johns Hopkins University School of Medicine, and has a masters degree in health services administration from the Harvard School of Public Health.

Appendix B
Quality Chasm Selected Bibliography

Berwick DM. 2002. A User's Guide for the IOM's *Quality Chasm* Report. *Health Affairs (Millwood, VA)* 21 (3):80–90.

Chassin MR, Galvin RW. 1998. The urgent need to improve health care quality. Institute of Medicine National Roundtable on Health Care Quality. *The Journal of the American Medical Association* 280 (11):1000–1005.

IOM (Institute of Medicine). 1999. *Ensuring Quality Cancer Care.* Hewitt M, Simone JV, eds. Washington, DC: National Academy Press.

IOM. 2000. *To Err Is Human: Building a Safer Health System.* Kohn LT, Corrigan JM, Donaldson MS, eds. Washington, DC: National Academy Press.

IOM. 2001. *Crossing the Quality Chasm: A New Health System for the 21st Century.* Washington, DC: National Academy Press.

IOM. 2002a. *Fostering Rapid Advances in Health Care: Learning from System Demonstrations.* Corrigan JM, Greiner AC, Erickson SM, eds. Washington, DC: National Academy Press.

IOM. 2002b. *Leadership by Example: Coordinating Government Roles in Improving Health Care Quality.* Corrigan JM, Eden J, Smith BM, eds. Washington, DC: National Academy Press.

IOM. 2003a. *Health Professions Education: A Bridge to Quality.* Greiner AC, Knebel E, eds. Washington, DC: National Academy Press.

IOM. 2003b. *Key Capabilities of an Electronic Health Record System: Letter Report.* Washington, DC: National Academy Press.

IOM. 2003c. *Patient Safety: Achieving a New Standard for Care.* Aspden P, Corrigan JM, Wolcott J, Erickson SM, eds. Washington, DC: National Academy Press.

IOM. 2003d. *Priority Areas for National Action: Transforming Health Care Quality.* Adams K, Corrigan JM, eds. Washington, DC: National Academy Press.

IOM. 2004a. *Keeping Patients Safe: Transforming the Work Environment of Nurses.* Page A, ed. Washington, DC: National Academy Press.

Quality Chasm Website

IOM (Institute of Medicine). 2004b. *Crossing the Quality Chasm: The IOM Health Care Quality Initiative.* [Online]. Available: http://www.iom.edu/focuson.asp?id=8089 [accessed June 29, 2004].

Appendix C
Descriptions of Summit Communities

ASTHMA COMMUNITIES

Children's Mercy Hospital/Kansas City Asthma Coalition

Children's Mercy Hospital (CMH) has developed an asthma registry with the goal of combining information from multiple sources to reduce fragmentation of care. Its disease management program includes an intensive asthma education program with 8 weeks of training on site in private physicians' offices—reimbursed by some health plans once the intervention has been completed, followed by ongoing support for asthma management. A complete culture change in health care delivery directed toward patient empowerment and self-management using a multidisciplinary team is emphasized. Home visits are conducted using technologies such as air sampling to optimize asthma treatment. Plans for an asthma coalition with multiple stakeholders are in progress, with the goal of identifying and efficiently allocating asthma resources where they are needed. CMH is one of six recipients nationwide of Improving Asthma Care for Children grants from The Robert Wood Johnson Foundation, which target children with asthma covered by Medicaid and State Children's Health Insurance Programs.

Controlling Asthma in the Richmond Metropolitan Area

Initiated in 2001, Controlling Asthma in the Richmond Metropolitan Area (CARMA) is one of seven initiatives selected for the Controlling Asthma in American Cities Project, funded by the Centers for Disease Control and Prevention. This project targets children aged 2–18 and their families, using community-based interventions that include education, intensive case management for high-risk children, and health care provider education. Project efforts include managed care collaboration and parish nurse/lay outreach partnerships. Also, linkages between obesity and asthma are being explored. The Bon Secours Richmond Health System, the University of Virginia Health System, and the Central Virginia Asthma Coalition are partners in this initiative, which includes annual assessments of effectiveness, cost, collaborative relationships, and feasibility of expansion. Long-term outcomes will be assessed by tracking hospitalizations and emergency department visits.

The Pediatric/Adult Asthma Coalition of New Jersey

The Pediatric/Adult Asthma Coalition of New Jersey (PACNJ), sponsored by the American Lung Association of New Jersey, is a state-level consumer-driven initiative formed in 2000 to provide the state with a clearinghouse for asthma programs and services. It currently uses six task forces to ensure that all public and private educational and child care facilities, physicians, and other providers comply with the National Heart, Lung, and Blood Guidelines for asthma management. PACNJ has been involved in the development of a state-mandated asthma action plan for any child carrying an inhaler in school and has provided school nurse education, with pre- and post-tests, via satellite broadcast. Its health insurance task force has developed guidelines for standards of care related to asthma treatment, based on findings from a conference on best practices for public and private New Jersey insurers. Current projects are focused on patient self-management tools for recognizing asthma severity and controlling asthma triggers in the home and school.

Philadelphia Department of Health

The Philadelphia Department of Health is one of 12 recipients nationwide of the Department of Health and Human Services' Steps to a HealthierUS grant. This initiative supports community-based programs designed "to help Americans live longer, better, and healthier lives" by reducing the burden of asthma, diabetes, and obesity. Steps funding will enhance programs already under way in Philadelphia, such as an asthma call center (Child Asthma Link Line) that links children who have presented at local pediatric emergency departments with acute asthma exacerbations to specialists and other community resources, such as asthma self-management education programs and programs to eliminate home environmental triggers. Future plans are to expand this care coordination model to other chronic diseases, starting with diabetes. The Asthma Call Center was established in partnership with the Philadelphia Allies Against Asthma Coalition and is funded by a grant from The Robert Wood Johnson Foundation.

DEPRESSION COMMUNITIES

Intermountain Health Care— Depression in Primary Care Initiative

Intermountain Health Care (IHC)—an integrated delivery system that includes providers, plans and hospitals—has focused on management of depression in primary care settings within the framework of the Chronic Care Model. This initiative provides the primary care clinician, patient, and family with the tools and organizational supports needed to identify, diagnose, treat, and manage depression. The effort, begun in 1999, has improved patient functional status and outcomes and enhanced physician satisfaction, and has not raised costs for employers or plans. In association with its community partners, IHC has developed an implementation plan for the delivery of evidence-based depression treatment in the primary care setting through a Mental Health Integration (MHI) model. As one of eight Robert Wood Johnson–funded Incentive Grant national sites for linking clinical improvement to economic strategies for depression care, this demonstration project includes a sustainable business plan that aims to link financial value to the delivery of improved clinical outcomes. Currently, the IHC initiative involves seven internal and eight community groups. By 2005, IHC hopes that a sustainable business model based on this community partnership effort will be fully implemented in 20 clinic sites, involving 85 physicians and more than 490,000 annual client visits.

Mid-America Coalition on Health Care Community Initiative on Depression

In 1998, the Mid-America Coalition on Health Care collaborated with eight Kansas City employers with the aim of identifying health risks to employees and their families. The Behavioral Risk Factor Surveillance System (BRFSS) was administered to a representative sample of 45,000 area residents, and the results were compared with Healthy People 2010 benchmarks. The group agreed to target depression in order to focus on creating community support for timely diagnosis and treatment, destigmatization, and identification of direct and indirect costs associated with the disorder. After an initial focus on designing the initiative and introducing it to regional employers, health plans, and physicians, the coalition has expanded to 15 employers and tripled the number of individuals impacted. Now in phase II, the coalition is studying barriers to diagnosis and treatment and best practices in benefit design, as well as supporting worksite educational programs and facilitating multidisciplinary communication. In phase III, increased community involvement through churches, schools, and health departments will expand the coalition's scope and enable redistribution and analysis of the BRFSS. The entire project will be documented to encourage duplication of regional collaboration for improving the community's health.

DIABETES COMMUNITIES

County of Santa Cruz, California

Santa Cruz County, California, a blend of urban and rural communities with a population of 260,000, faces the challenge of diabetes across all sectors of health care. A growing Latino population with a disproportionate prevalence of type 2 diabetes intensifies concern regarding the overall increase in this disorder. Two competing private medical groups and the Medi-Cal managed care program have joined the public health department in two collaborative approaches. The first, the Regional Diabetes Collaborative (RDC), has brought together front-line professionals from all disciplines and all sectors from three contiguous counties to create a coordinated approach to diabetes treatment, patient education, and policy advocacy. At the same time, an executive-level collaborative, the Santa Cruz Health Improvement Partnership (HIP), has selected common-ground issues that affect all health care interests, bridging silos and opening gates in competitive fences. HIP has chosen diabetes for its 2004 communitywide target, harmonizing its efforts with those of RDC. The vision for this effort involves preventive approaches to diabetes beginning in childhood, extending through guideline-driven, consistent care for diagnosed individuals using communitywide systems of care.

The Asheville Project

The Asheville Project began in 1997 as a collaborative effort involving Mission-St. Joseph's Hospitals; the City of Asheville, North Carolina; the North Carolina Association of Pharmacists; and the University of North Carolina. It focused initially on improving diabetes care for 47 Asheville city employees. The key elements of the program are financial incentives (waived medication copayments) to encourage patient participation, intense self-care education, and frequent one-on-one monitoring/assessment of patients by a care manager. Each patient's care is compared with guideline standards, and success is assessed frequently according to these standards. Collaborative goals are established, barriers identified, questions answered, and recommendations made to the patient's physician. Active participation qualifies patients for medication copay waivers, education is covered, care managers are paid, physicians are provided guideline recommendations on individual patients, and the health plan receives a positive return on investment. The project has resulted in annual net savings for 164 patients of $2,033/person/year for 5 years, a 50 percent reduction in sick days, increased patient self-testing from 70 to 99 percent, and significant improvement in clinical parameters. Today, 300 patients with diabetes are involved in the project, with another 400 patients in programs managing asthma, hypertension, and hyperlipidemia. Twelve other communities are replicating the Asheville Project.

Madigan Army Medical Center

Madigan Army Medical Center (MAMC) is an academic referral center that supports all Department of Defense direct health care and the TRICARE program, covering tertiary care for 460,000 beneficiaries in Washington, Oregon, and Alaska. Of the 103,000 beneficiaries who reside in the community served by MAMC, 76,000 are enrolled for primary care, including 3,000 individuals with adult-onset diabetes. MAMC's diabetes initiative uses an electronic scorecard keyed to evidence-based Diabetes Quality Improvement Project (DQIP) parameters, provider performance reports, and interactive patient surveys to facilitate care decisions, clinician teamwork, and patient engagement. Successful outcomes for this diabetic population include a 41 percent decrease in emergency department visits, a 16 percent decrease in bed days, and annual savings of $0.3 million.

The Washington State Diabetes Collaborative

The Washington State Diabetes Collaborative was established in 1999 to address the findings of a statewide project that identified significant gaps between existing and desirable diabetes care. Based on the Institute for Healthcare Improvement's Breakthrough Series approach, the collaborative has engaged more than 65 teams from urban and rural, public and private, and small to large care delivery systems and health plans in improving the delivery of patient-centered diabetes care. The collaborative is sponsored by Qualis Health, the Washington State Department of Health (DOH), and The Robert Wood Johnson Foundation–funded Improving Chronic Illness Care Program of the Sandy MacColl Institute. Qualis Health, a Seattle-based private, nonprofit organization, provides a broad range of services to consumers, employers, providers, managed care organizations, and government agencies aimed at improving the quality of health care delivery and health outcomes. It serves as the Medicare Quality Improvement Organization for Washington. The Washington DOH works to protect and improve the health of the people of Washington. The DOH Diabetes Prevention and Control Program supports this mission by improving the health care delivery system, enhancing health communications, and building active health communities.

HEART FAILURE COMMUNITIES

Grand Rapids Medical Education and Research Center

The Medical Education and Research Center (MERC), a consortium of health systems, health plans, the educational community, and other groups in Grand Rapids, Michigan, is dedicated to community improvement and education. Leaders involved in the MERC consortium meet twice monthly to discuss quality and health improvement initiatives. MERC's current efforts include a focus on care coordination, with an emphasis on improving patient flow across the community's entire health system, which builds upon a module in the Institute for Healthcare Improvement's Impact Program. Other efforts under way include collaboration on population-focused disease management, financial incentives at the physician level that have been targeting quality benchmarks since 1997, and placement of interdisciplinary "learner teams" that partner with neighborhood associations and parish nursing programs to conduct community health assessments and develop focused interventions. MERC also has dedicated staff who design and implement evaluations of each of these interventions.

Greater Flint Health Coalition

Established in 1992, the Greater Flint Health Coalition (GFHC) is a community/institutional partnership and a multifaceted collaboration involving government, hospitals, labor, business, insurers, physicians, educational systems, consumers, and faith-based organizations in Flint, Michigan. The United Auto Workers and General Motors joined GFHC in 1994, leading to the development of community-based initiatives focused on treatment and prevention of heart disease, diabetes, and depression and other health needs. The Guidelines Applied in Practice (GAP)-Heart Failure (HF) project is designed to facilitate both inpatient compliance with American College of Cardiology/American Heart Association guidelines and transfer of the patient from the hospital to the primary care physician. Hospitals participating in the GAP-HF program are provided with the following menu of resources: an intervention toolkit including standing orders, nursing critical pathways, and a discharge contract; a physician–nurse team trained in guideline implementation to work with hospital clinicians and administrators; and a report card outlining each institution's indicators of improved quality of care for heart failure.

The Oregon Heart Failure Project

The Oregon Heart Failure Project is a statewide effort aimed at improving the management of heart failure. This project was initiated in 2001 by the American College of Cardiology (ACC) as the ACC-HF-GAP program. In close partnership with the Oregon Medicare Quality Improvement Organization and The Robert Wood Johnson Foundation, the project was initially developed as a collaborative of cardiologists from diverse practice environments across a wide geographic area (the State of Oregon). Both the diversity and geographic dispersion of practice settings were intended to represent practice in the state. The project is focused on outpatient management and thus targets the majority of patients with heart failure—those not hospitalized. The project developed and tested a set of tools designed to make it easier to manage patients in the outpatient setting in compliance with the ACC/AHA guidelines. After establishing baseline data from all practices represented in the collaborative, the project is now poised to extend its work and disseminate its tools to the larger community of physicians and health systems that care for patients with heart failure in outpatient settings throughout Oregon.

PAIN CONTROL IN ADVANCED CANCER COMMUNITIES

Kaiser-Bellflower

The Kaiser Permanente (KP) TriCentral Palliative Care Program, an interdisciplinary home-based program that blends palliative and curative care, offers patients at the end of life enhanced pain control, symptom management, and psychosocial support. It was developed for patients with congestive heart failure, chronic obstructive pulmonary disease, and cancer in response to KP internal data indicating that 63 percent of patients in intensive care units and 54 percent of other hospitalized patients with these diagnoses died. The program currently provides a gradual transition for patients with a 12-month survival prognosis, allowing them to maintain their primary care physician while receiving home visits from a palliative care team. The program has met goals for pain control, receives high patient satisfaction scores, and in an initial study was found to have reduced costs by 45 percent. The program is developing web-based resources for its replication; expansion to other KP sites is planned.

Rochester Health Commission

Rochester Health Commission (RHC), created in 1996, is a nonprofit, community-based organization dedicated to improving the quality, access, and cost of health care in the community. RHC was identified by the RAND Corporation as one of three model health care coalitions in the United States. Comprised of key stakeholders, the commission has equal provider, consumer, and business representation on its board. Currently, RHC has 12 communitywide initiatives under its umbrella, including those addressing patient safety, communitywide clinical guidelines, and end-of-life/palliative care. Communitywide clinical guidelines were developed for asthma, diabetes, depression, congestive heart failure, pain, and other conditions. The end-of-life/palliative care initiative focuses on improving pain management for all types of pain in all care settings, from doctors' offices to nursing homes and hospices. RHC received a Robert Wood Johnson Rewarding Results grant for its work linking communitywide guidelines to incentives, and has long been involved in performance measurement, dating back to Health Plan Employer Data and Information Set (HEDIS)® reporting in 1999. RHC also developed the Rochester Model, a broad-based chronic disease proposal that focuses on restructuring the area's health care system to properly align incentives and provider/consumer/employer efforts to improve health care.

Appendix D
Community Selection Criteria

The IOM summit committee developed the following criteria for communities likely to be most successful in furthering the vision of the *Quality Chasm* at the local level:

- Care coordination
  - Is care coordinated across patient conditions, services, and settings over time?
  - Have interdisciplinary teams been formed that communicate with and across diverse health care settings, institutions, and the public/personal health care systems?

- Evidence-based practice
  - Have care processes been redesigned in accordance with best practices?
  - Have guidelines been implemented? Is there a mechanism in place to provide feedback on patient outcomes—effective/ineffective interventions?

- Information and communications technology
  - Are information and communications technologies in place to improve access to clinical information and support clinical decision making?
  - Has a disease registry been compiled? Are prompts and reminders incorporated for needed services? What types of decision support are in place for clinicians?

- Reimbursement
    - Are there any programs in place that reward or pay for quality?
    - Does financing support approaches to care that further the six aims set fourth in the *Quality Chasm* report—for example, group visits and non–visit-based care—and thus may better meet patient needs?
    - Has a business model been articulated that would make it possible for existing revenue streams to support the program in other settings and/or could serve as a model for reforming payment streams?

- Measurement
    - Has the community incorporated performance and outcome measures for improvement and accountability?
    - Has measurement of some elements been demonstrated consistent with the six aims of the *Quality Chasm*.

- Consumer engagement
    - Have all the necessary stakeholders been identified?
    - Have multistakeholder coalitions been formed, and are they functioning?
    - Will stakeholders in the community think the changes made will significantly help them (perceived benefit of the change)?

- Leadership
    - Is there strong senior leadership that supports this initiative and considers it a priority?

The following additional screening criteria were applied:

- Willingness/ability to provide evidence for the efficacy of efforts to address key barriers

- Ability to demonstrate an evaluation component—commitment to measurement and accountability

- Stated willingness/commitment to take lessons back from the summit

- Identification of at least two primary stakeholders who would be represented at the summit and are actively engaged in the program

- Inclusion of an assessment/communication strategy in the work plan
    - Are the changes relatively simple?
    - Can they be successfully piloted?
    - How can others watch and learn?

- Geographic diversity among represented communities

Approximately 90 communities from across the country were identified as possible summit participants by committee members and a diverse set of organizations. From this initial pool, 45 communities were further screened, from which 15 were selected for the summit.

The IOM committee's criteria specified that efforts must be focused on at least one of the five targeted priority areas and that stakeholders involved must include either a payer (e.g., health plan) or purchaser (public or private)—given their influence in shaping health care markets—and at least two of the following: hospital or health system, outpatient provider, consumer-based organization, and government. Coalitions that involved both the private and public sectors were viewed favorably, given their ability to influence care across the community.

The committee further sought to invite communities to the summit that took an evidence-based approach to their quality improvement work and focused on system interventions (e.g., development of information and communications technology or reimbursement innovations). Communities were sought that evaluated their progress through measurement, were willing to be frank about their experiences, had the support of top leaders in their local markets, and exhibited signs of viability for the longer term. In addition, the committee desired a mix of communities in terms of clinical conditions addressed, geography, and the lead stakeholder driving the initiative.

Appendix E
Summit Attendees

Kelly Acton
Indian Health Service
Albuquerque, NM

Karen Adams
Institute of Medicine
Washington, DC

Neal Adams
California Department of Mental Health
Sacramento, CA

Terri Ades
American Cancer Society
Atlanta, GA

David Adler
American Health Quality Association
Washington, DC

Gerard Anderson
Johns Hopkins Bloomberg School of Public
    Health, Johns Hopkins University
Baltimore, MD

Ron Anderson*
Parkland Memorial Health and Hospital System
Dallas, TX

Brian Austin◆
MacColl Institute for Health Care Innovation at
    Group Health Cooperative
Seattle, WA

Bruce Bagley
American Academy of Family Physicians
Leawood, KS

James Bailey
University of Tennessee Health Science Center
Memphis, TN

Stuart Baker
VHA, Inc.
Irving, TX

David Baker
Feinberg School of Medicine, Northwestern University
Chicago, IL

Richard Baron
Healthier Babies, Healthier Futures
Philadelphia, PA

Eugene Barrett
American Diabetes Association
Alexandria, VA

Michele Beard
Central Coast Alliance for Health
Santa Cruz, CA

Regina Benjamin*
Bayou La Batre Rural Health Clinic, Inc.
Bayou La Batre, AL

Donald Berwick◆
Institute for Healthcare Improvement
Boston, MA

Christina Bethell
The Kaiser Permanente Center for Health Research
Portland, OR

Maureen Bisognano◆
Institute for Healthcare Improvement
Boston, MA

Rachel Block
United Hospital Fund
New York, NY

Patricia Bomba
Excellus Blue Cross and Blue Shield
Rochester, NY

Robert Bonow
Feinberg School of Medicine, Northwestern University
Chicago, IL

Kent Bottles
Grand Rapids Medical Education and Research Center
Grand Rapids, MI

Bruce Bradley*
General Motors Corporation
Detroit, MI

David Brailer
Health Technology Center
San Francisco, CA

Shelby Brammer
Madigan Army Medical Center
Tacoma, WA

William Braun
Kaiser-Bellflower
Downey, CA

Richard Brumley
Kaiser-Bellflower
Downey, CA

William Bruning
Mid-America Coalition on Health Care Community Initiative on Depression
Kansas City, MO

Barry Bunting
Asheville Project, Mission St. Joseph's Hospital
Asheville, NC

Linda Burnes Bolton*
Cedars-Sinai Medical Center and Burns and Allen Research Institute
Los Angeles, CA

Clatie Campbell
Capital Health System
Trenton, NJ

Garry Carneal
URAC
Washington, DC

SUMMIT ATTENDEES

Collier Case
Sprint
Overland Park, KS

Christine Cassel
American Board of Internal Medicine
Philadelphia, PA

Barbara Cebuhar
American College of Surgeons
Chicago, IL

Jennifer Cernoch
Family Voices
Albuquerque, NM

Albert Charbonneau
Rochester Health Commission
Rochester, NY

Rebecca Chater
Kerr Drug
Asheville, NC

Leonard Christie
Oregon Health Sciences University
Medford, OR

Carolyn Clancy◆
Agency for Healthcare Research and Quality
Rockville, MD

Noreen Clark
University of Michigan School of Public Health
Ann Arbor, MI

Janet Corrigan
Institute of Medicine
Washington, DC

Vicki Cottrell
NAMI Utah
Salt Lake City, UT

Kathy Crispell
NW Kaiser Permanente
Clackamas, OR

June Dahl
University of Wisconsin Medical School
Madison, WI

Allen Daniels★
Alliance Behavioral Care, University of Cincinnati Department of Psychiatry
Cincinnati, OH

Helen Darling
National Business Group on Health
Washington, DC

Catherine Davis
UAW-Ford Community Health Care Initiatives
Kansas City, MO

Francois de Brantes
General Electric
Fairfield, CT

Anthony DeFranco
McLaren Regional Medical Center
Flint, MI

Carole DeSpain Magoffin
National Pharmaceutical Council
Reston, VA

Carol Diamond
Markle Foundation
New York, NY

Molla Sloane Donaldson
National Cancer Institute
Bethesda, MD

Denise Dougherty
Agency for Healthcare Research and Quality
Rockville, MD

Sylvia Drew Ivie
The Help Everyone Clinic, Inc.
Los Angeles, CA

Benjamin Druss
Emory University
Atlanta, GA

Michael Dunn
Madigan Army Medical Center
Tacoma, WA

Jack Ebeler
Alliance of Community Health Plans
Washington, DC

William Ellis
American Pharmacists Association Foundation
Washington, DC

Scott Ellsworth
Blue Cross and Blue Shield of the Rochester
  Region
Rochester, NY

Susan Enguidanos
Kaiser Permanente and Partners in Care
  Foundation
Burbank, CA

Shari Erickson
Institute of Medicine
Washington, DC

C. McCollister Evarts
University of Rochester
Rochester, NY

Wendy Everett
New England Healthcare Institute
Cambridge, MA

Adolph Falcon
The National Alliance for Hispanic Health
Washington, DC

Lucie Ferguson
Community Health Advocacy, Bon Secours
  Richmond Health System
Richmond, VA

Betty Ferrell
City of Hope National Medical Center
Duarte, CA

Harvey Fineberg
Institute of Medicine
Washington, DC

Arnold Finkel
Horizon/Mercy
West Trenton, NJ

Terri Flint
Intermountain Health Care
Salt Lake City, UT

Michael Friedman
Air Pollution and Respiratory Health Branch,
  National Center for Environmental Health,
  Centers for Disease Control and Prevention
Atlanta, GA

Martha Funnell
Michigan Diabetes Research and Training
  Center
Ann Arbor, MI

Henry Gaines
UAW/GM Community Health Initiatives
Flint, MI

Marcela Gaitan
The National Alliance for Hispanic Health
Washington, DC

Jerry Gardner
Intermountain Health Care, Physician Division
Ogden, UT

Lillee Gelinas*
VHA, Inc.
Irving, TX

Russell Glasgow
Kaiser Permanente Colorado
Penrose, CO

Joanne Godley
Health Commissioner's Office-Philadelphia
Philadelphia, PA

SUMMIT ATTENDEES

Augustus Grant
American Heart Association
Durham, NC

Liza Greenberg
URAC
Washington, DC

Ann Greiner
Institute of Medicine
Washington, DC

Oliver Grin
Champion Health and Fitness
Kentwood, MI

Suresh Gupta
Greater Flint Health Coalition
Grand Blanc, MI

David Guzick
University of Rochester's School of Medicine
 and Dentistry
Rochester, NY

Norma Hagenow
Genesys Health System
Grand Blanc, MI

Daniel Hawkins
National Association of Community Health
 Centers
Washington, DC

Maureen Hennessey
New Directions Behavioral Health
Shawnee Mission, KS

John Heryer
Blue Cross and Blue Shield of Kansas City
Kansas City, MO

Judith Hibbard
University of Oregon
Eugene, OR

Charles Homer*
National Initiative for Children's Healthcare
 Quality
Brookline, MA

Kim Horn
Priority Health
Grand Rapids, MI

Karen Ignagni
American Association of Health Plans
Washington, DC

David Introcaso
Agency for Healthcare Research and Quality
Rockville, MD

George Isham
HealthPartners, Inc.
Minneapolis, MN

Manoj Jain
QSouce, Center for Healthcare Quality
Memphis, TN

Paul Jarris
Vermont Department of Health
Burlington, VT

Stephen Jencks
Centers for Medicare and Medicaid Services
Baltimore, MD

Dave Johnson
Premera Blue Cross
Spokane, WA

Erika Jones
Children's Mercy Hospital
Kansas City, MO

Richard Kahn
American Diabetes Association
Alexandria, VA

Adrienne Keller
Psychiatric Medicine and Health Evaluation
    Sciences
Charlottesville, VA

David Kibbe*
American Academy of Family Physicians
Chapel Hill, NC

Kathleen King
Pajaso Valley Community Health Trust
Wetsonville, CA

Ken Kizer
National Quality Forum
Washington, DC

Ronald Knight
Harris Interactive, Inc.
Rochester, NY

Mary Anne Koda-Kimble*
University of California San Francisco
San Francisco, CA

Lisa Koonin◆
Centers for Disease Control and Prevention
Atlanta, GA

Allan Korn
Blue Cross and Blue Shield Association
Chicago, IL

Kathryn Kotula
National Association of State Medicaid
    Directors
Washington, DC

Marianne Kramer
Aetna National Quality Management
Blue Bell, PA

Harlan Krumholz
Yale University
New Haven, CT

Kim Kuebler
Emory University Hospital
Atlanta, GA

Teresa Lampmann
The Pediatric/Adult Asthma Coalition of New
    Jersey
Union, NJ

Sheila Leatherman
University of North Carolina
Minneapolis, MN

Peter Lee*
Pacific Business Group on Health
San Francisco, CA

Lauren LeRoy
Grantmakers in Health
Washington, DC

Joslyn Levy
New York City Department of Health and
    Mental Hygiene
New York, NY

Sandra Lewis
Portland Cardiovascular Institute
Portland, OR

Louise Liang
Kaiser Foundation Health Plan, Inc.
Oakland, CA

Anne Llewellyn
PRIME, Inc.
Miramar, FL

Kate Lorig*
Stanford University
Stanford, CA

John Lumpkin
The Robert Wood Johnson Foundation
Princeton, NJ

Beverly Lunsford
The Washington Home
Washington, DC

Summit Attendees

Joanne Lynn*
The Washington Home Center for Palliative Care Studies
Washington, DC

Ron Manderschied
Substance Abuse and Mental Health Services Administration
Rockville, MD

Sal Mangione
Jefferson Medical College
Philadelphia, PA

Elizabeth McCann
Medical Student at Columbia College of Physicians and Surgeons

LaMar McGinnis
American Cancer Society
Atlanta, GA

Elizabeth McGlynn
The RAND Corporation
Santa Monica, CA

Kevin McNally
New Jersey Department of Health and Senior Services
Trenton, NJ

Barbara McNeil
Harvard Medical School
Boston, MA

Ruth Medak
OMPRO-American College of Cardiology Foundation
Portland, OR

John Meyer
Madigan Army Medical Center
Tacoma, WA

John Miall
City of Ashville
Asheville, NC

Doriane Miller
American Hospital Association
Chicago, IL

Arnold Milstein
Pacific Business Group on Health
San Francisco, CA

Cecelia Montoye
Greater Flint Health Coalition
Grand Blanc, MI

Sydney Morss Dy
The Johns Hopkins Bloomberg School of Public Health
Baltimore, MD

Gordon Mosser
Institute for Clinical Systems Improvement
Bloomington, MN

Penny Mounce
Madigan Army Medical Center
Fort Lewis, WA

Mark Murray
Grand Valley State University
Allendale, MI

Woodrow Myers
Wellpoint Health Networks, Inc.
Thousand Oaks, CA

David Nathan*
Harvard Medical School
West Newton, MA

Don Nielsen
American Hospital Association
Chicago, IL

Jan Norman
Department of Health, State of Washington
Olympia, WA

Sam Nussbaum
Anthem Blue Cross and Blue Shield
Indianapolis, IN

Dennis O'Leary
Joint Commission on Accreditation of
　　Healthcare Organizations
Oakbrook Terrace, IL

Rita O'Neill
Kaiser-Bellflower
Downey, CA

Tracy Orleans
The Robert Wood Johnson Foundation
Princeton, NJ

William Pankey
FirstGuard Health Plan
Kansas City, MO

Ruth Parker
Emory University School of Medicine
Atlanta, GA

Barbara Paul
Centers for Medicare and Medicaid Services
Baltimore, MD

L. Gregory Pawlson
National Committee for Quality Assurance
Washington, DC

Harold Pincus
RAND-University of Pittsburgh Health Institute
Pittsburgh, PA

Thomas Platts-Mills
Asthma and Allergic Disease Center
Charlotte, VA

Jay Portnoy
Children's Mercy Hospital
Kansas City, MO

Christopher Queram
Employer Health Care Alliance Cooperative
Madison, WI

Timothy Quill
University of Rochester School of Medicine and
　　Dentistry
Rochester, NY

Helen Ragazzi
Controlling Asthma in the Richmond
　　Metropolitan Area
Richmond, VA

Donna Ramos
Health Improvement Partnership of Santa Cruz
　　County
Santa Cruz, CA

Brenda Reiss-Brennan
Intermountain Health Care
Salt Lake City, UT

Lawerence Reynolds
Mott Children's Health Center
Flint, MI

Lawrence Robinson
Health Commissioner's Office-Philadelphia
Philadelphia, PA

John Rother
American Association of Retired Persons
Washington, DC

Will Rowe
American Pain Foundation
Baltimore, MD

Barbara Rudolph
The Leapfrog Group
Madison, WI

John Rumsfeld
Denver VA Medical Center
Denver, CO

Judy Salerno
National Institute on Aging
Bethesda, MD

Cheryl Scott[*]
Group Health Cooperative
Seattle, WA

Hsien Seow
The Washington Home
Washington, DC

Summit Attendees

Wells Shoemaker
Physician Medical Group of Santa Cruz
Santa Cruz, CA

Steve Shortell
University of California, Berkeley
Berkeley, CA

Cameron Shultz
Greater Flint Health Coalition
Flint, MI

Lisa Simpson
University of South Florida
St. Petersburg, FL

Marie Sinioris
National Center for Healthcare Leadership
Chicago, IL

Stephen Skorcz
Greater Flint Health Coalition
Flint, MI

Thomas Smith
UAW/GM Community Health Initiatives
Flint, MI

Helen Smits
Eduardo Mondlane University
Old Saybrook, CT

Lynn Page Snyder
Institute of Medicine
Washington, DC

Shoshanna Sofaer
Baruch College
New York, NY

Dana Sommers
Grotenhuis Group
Grand Rapids, MI

John Spertus*
Mid America Heart Institute, University of Missouri
Kansas City, MO

Marilyn Stebbins
University of California, San Francisco and Catholic Healthcare West Medical Foundation
Rancho Cordova, CA

David Stevens
Agency for Healthcare Research and Quality
Rockville, MD

Susanne Stoiber
Institue of Medicine
Washington, DC

Dan Stryer♦
Agency for Healthcare Research and Quality
Rockville, MD

Jonathan Sugarman
Qualis Health
Seattle, WA

Thomas Sullivan
Massachusetts Medical Society
Waltham, MA

Sara Thier
The Robert Wood Johnson Foundation
Princeton, NJ

Stephen Thomas
Center for Minority Health, University of Pittsburgh
Pittsburgh, PA

Richard Tucker
Wenatchee Valley Medical Center
Wenatchee, WA

Reed Tuckson*
UnitedHealth Group
Minnetonka, MN

Sean Tunis
Centers for Medicare and Medicaid Services
Baltimore, MD

I. Steven Udvarhelyi*
Independence Blue Cross
Philadelphia, PA

Matthew Van Vranken
Spectrum Health Hospitals Grand Rapids
Grand Rapids, MI

Elias Vasquez
University of Maryland School of Nursing
Baltimore, MD

Frank Vinicor
National Center for Chronic Disease Prevention
 and Health Promotion, Centers for Disease
 Control and Prevention
Atlanta, GA

Ed Wagner◆
MacColl Institute for Health Care Innovation at
 Group Health Cooperative
Seattle, WA

Annette Watson
URAC
Washington, DC

Morris Weinberger
University of North Carolina
Chapell Hill, NC

Kevin Weiss
Hines VA Hospital
Hines, IL

Martha Whitecotton
Carolinas Medical Center
Charlotte, NC

Andrew Wiesenthal
The Permanente Federation
Oakland, CA

Anne Wilkinson
The RAND Corporation
Arlington, VA

Ellen Williams
Mission St. Joseph's Hospitals
Asheville, NC

Daniel Wolfson
American Board of Internal Medicine
Philadelphia, PA

William Yasnoff
Department of Health and Human Services
Washington, DC

Elaine Yuen
Jefferson Medical College
Philadelphia, PA

Stephanie Zaza◆
Centers for Disease Control and Prevention
Atlanta, GA

Jonathan Zimmerman
Siemens Medical Solutions Health Services
Malvern, PA

---

* Committee Member
◆ Liaison Member

Appendix F
Conference Prework and Sample Matrices

The following letter and accompanying matrices were sent to the community participants in advance of the summit.

Dear Community Participant:

As a participating community at the Institute of Medicine's Quality Chasm Summit on January 6-7, 2004, you will be actively involved in developing high-level work plans (including metrics) to redesign care in one of the following five clinical areas: asthma, depression, diabetes, chronic heart failure, and pain control in advanced cancer. Prior to the Summit, as shared with you in your invitation letter, your group will need to complete some preparatory work so that the condition-specific working groups can be as productive as possible. We will make every effort to facilitate this process in a manner that is sensitive to your time constraints. Your commitment will be as follows:

- Participation by at least one member of your community team in a conference call to receive guidance in completion of pre-work materials.
- Completion of two matrices to assess gaps in care and barriers/opportunities for improvement.
- Follow-up conference call with committee content experts to agree upon assumptions derived from the data that will help inform the Summit work plans.

The IOM Next Steps Summit is intended to support communities of care providers in "Crossing the Chasm" to delivering high-quality care in one or more of the aforementioned five priority areas. This document lays the foundation for the condition-specific working groups. By investing in a modest amount of preparatory work, the participants should be able to maximize their time at the conference so that unique and valuable insights into how best to improve care within each community can be learned and deployed.

The first step towards optimizing the quality of care for the five conditions being targeted is to visualize the process of ideal care and to understand potential impediments to delivering that care. Figure 1 below represents the cycle of "ideal" care.

Using chronic heart failure as an example, the initial step is to recognize that the patient suffers from the syndrome of heart failure and to make a proper diagnosis. These diagnostic steps are outlined in the first column of the attached grids and include an assessment of left ventricular function, the use of laboratory tests to exclude other etiologies for these symptoms, and the exclusion of significant ischemic coronary disease. The next step of the care process is to educate patients about the nature of heart failure and what to expect regarding treatment (including lifestyle interventions) and prognosis. The third phase of care is to recommend initial treatment. Current standards of care for patients with left ventricular dysfunction include the use of angiotensin converting enzyme inhibitors, beta-blockers and anti-coagulation for those with atrial fibrillation. Ensuring that treatment recommendations are followed is the next step along the path of ideal care and includes teaching patients techniques of self-management such as monitoring weight and medication compliance. Finally, serial assessments of patients' responses to treatment and monitoring the status of their heart failure are needed to continually optimize the other aspects of their heart failure care. This can be done through the serial assessment of patients' symptoms, function and quality of life. Sub-optimal health status (symptoms, function and quality of life) should trigger a repeated pursuit, using the same steps outlined above, of opportunities to improve the patient's condition. Naturally, it should be emphasized that this pursuit is one of shared management.

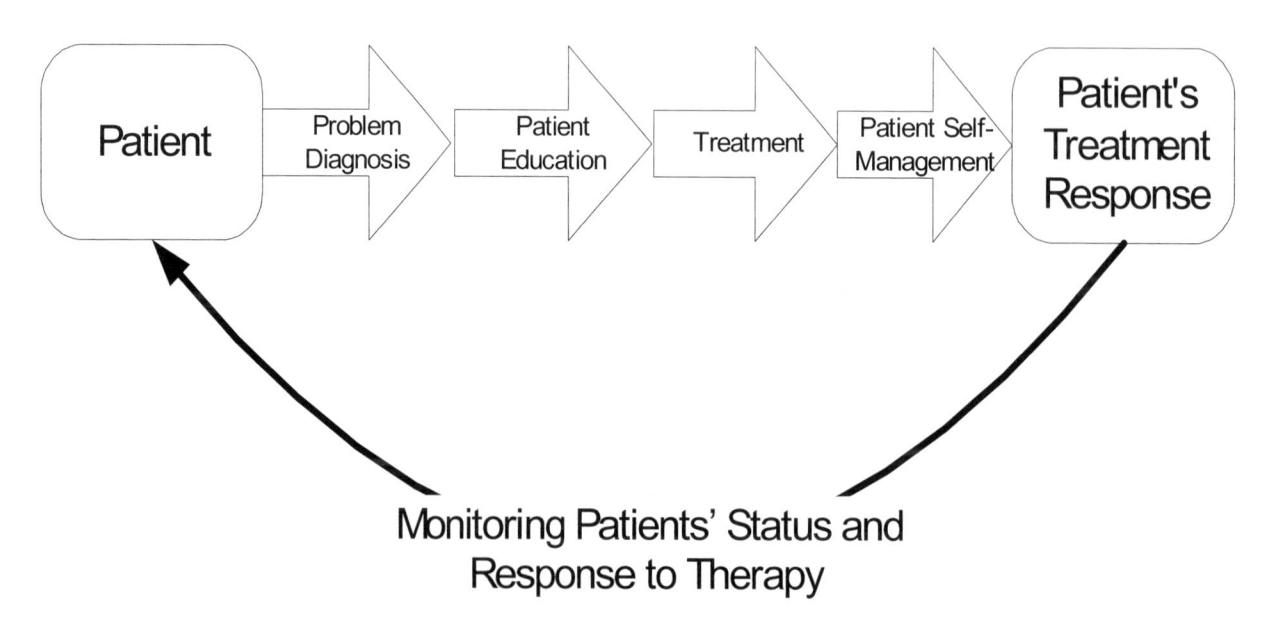

Figure F-1. Cycle of "Ideal" Care

Rendering optimal care for patients with chronic conditions requires the efficient coordination of multiple components of the health care system and its environment. Towards that end, the Next Steps Summit is designed to identify those aspects of care that are most rate limiting in achieving a system that is safe, effective, patient-centered, timely, efficient and equitable. To identify the most pressing components of care for emphasis during the summit, we have designed the first of the attached worksheets. This matrix aligns each component of the process of "ideal" care against the six aims of high-quality healthcare described in the IOM's *Crossing the Quality Chasm*. Please rank each process of care from 1-5, where a score of 5 indicates complete satisfaction of the goal and lower scores represent an increasing gap between current and ideal care. We will use these scores to identify the areas most in need of improvement.

The second matrix is designed to illuminate strategies currently being implemented at your institution to support high-quality care in each of these aspects of the desired "ideal" care process. We intend to share strategies from communities successful in certain aspects of care delivery with those struggling in those areas. Conversely, we hope to identify areas where all are suffering and to brainstorm solutions, through the use of national experts, for how to overcome these challenges. Your thoughtful and detailed completion of these grids is very much appreciated and the best possible investment that you could make in ensuring a successful conference in January. Thank you again for your participation and commitment to this process.

Sincerely,

John Spertus, M.D., M.P.H.
Chair, Community Pre-work Subgroup
Quality Chasm Summit

MATRIX # 1
CHRONIC HEART FAILURE

Please list each of the components of ideal chronic heart failure care below and rate on a scale of 1-5 (where 5 means that the aim is completely satisfied and 1 represents an enormous gap) how well each component is performing in your community* in attaining each of the IOM 6 Aims for healthcare. We have provided examples under each heading. You may enter not applicable "N/A" where appropriate.

"Ideal" CHF Care	IOM 6 Aims for Health Care					
	Safe	Effective	Pt-Centered	Timely	Efficient	Equitable
Diagnosis						
• EF assessed						
• Lab tests						
• Ischemia excluded						
• Others?						
Pt Education						
• Disease knowledge						
• Prognosis						
• Treatment plan						
• Others?						
Treatment						
• ACE-I						
• BBs						
• A-coag for Afib						
• Others?						
Self-management						
• Monitoring weight						
• Taking meds						
• Others?						
Monitoring Disease Status						
• Document symptoms/activity, NYHA, KCCQ						
• Others?						

*Please define your community for us. For example: # individuals; # privately insured; #uninsured etc.

Institute of Medicine Aims for the 21st-Century Health Care System

Health care should be:

- **Safe**—avoiding injuries to patients from the care that is intended to help them.

- **Effective**—providing services based on scientific knowledge to all who could benefit and refraining from providing services to those not likely to benefit (avoiding underuse and overuse, respectively).

- **Patient-centered**—providing care that is respectful of and responsive to individual patient preferences, needs, and values and ensuring that patient values guide all clinical decisions.

- **Timely**—reducing waits and sometimes harmful delays for both those who receive and those who give care.

- **Efficient**—avoiding waste, including waste of equipment, supplies, ideas, and energy.

- **Equitable**—providing care that does not vary in quality because of personal characteristics such as gender, ethnicity, geographic location, and socioeconomic status.

MATRIX # 2
Strategies for Achieving High-Quality CHF Care

This grid is to illustrate how improving CHF outcomes relates to five areas in need of "System Improvement." We have purposefully written it as a series of questions to help in defining various system interventions. For many, there is no single "right answer." Rather, these are suggestions your community** should use to guide your responses to the worksheet accompanying this grid.

"Ideal" care	Examples	Clinical Information Systems	Delivery System Redesign	Decision Support	Self-management Support	Community Resources and Policies
Diagnosis	1. EF Assessment* 2. Exclusion of active ischemia* 3. Exclusion of other etiologies through lab work*	Does your community have a database to identify patients with heart failure? Does your community have a mechanism for enrolling heart failure patients into a database so that the processes and results of their care can be measured? How do you track test results?	Who reviews the registry to insure complete workup? How does an efficient work-up, convenient to patients occur?	Does your community have an evidence-based guideline for heart failure diagnosis? How is the guideline disseminated to providers? How is the guideline "embedded" into your system? How are recommendations for further care (Patient education, treatment, self-management, monitoring) facilitated? For Group A patients, at risk for but without HF, how are primary prevention practices supported?	How is the import of a complete work-up communicated to patients?	What links does your community have set up to provide information for patients about heart failure diagnoses?
Patient Education	1. Disease Knowledge 2. Treatment plan 3. Prognosis	How is it known whether patients have an adequate understanding of HF, its treatment and their prognosis?	Are 'education clinics' available to provide this information? Are patient groups so that newly diagnosed patients can learn form other patients available?	What tools are available to allow patients to select among different therapies and treatment environments? What process is in place to facilitate patient decisions about living wills and end of life care?	Is there support for patients to create living wills? How are lifestyle changes (smoking cessation, exercise programs, etc.) supported?	What links does your community have set up to provide information for patients about treatment?

Adapted w/ permission from Ed Wagner, MacColl Institute for Health Care Innovation at Group Health Cooperative

Conference Prework and Sample Matrices

"Ideal" care	Examples	Clinical Information Systems	Delivery System Redesign	Decision Support	Self-management Support	Community Resources and Policies
Treatment for systolic left ventricular dysfunction (i.e. EF < 40-45%, moderate LV dysfunction or worse by qualitative assessment)	1. General measures (diet, exercise, smoking cessation, etc. 2. ACE-I* 3. Beta blockers* 4. Anti-coagulation for Atrial Fibrillation*	How does your community track general measures, such as diet, physical activity, and immunizations? How does your community monitor the initiation and titration of needed medications? How are contraindications for certain medicines identified? How are medication dosages and medication changes tracked?	Who reviews the registry for these general aspects of care? Are titration clinics available to adjust and monitor medications? Who provides patients with the means to monitor and follow treatment plans at home?	Does your community have an evidence-based guideline for general measures in heart failure management, such as sodium restriction, fluid intake, physical activity, immunizations and avoidance of NSAIDs? Do guidelines describe optimal doses of ACE inhibitors (ex: captopril 150 mg/d, enalapril 20 mg/d or equivalent) and substitutes for ACE inhibitors? Beta blockers? Anti-coagulation? Do guidelines address the role of diuretics in maintaining euvolemia and minimizing symptoms? Do guidelines address the use of digoxin? How is the guideline disseminated to providers? How is the guideline "embedded" into your community system?	Do you have documentation of collaborative goal setting and shared treatment plans for general measures? What ways and means are available to provide self-management support to patients? What incentives does your community have to encourage patients? What methods are there to assist patients with medication management? What methods are used in teaching patients about medication adjustments? Are patients encouraged to report medication effects?	What links does your community have set up to: Financial support for medications? Transportation to appointments? Home health agencies? What programs are available to assist patients in obtaining medications? What programs are available to assist the patient and caregiver in medication management?
Treatment for Diastolic Heart Failure (LVEF > or = 45%, normal or mild LV dysfunction by qualitative assessment)	1. General measures 2. Control of hypertension	How are medication dosages and changes tracked?	Who monitors medication adjustment? What intervals are established to review medications? How is care for underlying illnesses coordinated with heart failure care?	Do guidelines address optimization of BP control (140/90 or less), aggressive treatment of coronary artery disease and maintenance of sinus rhythm? Do guidelines address the role of diuretics in maintaining euvolemia and minimizing symptoms, nitrates for preload reduction, other therapeutic options (such as ACE inhibitors, beta blockers, calcium channel blockers and ARBs) and digoxin in patients who continue to have symptoms despite the above?	What methods are there to assist patients with medication management? What methods are used in teaching patients about medication adjustments? Are patients encouraged to report medication effects?	What programs are available to assist patients in obtaining medications? What programs are available to assist the patient and caregiver in medication management?

Adapted w/ permission from Ed Wagner, MacColl Institute for Health Care Innovation at Group Health Cooperative

"Ideal" care	Examples	Clinical Information Systems	Delivery System Redesign	Decision Support	Self-management Support	Community Resources and Policies
Treatment for Refractory Heart Failure		How does your community track which heart failure patients need referral?	How do case managers, primary care providers and cardiologists interact?	Does the guideline include the decision to refer?	How is care coordinated from the patient's perspective?	What assistance is provided to complete referrals?
Self-management	1. Monitoring weight 2. Complying with medications	How is it known whether patients have an adequate understanding of HF and their role in managing their disease? How do you document changes to the care plan? How is the need for case management identified? How is information shared across practice settings?	Are 'education clinics' available to provide this information? Who reviews the collaborative goals? Who calls the patients to discuss monitoring, diet, exercise, medication use? Who determines discharge from follow-up care? How do case managers interact with primary care providers and specialists? What methods and schedules are used to contact patients?	What techniques for teaching patients appropriate guidelines for how to adjust diuretics, when to call for additional input, and how to arrange follow-up appointments for changes in their condition? Do you utilize behavior change and motivational techniques in patient interactions? How are providers trained in motivational techniques? How are patients assisted to make informed decisions about their care? Does your community have evidence-based protocols for the case managers? How are the protocols disseminated to case managers? How is the protocol "embedded" into your community's system?	Is there a mechanism for patients to make appointments promptly? What tools are available to assist patients with their self-management? What "menus" of self-management support are available to patients? (Class, telephone, peer, case management.) What incentives does your community have to encourage patients? Does self-management support address all conditions experienced by the patient and their interactions?	What assistance is provided to patients for ensuring home monitoring, such as scales or caregivers? What links does your community have set up to: Home health programs? Support groups? Internet links? Transportation programs? Financial assistance? When one is involved, how does the case manager interact with other health care providers in the community?
Monitoring	1. Formal assessment of signs and symptoms through use of explicit descriptions, NYHA of health status measures (e.g. Kansas City Cardiomyopathy Questionnaire)* 2. Laboratory testing to monitor potential electrolyte imbalances from medications	How does your community track periodic assessments of symptoms and function? How do you track laboratory tests? What ICT tools are available to facilitate the use of patient-centered health status measures?	Who monitors signs, symptoms, medication side effects and daily weights? What intervals are established to review laboratory tests? What methods are used to monitor patients (phone, fax, email)?	Do guidelines include periodic assessment of signs, symptoms, weight and medications? Do guidelines include intervals for monitoring laboratory tests?	What methods are there to assist patients with monitoring? What methods are used in teaching patients about monitoring?	What assistance is provided to patients for ensuring home monitoring, such as scales or caregivers?

Adapted w/ permission from Ed Wagner, MacColl Institute for Health Care Innovation at Group Health Cooperative

CONFERENCE PREWORK AND SAMPLE MATRICES

"Ideal" care	Examples	Clinical Information Systems	Delivery System Redesign	Decision Support	Self-management Support	Community Resources and Policies
End of Life Issues	When no other options are available to improve the health status of severely debilitated patients, end of life care should be pursued	How do you track patient preferences for end of life care? Is this information available across multiple settings?	Who discusses end of life issues with patients? When and where do discussions occur? Which team members can be helpful to the patient and family and how are they involved?	Do protocols and guidelines address advance planning such as living will, durable power of attorney for health care or other appropriate legal documents?	How are patient and family members provided with helpful information and support?	What links do you have set up to community programs to assist patients, such as legal aid?
Sharing successes/ failures across institutions						
Engendering involvement of practitioners						
Care delivery by clinicians other than cardiologists						
Other Please consider any unique attributes of your community initiative not addressed above, and capture those efforts in the worksheet.						

*Indicates a performance measure as proposed by the ACC/AHA/AMA's Physician Consortium on Performance Improvement Clinical Performance Measures for Heart Failure
**Community is defined as: geographic region, integrated delivery system, collection of providers, coalition, & others.

Adapted w/ permission from Ed Wagner, MacColl Institute for Health Care Innovation at Group Health Cooperative

Appendix G
Summit Planning

The summit committee was organized into subgroups to carry out the extensive planning required. The six subgroups focused on the agenda, the summit participants list, community selection, prework with participating communities, summit cross-cutting sessions, and facilitation of the summit working groups. Over a 6-month period leading up to the summit, the full committee met four times—twice in face-to-face meetings and twice in full committee conference calls. The committee also met before, during, and directly after the summit to monitor progress and assess outcomes.

The committee benefited greatly from the input and advice of key liaisons, including Lisa Koonin and Stephanie Zaza from the Centers for Disease Control and Prevention; Don Berwick and Maureen Bisognano from the Institute for Healthcare Improvement; Ed Wagner and Brian Austin from the MacColl Institute for Healthcare Innovation at Group Health Cooperative; and Carolyn Clancy and Dan Stryer from the Agency for Healthcare Research and Quality. These individuals apprised the committee of care delivery innovations and challenges, as well as emerging federal programs and priorities to support local innovation. Paul Tarini and Tracy Orleans from The Robert Wood Johnson Foundation also provided important input.

The committee worked with IOM staff to develop background papers on each of the five priority areas targeted for the summit. Before the summit took place, all participants received a copy of *Crossing the Quality Chasm: A New Health System for the 21st Century* and had an opportunity to participate in a teleconference focused on reviewing the report's major findings and recommendations, led by George Isham from HealthPartners, Inc.

Appendix H
Summit Agenda

JANUARY 7, 2004

8:00	**Continental Breakfast** – NAS Great Hall

Plenary Session – NAS Auditorium

8:30	**Welcome and Introductions**

　　　　Reed V. Tuckson, M.D., Chair, Quality Chasm Summit Committee
　　　　Harvey V. Fineberg, M.D., President, Institute of Medicine
　　　　John R. Lumpkin, M.D., Senior Vice President, The Robert Wood Johnson Foundation

9:00	**A Call for a Better Health System:**

How to Make Success the Norm in America
　　　　Consumer speaker relates experiences dealing with the broken health
　　　　care system. Interactive community panel share success stories—as well
　　　　as failures—in overcoming barriers to improving quality care in each of the
　　　　5 targeted priority areas.

Moderator:
　　　　Allen Daniels, LISW, Ed.D., CEO Alliance Behavioral Care and Quality Chasm Summit
　　　　　　Committee Member

Consumer Speaker:
　　　　Martha Whitecotton, R.N., Vice President and Chief Nurse Executive Officer, Carolinas
　　　　　　Medical Center, Charlotte, NC

Community Panel:
　　　　William Bruning, J.D., Mid-America Coalition on Health Care Community Initiative on
　　　　　　Depression
　　　　Henry Gaines, Regional Coordinator, Greater Flint Health Coalition
　　　　Jay Portnoy, M.D., Children's Mercy Hospital/Kansas City Asthma Coalition

JANUARY 7, 2004 (Continued)

10:30	**Articulating the Gap:** **Laying the Issues on the Doorsteps of Leadership** **Keynote Speaker:** Donald M. Berwick, M.D., CEO, Institute for Healthcare Improvement, Boston, MA
11:15	**Question & Answer Session for Keynote Speaker**
11:30	**Overview of Afternoon Session** Reed V. Tuckson, M.D. provides an overview of post-lunch crosscutting strategy sessions and briefly describes condition-specific working group assignments.

Remaining session open only to pre-registered participants due to space constraints.

11:45	**Working Lunch** Note: Participants were assigned to lunchtime working groups in advance of the Summit. Please attend only your assigned working groups as care was taken to have a mix of stakeholders represented. Pick up a lunch box in the Great Hall. **Asthma Group** – Members' Room **Depression Group** – Room 180 **Diabetes Group** – Lecture Room **Heart Failure Group** – Room 150 **Pain Control Group** – Board Room **National Champions** – Executive Dining Room
12:45	**Cross Cutting Strategy Sessions I** Note: Each strategy session will be repeated. Participants were provided the opportunity to select their sessions in advance of the Summit. Again, please attend only your assigned working groups as care was taken to have a mix of stakeholders represented. Logistical information below.

2:15	**Cross Cutting Strategy Sessions II**
	
	Care Coordination – Room 180
	    Co-facilitators: Gerard Anderson, Ph.D. & Christine Cassel, M.D.
	    Community examples: Kaiser Bellflower & Philadelphia Department of Health
	Community Activation/Leadership – Room 150
	    Co-facilitators: Shoshanna Sofaer, Dr.P.H. & David Stevens, M.D.
	    Community examples: The Pediatric/Adult Asthma Coalition of New Jersey & Rochester Health Commission
	Finance – Members' Room
	    Co-facilitators: Peter Lee, J.D. & Steve Udvarhelyi, M.D.
	    Community examples: Grand Rapids Medical Education & Research Center & Mission-St. Joseph's Health System Asheville Project
	Information and Communications Technology – Room 280 (second floor)
	    Co-facilitators: David Kibbe, M.D. & David Brailer, M.D., Ph.D.
	    Community examples: County of Santa Cruz, CA & Madigan Army Medical Center
	Measurement – Board Room
	    Co-facilitators: Judith Hibbard, Ph.D. & Arnold Milstein, M.D.
	    Community examples: Intermountain Health Care Depression in Primary Care Initiative & The Washington State Diabetes Collaborative
	Patient-Self Management – Lecture Room
	    Co-facilitators: Kate Lorig, R.N., Ph.D. & Russell Glasgow, Ph.D.
	    Community examples: Controlling Asthma in Richmond Metropolitan Area & The Oregon Heart Failure Project

JANUARY 7, 2004 (Continued)

3:45	**Change Over Break**

4:00	**Condition Specific Working Groups Break Out Sessions**
	Facilitated working groups identity strategies and develop action plans for "Crossing the Chasm". Although participants will assemble by condition, an emphasis will be placed on crosscutting strategies and co-morbidities.
	
	Asthma Group – Members Room
	    Co-facilitators: Linda Burnes-Bolton, R.N., Dr.P.H. & Charlie Homer, M.D.
	Depression Group – Room 180
	    Co-facilitators: Cheryl Scott, M.H.A. & Allen Daniels, LISW, Ed.D.
	Diabetes Group – Lecture Room
	    Co-facilitators: Ron Anderson, M.D., Regina Benjamin, M.D. & David Nathan, M.D.
	Heart Failure Group – Room 150
	    Co-facilitators: Lillee Gelinas, R.N., M.S.N. & John Spertus, M.D.
	Pain Control Group – Board Room
	    Co-facilitators: Mary Anne Koda-Kimble, Pharm.D & Joanne Lynn, M.D.

6:30	**Reception & Networking – NAS Great Hall**

1st Annual Crossing the Quality Chasm Summit

JANUARY 8, 2004

8:00	**Continental Breakfast** – NAS Great Hall
8:30	**Condition Specific Working Groups Finalize Action Plans**

Asthma Group – Members' Room
Depression Group – Room 180
Diabetes Group – Lecture Room
Heart Failure Group – Room 150
Pain Control Group – Board Room

Plenary Session – NAS Auditorium

10:15 **Working Groups Report Synopsis of Key Strategies**
Note: After each working group presentation there will be a 10 minute time frame for the audience to offer suggestions and build upon summit action plans.

Open only to pre-registered participants due to space constraints.

12:00 **Working Lunch**
Condition specific groups fine-tune reports
Working group facilitators have "heads-up" session with Reactor Panel participants
National Champions debrief with the IOM Committee Chair

Asthma Group – Members Room
Depression Group – Room 180
Diabetes Group – Lecture Room
Heart Failure Group – Room 150
Pain Control Group – Board Room
National Champions – Executive Dining Room
Reactor Panel – Room 280 (Second Floor)

Plenary Session – NAS Auditorium

1:30 **Reactor Panel Discussion**
Panelists & community leaders candidly react to major themes that surfaced in the action plans presented.

Moderator:
Bruce Bradley, M.B.A., Director, Health Plan Strategy & Public Policy, General Motors Corporation and Quality Chasm Summit Committee Member
Al Charbonneau, President and CEO, Rochester Health Commission, Rochester, N.Y.
Helen Darling, President, National Business Group on Health, Washington, D.C.
Sylvia Drew-Ivie, J.D., The Help Everyone Clinic, Los Angeles, CA
George J. Isham, M.D., Medical Director & Chief Health Officer, HealthPartners, Inc., Minneapolis MN

2:30 **Audience Suggestions for Building on Action Plans**

3:00 **Commitments from National Champions**
Reed V. Tuckson, M.D., Quality Chasm Summit Committee Chair

4:15 **Closing Remarks**
Reed V. Tuckson, M.D., Quality Chasm Summit Committee Chair

4:30 **Summit Adjourns**

Appendix I
Facilitating the Summit Working Groups

Committee members provided guidance to the condition-specific working groups in using a number of facilitation tools to generate their action plans. Within each of these five condition-specific groups, the participants worked in subgroups of six to eight individuals. Each of these subgroups focused on generating and prioritizing strategies for use of a key cross-cutting intervention (e.g., financing, information and communications technology) to improve care for a particular condition. "Brainwriting," a technique employed in silence, was used to generate ideas at each table, which were then categorized and prioritized using affinity diagrams (Brassard and Ritter, 1994). On day two, each of the condition-specific working groups developed an affinity diagram for the entire group, which identified the top two or three key leverage points. The condition-specific groups then developed action plans focused on these leverage points, which included strategies at the national and local levels, implementation timelines, and measures for evaluating progress.

REFERENCES

Brassard M, Ritter D. 1994. *The Memory Jogger II.* Salem, NH: Goal QPC.

Appendix J
Condition-Specific Working Group Questions

Asthma Working Group Questions

1. Measurement: What can we do to enhance asthma performance measures and further the adoption of useful measures?

2. Information and Communications Technology: What steps can be taken to promote the widespread use of clinical information systems for asthma care that support not only tracking and decision support, but also communication and patient involvement?

3. Care Delivery: What strategies might be adopted to change care delivery at the clinician/ microsystem level to enable the right care at the right time?

4. Patient Self-Management: What are the highest-priority steps for promoting the widespread development of self-management capabilities for patients with asthma (and their families)?

5. Finance: What are the components of a model insurance benefits package for essential asthma services? What strategies could be used to foster widespread adoption of such a package?

6. Community Activation: What strategies would create and foster a seamless web of asthma care for children and families, as well as adult patients, across the community—including the health, welfare, school, and work environments?

Depression Working Group Questions

1. Measurement: How can we establish a common set of performance measures for depression, incorporating consumer satisfaction as well as outcomes?

2. Information and Communications Technology: Given issues of stigma, confidentiality, and anonymity, how can we incorporate behavioral health information into patients' electronic health records and registries?

3. Care Coordination: What strategies can we implement to enhance communication between primary care physicians and specialists, including multiple behavioral health providers?

4. Policy: What can be done to address gaps in policy to support the evidence-based treatment of major depression in both the private and public sectors (i.e. screening, care management, follow-up)?

5. Finance: How can we align financial incentives to support an integrated approach among primary and specialty care, employers, and payers for the assessment and treatment of major depression?

6. Community Activation: How can we foster community linkages to support patients (consumers) and families facing the challenges of major depression?

Diabetes Working Group Questions

1. Measurement: What strategies can be used to further adoption of diabetes measures and better performance among those already collecting and reporting such measures?

2. Information and Communications Technology: What is the highest-leverage focus for information and communications technology to improve diabetes care (e.g., to support tracking, decision support, communications, measurement/accountability), and what are the key strategies for furthering its implementation?

3. Care Coordination: What are the highest-leverage strategies to support coordination of care between individual practitioners and organizations, with the goal of improving care for those with diabetes?

4. Patient Self-Management: What are the key steps clinicians, health care organizations, and community organizations can take to create and foster patient self-management?

5. Finance: What strategies can be used to make the business case to payers for supporting patient self-management and care management activities for those with diabetes?

6. Community Activation: What are the most effective ways of activating the major stakeholders in a community to focus on diabetes care?

Heart Failure Working Group Questions

1. Measurement: How can we best measure care processes (i.e., adherence to guidelines) and outcomes (e.g., health status, hospitalizations)?

2. Information and Communications Technology: Why has the promise of information and communications technology not been realized in heart failure care?

3. Care Coordination: Breakdowns in care coordination (both inpatient to outpatient care and across multiple providers) are rampant. What strategies can we implement to support care coordination?

4. Clinical Engagement: Physicians need to have a sense of personal commitment to optimizing their patients' care and outcomes. How do we encourage clinicians to use tools and systems to consistently deliver and monitor quality care?

5. Finance: Several aspects of care are not reimbursed, including patient education, monitoring of health status, dietary management, community coordination, and end-of-life planning. How do we redesign the reimbursement system (Medicare and the major payers) to support quality in heart failure care?

6. Clinical Leadership: Physician ownership of quality assurance/quality improvement efforts is critical to their success. How do we inspire clinician leadership in quality assessment and improvement?

Pain Control in Advanced Cancer Working Group Questions

1. Measurement: Who could undertake what specific actions to measure performance in the prevention and management of advanced cancer pain, both to motivate improvement and to monitor the effectiveness of progress overall and in key subpopulations?

2. Abandoning Policy/Forging Will: What specific actions could be undertaken by various stakeholder groups (i.e., political leaders, public and private payers, cancer organizations, pharmaceutical companies, providers) that would eliminate the commonplace practice of tolerating serious cancer pain and instead forge the will to achieve reliable prevention and relief of cancer pain?

3. Care Coordination: What improvements would create seamless and reliable care plans for the prevention and relief of cancer pain, from diagnosis to death, as patients change settings of care (i.e., hospital, home, nursing home) and provider organizations (i.e., cancer center, primary care physician, home care, hospice)?

4. Regulatory: What changes in federal, state, and local regulations and enforcement would facilitate excellent prevention and management of the pain of advanced cancer? How could those changes be achieved?

5. Assessment and Treatment: What strategies would ensure reliable assessment and prescribing practices so that clinicians will be effective in preventing and relieving pain for patients living with advanced cancer?